Great Discoveries in Psychiatry

Great Discoveries in Psychiatry

Ronald Chase

Cover image: Dissection illustrating the brain's meninges.
In 1822, Antoine Bayle discovered inflamed arachnoid membranes (shown at left) in a certain type of mental patient. Drawn by Gerard de Lairesse for Govard Bidloo's *Anatomia humani corporis*, 1685.
[National Library of Medicine, USA]

Logos Verlag Berlin

Bibliographic information published by the Deutsche Nationalbibliothek

The Deutsche Nationalbibliothek lists this publication in the Deutsche Nationalbibliografie; detailed bibliographic data are available on the Internet at http://dnb.d-nb.de .

ISBN 978-3-8325-5347-0

Logos Verlag Berlin GmbH
Georg-Knorr-Str. 4, Geb. 10
12681 Berlin
Germany
Tel.: +49 (0)30 42 85 10 90
Fax: +49 (0)30 42 85 10 92
INTERNET: https://www.logos-verlag.com

Discovery consists of seeing what everybody has seen and thinking what nobody has thought
Albert Szent-Gyorgyi

Contents

Introduction

This is a history of psychiatry told in stories of discovery. Historians generally agree that psychiatry began as a medical speciality in 1801, when Phillipe Pinel published his *Traité médico-philosophique sur l'aliénation mentale*. There were no psychiatrists at the time—only physicians—but Pinel was insightful about mental illnesses. He wrote his treatise shortly after becoming chief physician at the Salpêtrière hospital in Paris. Although officially responsible for all 7,000 female patients, Pinel worked almost exclusively in a ward of 200 mental patients. He was a compassionate caretaker who famously cut the chains that bound the most seriously ill. Beyond that, he experimented with physical and psychological treatments, defined the six most common types of mental illness, addressed causes and used statistical analysis. In short, Pinel was an intellectual, an innovator and a creative explorer in the strange world of psychiatric disorders. This book is about discoveries made by people like Phillipe Pinel.

The chapters follow a rough chronological order beginning around the year 1800 and continuing right through to the present. The subject matter varies from care and treatments to diagnostics, biomarkers and neuroscience. Some chapters recount a single discovery, whereas others summarize a series of connected discoveries. My definition of discovery includes not only scientific findings but also discoveries of an intellectual or intuitive nature. Science-based research offers our best hope for better treatments going forward, but good ideas help too.

The first chapter (Kindness) begins with a description of psychiatric care at Britain's oldest institution for mental patients, the Bethlem Hospital in London. At the turn of the nineteenth century, the buildings were in a state of collapse and patient care was generally dreadful. Progress was made when Samuel Tuke in York and Phillipe Pinel in Paris simultaneously discovered that kindness works better than harshness. The next two chapters are about early biomarkers of mental illness. A young physician performing autopsies at an asylum that held several Napoleon Bonapartes and the Marquis de Sade found inflamed cerebral membranes in a group of deceased patients who had claimed fabulous wealth and incredible fame.

Elsewhere, at a later time, a pair of psychiatrists found swollen ventricles in the brains of schizophrenia patients. Chapter 4 tells of how one woman's horror at seeing a dog drink water from a glass led Sigmund Freud to discover psychoanalysis.

Chapter 5 recounts how heredity came to be understood as a major risk factor for mental illness. The following chapter begins with the discovery of multiple mental illnesses in a Scottish family of 77 individuals and continues by tracing the early history of psychiatric genetics. With chapter 6 we move into the twentieth century with accounts of two child psychiatrists on two continents, both taking credit for the discovery of autism. The next four chapters (numbers 8–11) describe the discovery of new treatments: the dramatic introduction of electroconvulsive therapy, John Cade's single-handed discovery of lithium as a treatment for mania, and the chemical tinkering that produced the first effective treatments for schizophrenia and mania.

Modern neuroscientific findings in four key areas of research are described next. Chapters 12 and 13 focus on defects that constitute endophenotypes for one or another of the major mental illnesses, that is, biomarkers that lie intermediate between genes and symptoms. You will learn about the loss of gray matter in the brain, eye movement abnormalities and leaky nerve cell axons. Chapter 14 considers the role of memory in mental illness and discusses experiments in which harmful memories are either modified or removed. The final chapter is somewhat different in that it is about discoveries that bring into question traditional methods for diagnosing mental illnesses.

The reader will note a variety of story lines. Not every discovery arrives in a flash of lightning accompanied by a shout of joy. The discoveries of lithium therapy for mania and chlorpromazine for schizophrenia come closest to that romantic ideal, but the majority of discoveries featured here required years of effort. A few were made by individuals working alone (transcranial electrical stimulation, diffusion magnetic resonance imaging). The rest came from cooperative work by multiple investigators, often when in competition with other equally motivated teams. And finally, there is room in this book for discoveries (X-rays, insulin shock therapy) made through pure serendipity, defined as a chance event that carries unforeseen significance.

The Perspective sections at the end of each chapter go beyond the factual accounts to provide updates, additional interpretations and opinionated commentary. Each chapter also contains a short list of suggested readings.

1 Kindness

Kindness toward people with mental illness was not discovered at any particular moment, but rather around the year 1800. Even so, it happened almost simultaneously in London and Paris. To be clear, that was when *institutions* first acknowledged kindness, for there must have been at least some kind caretakers from the start. We assume that to be true even though we know very little about the care of mentally ill persons in earlier times.

Most people with mental disorders were kept at home, but others were outcast and occasionally brutalized. In the middle ages, some communities resorted to chaining troublesome individuals to posts. People were thought to be possessed by the devil if they acted strangely and had hallucinations. Church records from the fifteenth century tell of women claiming to have been transported over vast distances at night. Heinrich Kramer, a Catholic clergyman, explained the origin of the phenomenon, 'The art of riding abroad may be merely illusory, since the devil has extraordinary power over the minds of those who have given themselves up to him, so that what they do in pure imagination, they believe they have actually and really done in the body.'[1] Acting on this line of thinking, women who admitted to 'riding abroad' were accused of witchcraft and, when found guilty, condemned to death. They were usually tied to a stake and burned.

As cities grew in size and density, concerns arose over public security, so places were set aside as refuges for persons considered suspicious or dangerous. Perhaps the first such institution was the Priory of Saint Mary of Bethlehem in London. Founded in 1247, it initially served all manner of misfits, be they sick, wounded, deranged or simply poor. Gradually, over centuries, it became increasingly specialized in caring for the insane. Even as witchcraft and their attendant punishments were sweeping across Europe, the small Priory in London offered safe housing for the insane. The name Bethlem gradually morphed into Bedlam, and while bedlam was a verbal corruption, not a true name of anything, it became associated with

---

[1] Heinrich Kramer and James Sprenger, *Malleus Maleficarum (The Hammer of Witches)*. First published in 1486. Translation by Montague Summers, 1928. Quote in Part I, Question I.

madness, chaos and irrationality. Moved three times, the Priory first established in 1247 is today operating as the Bethlem Royal Hospital located in South London.

Let's take a look at the Bethlem hospital around the year 1800, at the time when kindness was just beginning to root in Britain. The hospital building, then located at Moorfields just north of London, was in such a state of physical dilapidation that wealthy citizens had begun collecting funds for a new building. Built on rubble, the walls were buckling, the roof was leaking and the whole place reeked of (mostly) human filth. A sense of what occurred at Bethlem and at similar asylums in England can be gleaned from historical documents such as the 'Report from Committee on Madness', submitted to the British House of Commons in 1815. The picture that emerges is one of unkindness bordering at times on outright brutality. However, we should not assume that the caretakers were inherently evil or sadistic. They were mostly uneducated, underprivileged men desperate for work. One can understand that they might have occasionally vent their frustrations, given that they had been placed in a situation where there were far too many patients, very few workers and no real prospects of recovery.

Consider also the lack of sanitation. On the very first page of the government report, George Higgins describes his experience upon visiting the York Lunatic Asylum, where Higgins himself was a governor. 'When the door was opened ... I found four cells of about eight feet square, in a very horrid and filthy situation; the straw appeared to be almost saturated with urine and excrement ... the walls were daubed with excrement; the air holes, of which there [was] one in each cell, were partly filled with it; in one cell there were two pewter chamber-pots loose.'[2] Another witness was George Wallet, the steward at Bethlem. He described the smells in the infirmary as 'very offensive'. Asked if the odor came from the sewers, he replied that it 'proceeded more from dirty patients.'[3]

All types of patients were thrown in together. Mild cases were mixed with severe cases, calm patients with excited patients, young with old. There are documented examples of epileptics, demented elders, intellectually handicapped and psychotic persons all occupying the same hospital unit. The mental patients were never formally diagnosed, but they would have been described as either melancholic or manic, these being the two grand categories of mental illness commonly acknowledged since ancient

---

[2] House of Commons, *First Report from the Select Committee on Madhouses* (1815), p. 1.
[3] Ibid, pp. 36, 37.

Grecian times. Early in the seventeenth century, the Oxford cleric Robert Burton said of melancholic persons, 'I think I may truly conclude that they are not always sad and fearful, but usually so ... Some are afraid that heaven will fall on their heads; some afraid they are damned, or shall be.'[4] Thus, melancholia implied depression, but also delusions and anxiety. Mania meant extreme excitement and delusions. In common parlance toward the end of the eighteenth century, all patients, whether melancholic or manic, were simply 'mad'.

Sculpture depicting 'Melancholy' (left) and 'Raving Madness' (right), at Bethlem Hospital. Engraving by C. Warren, 1805 [Wellcome Library]

Patients who were highly excited, violent or dangerous posed a special problem because, at the Bethlem hospital, there were just 4 caretakers looking after 120 patients. Under the circumstances, caretakers routinely resorted to mechanical restraint by means of chains, wrist manacles, leg manacles and straitjackets. One outrageous use of these devices came to light in 1814 when Edward Wakefield, a real estate agent from the city of York, managed to inspect the Bethlem hospital at Moorfields. There he found a patient, aged 55, who had been held at the hospital for fourteen years. Wakefield described what he saw,

---

[4] Robert Burton, *The Anatomy of Melancholy. Quote from Edward Shorter, A Historical Dictionary of Psychiatry.* New York: Oxford University Press (2005), p. 175.

WILLIAM NORRIS:

Confined in this Manner in Bethlem Hospital

Handout publicizing harsh treatment of James Norris [G. Arnald, artist]

A stout iron ring was riveted about his neck, from which a short chain passed to a ring made to slide upwards and downwards on an upright massive iron bar, more than six feet high, inserted into the wall. Round his body a strong iron bar about two inches wide was riveted; on each side of the bar was a circular projection, which being fashioned to and enclosing each of his arms, pinioned them close to his sides. This waist bar was secured by two similar iron bars which, passing over his shoulders, were riveted to the waist both before and behind. The iron ring about his neck was connected to the bars on his shoulders by a double link. From each of these bars another short chain passed to the ring on the upright iron bar.[5]

The patient's name was James Norris, an American who had been sent to Bethlem by the Office for Sick and Wounded Seamen. Various reports differ

---

[5] Jonathan Andrews et al. (1997), p. 424. See suggested readings.

with respect to the length of time that he was restrained in the described manner, but it was somewhere between nine and twelve years. Norris's case may have been exceptional in that no other patient was so heavily restrained for so long, but it shows the lengths to which the hospital would go in managing difficult patients.

Bethlem Hospital aimed to cure its patients, and many were discharged, but few if any were actually cured. Even the treatments were unkind. Probably the most common treatment was the cold water bath, used for centuries on the idea that it slowed the delivery of blood to the brain. Patients were immersed in cold water twice weekly from July to the onset of winter. In some cases, the water spilled down onto the patient from a spout placed a meter or so above the patient's head.

A second type of treatment was adapted from ancient practices going back at least as far as Hippocrates in the fourth century B.C. Hippocrates stated that madness is caused by poisonous substances circulating within the brain. In his time and later, physicians devised various methods for ridding the body of such substances. At Bethlem, the methods of choice were bloodletting, induced vomiting and diarrhea. The goal was chemical purification, but the experience itself was hellish. Thomas Monro, the sole physician at Bethlem, described the practice,

> In the months of May, June, July, August and September, we generally administer medicines; we do not in the winter season, because the house is so excessively cold that it is not thought proper ... We apply generally bleeding, purging and vomit; those are the general remedies we apply ... all the patients who require bleeding are generally bled on a particular day, and they are purged on a particular day ... after they have been bled they take vomits once a week for a certain number of weeks, after that we purge the patients.[6]

If the House of Commons ordered a survey of British madhouses, its parliamentarians must have already known that all was not right in those institutions. Among the numerous witnesses who confirmed their suspicions was the aforementioned Edward Wakefield who reported on the iron-clad patient, James Norris. The committee minutes list Wakefield as a 'land agent', but he was also an active member of the Quaker community. He and a small group of friends were battling to reform Britain's prisons and mental asylums. After encountering patient James Norris at Bethlem, Wakefield hired

---

[6] David Russell, *Scenes from Bedlam*. London: Harcourt Brace (1997), p. 64.

an artist to accompany him on a subsequent visit so that the artist could draw a portrait of Norris. Taking full advantage of the opportunity made possible by the intervention, Wakefield and his fellow reformers printed copies of the portrait and distributed them in public places (illustration, p. 13).

As part of his testimony before the parliamentary committee, Wakefield remarked, 'At this time there are Quakers who are neither medical men or of any professional class who are conspicuous for the extraordinary treatment of insane persons, by the attention and kindness which they pay to them.'[7] He was speaking of a new type of mental asylum, recently opened in the city of York. We will examine why Wakefield thought the treatments at York were 'extraordinary', and how kindness played into all of that. But we begin with how the Quakers came to be involved in caring for mental patients.

The men who started the York asylum knew about the conditions at Bethlem and other asylums. They understood why the institutional managers saw safekeeping as their chief mandate. Even though the managers paid lip to the possibility of cures, in reality they had no treatment that could deliver on the promise. Besides, the managers had responsibilities unrelated to treatments, such as supervising visitations. As late as 1770, the general public was allowed into the Bethlem hospital—after paying an entrance fee—to view a kind of freak show featuring the miserable patients and their mad behaviors. The zoo-like nature of these exhibitions left visitors with the impression that mental patients are less than human. Underlying that attitude were beliefs equating madness with corrupted souls and moral depravity. At any rate, mad persons were rarely considered ill. At best, they were annoying and troublesome; at worse, dangerous. There was little that could be done apart from preventing them from doing harm to themselves or others. In other words, safekeeping.

Attitudes began to change in the eighteenth century. It was the era of the enlightenment, led in Europe by the likes of Voltaire, René Descartes, David Hume, and Immanuel Kant. Across the Atlantic, Benjamin Franklin and Thomas Jefferson led the charge. As authoritarian and morality-based attitudes came under fire, the emphasis shifted toward rational, scientific ways of thinking. Consequently, at the turn of the century, madness was no longer seen as moral failure, even if it was not yet an illness. Many observers equated madness with the loss of reason. In the words of the French intellectual Blaise Pascal, 'I can well conceive of a man without

---

[7] *First Report from the Select Committee on Madhouses* (1815), p. 24.

Portrait of a madman [Charles Bell, 1806]

hands, feet, head ... But I cannot conceive man without thought; he would be a stone or a brute.'[8] John Monro, the physician at Bethlem in the latter half of the eighteenth century, wrote that madness is 'a total suspension of every rational faculty.'[9] At this time also, the philosopher John Locke was explaining how humans acquire knowledge by associating ideas. It was easy to imagine how madness could arise from a faulty association of ideas.

These intellectual developments had practical consequences, one of which was the founding of a second mental hospital in London, named the St. Luke's Hospital for Lunatics. Led by its enlightened chief physician, William Battie, St. Luke's quickly became the progressive counterpart to Bethlem. Battie insisted that 'madness is, contrary to the opinion of some unthinking persons, as manageable as many other distempers, which are equally dreadful and obstinate, and yet are not looked upon as incurable: and that

---

[8] Blaise Pascal, *Pensées* (1669).
[9] John Monro, *Remarks on Dr. Battle's Treatise on Madness.* London: Clarke (1758).

such unhappy objects ought by no means to be abandoned, much less shut up in loathsome prisons as criminals or nuisances to society.'[10]

Hospital custodians gradually discarded their harsh (and useless) physical treatments in favor of psychological approaches. After all, if madness was due to the absence of reason or the incorrect association of ideas, perhaps it could be overcome by ignoring the patient's poisoned fluids and focusing instead on his or her mind. Mental manipulation became the new treatment of choice.

Physicians experimented with various techniques, including intimidation. Intended as a means of encouraging compliance to rules, intimidation was easily administered and sometimes successful. When patients failed to behave as they were told, the doctors attempted to 'tame' them. In some cases this meant staring straight into the patient's eyes for many long minutes without saying a word. Benjamin Rush, a renowned American physician, recommended a technique that he borrowed from the management of horses in England. He made his patients stand all day on their feet. In the hands of other doctors, intimidation required physical blows.

In the midst of these developments, a new mental asylum opened its doors at York in northeast England. Intentions notwithstanding, conditions at this asylum did not live up to expectations. Inside the grandiose structure, patients lived in squalor and many were beaten or underfed. When suspicions arose following the unexplained death of a patient who happened to be a member of the Quaker Church, the local Quaker community reacted. In 1796, it founded its own asylum, named The Retreat (later the York Retreat). It was an early example of the many philanthropic and humanitarian ventures for which the Quakers later became famous.

George Fox and friends founded the Society of Friends in 1650 as an alternative to the Church of England. Its members were called Quakers because they 'trembled at the word of the Lord.' They had no ordained clergy because everyone had direct access to God. Their practices were simple, in line with contemporary attitudes during the Age of Reason. Although the group initially attracted mostly English and Welch adherents, its teachings were admired by the French philosopher Voltaire, and it successfully spread to North America despite early persecutions. William Tuke, a Quaker and local tea merchant, proposed the original plan for the new asylum at York. Beside raising funds and overseeing construction, he also gave voice to the moral principles that were to underlie practices at The Retreat. William Tuke was the first head of the asylum. After him, three later generations of

---

[10] William Battie, *A Treatise on Madness*. London: J. Whiston and B. White (1758).

William Tuke [Wellcome Collection]

Tuke men assumed the position. William's great-grandson told of the decisive event that led to the creation of the asylum. It happened while William was visiting St. Luke's Hospital in London, then the second largest mental institution in England. There, he encountered 'a young woman, whose condition especially arrested his attention, and excited his compassion. She was without clothing, and lay in some loose, dirty straw, chained to the wall.' William was saddened and dumbfounded. Yes, he thought, some unruly patients need to be restrained, and the caretakers' work is stressful, but why abuse the patients? The patients, he concluded, were 'miserably coerced not from intentional cruelty, but from a conviction of the superiority of such a course of treatment over any other.' William's grandson further remarks, 'The form of this unhappy patient haunted him afterwards, and redoubled his exertions, until his plans were carried into practical effect.'[11] And so it was that kindness was discovered though charitable work at a local asylum, aided and abetted by religious faith.

---

[11] D.H. Tuke, 'William Tuke, the founder of the York Retreat.' *Journal of Psychological Medicine and Mental Pathology* 8:507–512 (1855). All quotes are those of D.H. Tuke, p. 509.

The Retreat at York [Gemälde von Carve, c. 1796]

The Retreat was meant to be a quiet place where one could rest the mind, so it was designed—so far as practical—to resemble a home. In addition to the residence, it had a bakehouse, a brew-house and a laundry. There were beautiful gardens at the rear of the main structure and a few small farm buildings scattered around eleven acres of tranquil grounds. Still, concerns over security necessitated precautions. The bedroom doors, for example, were fitted with bolts, but the bolts were encased in leather so the attendants could close the doors at night without waking the patients. The glazed windows looked ordinary, but the wooden sashes had iron bars embedded within them, and the glass panes were so small that no patient could escape through them.

Unlike at Bethlem and similar institutions elsewhere in Britain, where custody and security were prioritized above all else, the York Retreat earnestly aimed for cures. The men and women running the Retreat blamed mental disturbance on life circumstances and bad decisions. They recognized that no good could possibly come from hurtful treatments, so they chose treatments based entirely on their likely efficacy. Instead of cold baths, they gave warm baths; instead of bloodletting and forced vomiting, they provided restful sleep and abundant food. Chains and beatings were prohibited. Only if a patient became violent, was he or she put in a straight-jacket or strapped to a specially constructed bed. Overlying all of this was a psychological approach for changing the patients' minds. Later known as 'moral therapy', it mixed religious idealism with Enlightenment philosophy and tempered the whole with common sense. Taken as a whole, these measures constituted a variety of kindness.

The Retreat encouraged change through the voluntary adoption of moral behaviors. Patients were told in no uncertain terms which behaviors were acceptable and which were not, and they were expected to act accordingly. Good behaviors were rewarded with praise and bad behaviors were criticized, but there was no corporal punishment. Caretakers confronted agitated patients with a show of force, and only when that did not work did they sometimes resort to mechanical constraints. Patients were told that they alone could curb incorrect behaviors, and they were encouraged to practice self-control. Initially designed and supervised by a lay member of the Quaker community, the treatment program was later directed by medical doctors.

According to the Quaker way of thinking, patients at The Retreat acted the way they did because they had not internalized rules of behavior. They should have done that in their youth, but apparently they had not. Implicitly, therefore, the patients were not yet fully adult. To correct the situation, the caretakers adopted the same forms of psychological manipulation used by parents in raising children. A visiting doctor from Switzerland surmised the strategy,

> They [Retreat staffers] do not consider them [the patients] as absolutely deprived of reason; or, in other words, as inaccessible to the motives of fear, hope, feeling and honor. It appears that they consider them rather as children ... Their punishments and rewards must be immediate, since that which is distant has no effect upon them ... Subject them first; encourage them afterwards, employ them, and render their employment agreeable by attractive means.[12]

We can flesh out the visitor's concluding sentence by noting that 'subject them' refers to verbal intimidation, and 'encourage them' refers to the caretakers' kindly manners, the occasional tea party and walks into neighboring villages. The 'employment' differed according to sex. For female patients,

---

[12] Samuel Tuke, *Description of the Retreat* (1813), p. 223.

Cutting the chains at La Salpêtrière [Tony Robert-Fleury, 1795]

it consisted of polishing furniture, assisting in the kitchen, churning butter and ironing. The men pumped water, chopped wood and cleaned shoes.

Historians disagree about the success of moral therapy at The Retreat. According to some, cure rates were higher there than at other psychiatric institutions, but given differences in patient characteristics, the various meanings of 'cure' and the incompleteness of records, the statistical evidence is shaky. Nevertheless, even without registering more cures, the care was certainly more humane. The Retreat still operates as a mental health facility. Although no longer in the hands of the Quakers, it seeks to 'reflect the tolerance, humanity and values of our Quaker roots.'[13]

While quiet prevailed at the modest retreat in York, a distinctive rattle could be heard within the prison-like confines of France's largest hospital, La Salpêtrière in Paris. It was the sound of chains being cut away from a female lunatic as fellow patients watched in dulled awe. The historically significant moment was recreated 80 years later in a famous painting that shows Dr. Philippe Pinel ordering the removal. If truth be known, however,

---

[13] https://www.theretreatyork.org.uk/about-us/

Pinel's assistant, Jean-Baptiste Pussin, cut the chains himself, on his own accord.

Whereas Philippe Pinel was then the chief physician at La Salpêtrière, his assistant was a former tanner with no medical training. Pinel and Pussin first met at the La Bicêtre Hospital, also in Paris. That hospital held about four thousand men, mostly petty criminals and pensioners but also several hundred mental patients. After landing there with a serious neck infection, Pussin enjoyed mingling with his fellow patients, and after recovering from his infection, he accepted an offer to work as a *concierge* (superintendent) at the same hospital. Pinel arrived at La Bicêtre in 1793 as 'physician of the infirmaries.' Two years later, he was appointed chief physician at La Salpêtrière, a hospital complex with approximately seven thousand female patients suffering from a variety of illnesses. The vast majority of the women were elderly and poor. Pinel took personal charge of an infirmary holding about 200 mental patients. In the beginning, he visited every patient once or more each day. Then, realizing that he could not continue at the same pace while also keeping up with his administrative responsibilities, he sought an assistant. Recalling Pussin's excellent work La Bicêtre, Pinel invited Pussin to join him at La Salpêtrière. His choice of Pussin is significant because it speaks to Pinel's grounded approach to psychiatry. In his famous textbook, Pinel explains why he so much admired men like Pussin who,

> strangers to medical principles, and only guided by sound judgment or some obscure tradition, have devoted themselves to the treatment of psychiatric patients. They have brought about the cure of a large number, either by playing for time, or forcing regular work on them, or by exercising gentleness or energetic discipline in a timely way ... The practice of constantly living in the midst of psychiatric patients, of studying their behaviour, their diverse characters, the objects of their pleasure or their dislikes, the advantage of following the course of their aberrations by day and night and in different seasons of the year, the art of controlling them and sparing them fits of anger and grumbling, the skill of adopting, at the right time, a tone of kindliness with them or an imposing air, and of subduing them by force when gentleness does not suffice ... must of necessity convey to intelligent and zealous men a great deal of knowledge and detailed insights ...[14]

---

[14] Philippe Pinel (1809, 2008), p. xxx. See suggested readings.

Pinel saw in Pussin the very qualities that he himself possessed or strove to emulate. Rather than disparaging Pussin for his lack of professional training, Pinel considered it a bonus, for Pinel was a revolutionary. He didn't actually participate in the French Revolution, but he was friendly with some of the men who did. With youthful experience as a writer, medical editor and naturalist, Pinel favored practical knowledge over the abstract learning flaunted by elite intellectuals. Pussin, in short, was Pinel's kind of man. In keeping with revolutionary custom, Pinel addressed his subordinate as Citizen Pussin.

Jean Baptiste Pussin (left) and Philippe Pinel [Wellcome Collection]

Pinel, encouraged by Pussin, gradually moved away from bloodletting, purgation, chaining and shackling. In the second edition of his textbook, published in 1809, he wrote that 'experience every day bears out the success achieved from consoling talks and the happy device of reawakening the patient's hope and gaining his confidence. But using bad treatments or restraint methods which are too harsh aggravates the illness and often makes it incurable.'

When dealing with difficult cases, Pinel supplemented kindness with psychological tactics. He advised physicians to 'subject them first; encourage them afterwards.'[15] These words, which Pinel quoted from the 'Bibliothèque britannique', may sound familiar to readers of this book, because they are the exact words used by the Swiss doctor in his report on the York

---

[15] Ibid., quotes on pp. 81, 82.

Retreat (quoted on page 22). Several remarkable cases recorded by Pinel illustrate the prescribed method.

One case involved a soldier who became violent at La Bicêtre.[16] The man was physically restrained because he was tearing things up and verbally attacking Pinel. Unexpectantly one morning, Pinel found the patient dramatically different. The man kissed Pinel's hand and reminded him, 'You promised me freedom inside the hospital if I remain calm. I call upon you to keep your word.' Speaking softly and with reassurance, Pinel released him from his restraints. Seven months later, the man left the hospital completely cured.

In other situations, Pinel resorted to a display of authority or a touch of terror. While not exactly kindly, these psychological tricks often worked with agitated patients, just as they did at the York Retreat. He and Pussin staged little make-believe shows designed to nudge a patient into a certain way of thinking. For example, a religious fanatic refused to eat his meals. One evening, Pussin and several hospital attendants surprised the patient in his room. The men were all carrying heavy chains, and they rattled them loudly, startling the patient. Pussin looked straight into the fellow's eyes and sternly warned him that he would face severe punishment if he did not eat his soup. Sure enough, the patient did eat his soup, he relented on his fast, and he regained his sanity.

Pinel also used theatrical shows to, in his words, 'combat and destroy' delusions. One patient, a watchmaker, was obsessed with perpetual motion machines. He also came to believe that his head had been removed by the guillotine, tossed into a pile and lost. In its place, the patient had been given a new, particularly ugly, head. To cure him, Pinel obtained the assistance of a convalescing fellow lunatic. This man began discussing with the watchmaker the miracle of Saint Denis, who supposedly picked up his decapitated head, kissed it and carried it to his burial place. 'How do you suppose Saint Denis kissed his own head?' asked the actor of the watchmaker. 'Do you think it was with his heels?' Before the clockmaker could respond, the actor burst out laughing. Sensitive to the ridicule, the clockmaker walked hurriedly away and never afterwards mentioned losing his head. He returned to his family 'in perfect health' and reopened his watchmaking business.[17]

---

[16] Pinel wrote about these cases while at La Salpêtrière, but they originate from La Bicêtre, hence the male patients.

[17] Philippe Pinel, *A Treatise on Insanity*. Translated by D.D. Davis, Sheffield England: W. Todd (1801, 1806), p. 72.

Another patient, a tailor, was convinced that his critical comments during the violent phase of the Revolution had led to his condemnation, and that he was facing death by guillotine. Pussin arranged for three physicians to approach him dressed in black suits like those worn by magistrates. Acting as though they were conducting a trial, the fake magistrates interrogated the patient about his opinions and his activities. Then, after briefly discussing his case, they formally declared him innocent. The tailor's symptoms disappeared almost immediately, but they later returned. Despite the dubious result in this particular case, Pinel claimed that the religious fanatic who refused to eat, as well as the watchmaker whose head had been replaced, were completely cured by a single theatrical stunt. Such results are hard to believe—given that these men were obviously psychotic—but who knows.

Seven years passed between the first and second editions Pinel's textbook. Notable in the latter is the addition of a lengthy section titled, 'Results of observations and construction of tables for determining the degree of probability of curing mentally ill patients.' Pinel considered it a scientific experiment, and he filled that part of the textbook with tables and statistics. The data relate to a period of four years during which 1004 women were admitted to Salpêtrière. Using hospital records, he calculated the cure rate for melancholy at 62%, and for mania 51%.

He also compared cure rates for patients who came to Salpêtrière from other institutions with rates for patients who came directly to Salpêtrière. In the former case (presumably long-term illnesses), the cure rate was 15%, whereas for patients not transferred from elsewhere (short-term illnesses), the cure rate was 93%. Ninety-three percent is an extraordinarily high rate of success relative to modern experience with psychotic illnesses, but like the results claimed for the York Retreat, they must be taken with a large grain of salt. First, it is impossible to know just how sick were the patients when first admitted, and second, Pinel does not explain what he means by 'cured'. Since his experiment rested entirely on written notes of admissions and releases, he probably understood patients to be cured if they were released from the hospital, but the records themselves belie the definition, because 16% of the 'cured' patients were re-admitted during the 4-year period covered by the investigation.

Clearly, Philippe Pinel's methods in Paris had a lot in common with those employed by the Tukes at York. The type of treatment dispensed at La Salpêtrière came to be known as *traitement moral*—close to the 'moral treatment' practiced at York—but the linguist equivalence is less than it appears. The Quakers in York understood 'moral' in the same way as English speakers understand the word today, referring to right and wrong. For nineteenth century French psychiatrists, however, *traitement moral* had a broader, more nuanced meaning. While incorporating ethical principles in the Quaker sense, the French term referred specifically to treatments that appealed to the patient's thoughts and emotions, as opposed to treatments directed at the body.

Given the similarity of therapeutic methods in York and Paris, and because the two strategies were developed at roughly the same time, one could easily imagine the innovators sharing ideas across the English Channel. However, the only evidence in support of the supposition is Pinel's quotation from the Swiss doctor's report, which occurs in the second edition of his textbook (1809), but not in the first edition (1801) when he was already practicing *traitement moral*. It is possible, therefore, that kindness was discovered independently in York and Paris.

Perspective

Kindness is an unusual type of discovery, yet in some respects it resembles familiar scientific discoveries. Like the hypotheses that generate scientific experiments, the principle of kind treatment grew from intuitions grasped by two creative individuals. It was a solution to a vexing problem, how to deal with large numbers of incurable and occasionally unmanageable patients. Also as in science, kindness underwent a trial phase—an experimental phase, if you will—during which key data were recorded. As results accumulated and were analyzed, the methods were revised accordingly. We can question the accuracy of those data, but not the scientific intent of either William Tuke or Philippe Pinel.

Everyone would agree that kindness is better than humiliation and brutality, but kindness is not simply a matter of ethics. It actually improved the mental health of patients, and this fact alone forever changed the practice of psychiatry. Moral treatment did not completely stop inhumane practices, but it did establish a standard of treatment that has been widely—practically universally—adopted.

Moral treatment was wholly different from earlier treatment methods (baths, bloodletting and purgatives) because it was psychological rather than physical. In this respect, moral treatment paved the way for psychotherapy, currently the most widely practiced therapeutic method in psychiatry apart from drugs. The Tukes and Philippe Pinel appreciated the unique problems besetting each patient. It was the individual with his or her life history and present circumstances that mattered, not some abstract notion of mental disorder. These men found their patients' stories interesting, and Pinel in particular succeeded in making them interesting for his readers as well. Pinel custom-made his theatrical shows for specific individuals. The Tukes allowed each patient to choose the work that he or she preferred and the recreations that suited his or her interests. The end result of these measures was therapies tailored to individual patients, but the process depended on the doctor gaining insights into the patient's needs, and this drew them into meaningful conversations. It was the same strategy ultimately adopted by present day psychotherapists.

Suggested readings

Jonathan Andrews et al., *The History of Bethlem.* London: Routledge (1997).

Anne Digby, *Madness, Morality, and Medicine: A Study of the York Retreat, 1796– 1914.* New York: Cambridge University Press (1985).

Ayisha A. Kibria and Neil H. Metcalfe, 'A biography of William Tuke (1732– 1822): Founder of the modern mental asylum.' *Journal of Medical Biography* 24:383–388 (2014).

Philippe Pinel, *Medico-Philosophical Treatise on Mental Alienation.* Second edition, translated by Gordon Hickish, David Healy and Louis C. Charland, Chichester UK: John Wiley & Sons (1809, 2008).

2 Cobwebs on the brain

We call them mental illnesses, but equally, they are brain illnesses because the brain generates the mind. *How* the brain generates the mind is a thorny, unsolved problem that is of no immediate concern to psychiatry. But what goes wrong in the brains of mental ill patients is crucial for designing physical treatments, whether they be pharmaceutical or electrical. Thus, the search for brain correlates, or biomarkers, of mental illness is a central theme in the history of psychiatry. The first significant finding was made by a young French doctor working in suburban Paris at an asylum not far from Philippe Pinel's hospital. His discovery followed a long line of speculation.

The ancients knew that inside the head there lies a bulky, wrinkled structure. They knew, too, that people behave oddly after suffering a blow to the head. Some cannot speak properly, others have trouble walking or remembering things. And, the ancients knew about epilepsy. In the time of Hippocrates, around 400 B.C., it was the 'sacred disease'. Most people thought that it had a supernatural, or divine, origin. One author—possibly Hippocrates himself— contested that opinion. In a work titled, 'On the Sacred Disease,' the author wrote,

> Men ought to know that from nothing else but the brain come joys, delights, laughter and sports, and sorrows, griefs, despondency, and lamentations. And by this, in an especial manner, we acquire wisdom and knowledge, and see and hear, and know what are foul and what are fair, what are bad and what are good, what are sweet, and what unsavory.[18]

Hippocrates went even further in his account of the brain by specifically addressing not only the sacred disease, but other illnesses now said to be mental,

> And by same organ [the brain] we become mad and delirious, and fears and terrors assail us, some by night, and some by

---

[18] Translation by Francis Adams. http://classics.mit.edu/Hippocrates/sacred.html

day, and dreams and untimely wanderings, and cares that are not suitable, and ignorance of present circumstances, desuetude, and unskillfulness. All these things we endure from the brain, when it is not healthy ...

Hippocrates blamed excessive levels of certain biological substances—humors—as the causal agents. Each humor creates its own set of symptoms, and each acts through a different mechanism,

> [T]he depravement of the brain arises from phlegm and bile, either of which you may recognize in this manner: Those who are mad from phlegm are quiet, and do not cry out nor make a noise; but those from bile are vociferous, malignant, and will not be quiet, but are always doing something improper. If the madness be constant, these are the causes thereof. But if terrors and fears assail, they are connected with derangement of the brain, and derangement is owing to its being heated ... He is grieved and troubled when the brain is unseasonably cooled and contracted beyond its wont. This it suffers from phlegm, and from the same affection the patient becomes oblivious.

Leaving aside such details as phlegm, bile and brain temperature, the overall intent of the argument has a modern flavor. It is specific in its identification of causes and plausible in its description of mechanisms. The only problem: no proof. It would be another two thousand years before writers proposed alternatives to the humoral model of insanity, and even then, the ideas were based on the claims of a physician, Galen, who lived 1500 years earlier. Galen believed that brain fibers (nerves) are filled with 'animal spirits', a kind of ethereal gas. Even as late as the seventeenth century, physicians held to the belief that muscle contractions and sensory experiences are triggered by messages carried by animal spirits. Thus, the French theologian and philosopher Nicholas Malebranche proposed that hallucinations, a common symptom of psychosis, are caused by exceptional agitation of animal spirits. In a similar vein, the English doctor Thomas Willis wrote that mental illness is the result of brain damage that follows from tiny internal explosions.

At the turn of the nineteenth century, when psychiatry was waking up to the advantages of kindness, knowledge of the brain had hardly progressed from the days of Malebranche and Willis, which is to say, doctors still knew very little. Although there were a few microscopes around, they were not very powerful. The smallest biological objects brought to the human eye were the walls of certain plant cells, and no one had yet looked at a nerve cell. Few doctors accepted Aristotle's teaching that rational thought comes from the heart, but some clung to the fantasy of animal spirits.

Even if the majority of physicians assumed that the brain is somehow implicated in madness, they saw no signs of abnormality. The spirits were not visible. And besides, many prominent physicians, including Philippe Pinel, attributed brain-related mental disorders to diseases elsewhere in the body. Pinel told his students that mania originates in the stomach or the intestine, and spreads from there to the brain. For the most part, however, Pinel did not concern himself with biological mechanisms. For him, these mysteries were unhelpful in the practical business of diagnosis and treatment. He diagnosed patients entirely from observation of their symptoms, and his treatments—apart from baths—were psychological. If a woman was excited, delusionary and disoriented, she suffered from mania and was given a bath, preferably very cold. If, on the other hand, she was sullen and inactive, she was diagnosed as melancholic and given moral therapy.

Interest in the brain picked up in the second decade of the nineteenth century. However, the research that drew the most public attention involved a false claim. It was said that the barely perceptible bumps on the skull are due to local swellings in the underlying brain, and every bump—depending on its location— indicates a particular personality trait. A bump here meant that you have deep religious beliefs, a bump there meant that you love money. It could imply a heightened sense of smell or a tendency for violence. From this fantasy grew the pseudo-science of phrenology. By the time they finished, the phrenologists had mapped out nearly forty bumps representing an equal number of personality traits. It became big business for physicians, psychiatrists and outright fraudsters, all seeking to cash in on brain 'science'.

A few men with brighter minds and better technical skills challenged the phrenologists' claims. One was an Italian named Luigi Rolando whose anatomical investigations showed that the phrenologists' bumps are simply places of intersecting sulci,[19] and the size and position of the sulci does not differ between brains. In France, a French doctor named Jean Pierre Flourens conducted experiments to answer the question whether different

---

[19] A sulcus is a normally occurring groove in the cerebral cortex. Collectively, sulci have the effect of expanding the surface area of the brain, thus allowing for additional neuronal circuits.

parts of the brain have different functions. After brutally removing the cerebral hemispheres in living rabbits, he found that the animals could no longer see or hear, nor move their limbs. Removal of the cerebellum caused them to stumble and fall down. Together, the pioneering studies of Rolando and Flourens destroyed phrenology, while also putting to rest Aristotle's contention that the brain is nothing but an organ for cooling the blood.

Not before the second decade of the nineteenth century were researchers able to examine in any detail the interior of the brain. While living brains have the look and feel of tofu, dead brains left untreated quickly turn to mush, rendering them useless for anatomical observations. It was a big problem for anatomists until Johann Christian Reil discovered a method for hardening the brain. He began by immersing it in alcohol for a few days. Next, he put it into a solution of potash (a mixture potassium-containing compounds) for several more days, then back into alcohol. This simple innovation had enormous consequences because it allowed anatomists to slice the brain into thin sections, which in turn enabled examinations aided by the microscope. As it happens, Johann Christian Reil, the brain anatomist, was also Dr. Reil, the psychiatrist. In fact, you might say that Reil was the *first* psychiatrist, because he coined the word 'psychiatry'.

It was around this time that a young physician by the name of Antoine Laurent Jessé Bayle took a job at an insane asylum on the southeastern edge of Paris. Founded by a friend of King Louis XIII in 1641, the *Maison Royale de Charenton* was much smaller than either La Bicêtre or La Salpêtrière, but like them it had a long history. Soon after its opening, it was taken over by a religious group, the Order of Saint-Jean-de-Dieu. In the beginning, it served as both a hospice for poor mental patients and a prison. Persons deemed to be a threat to public security—or simply troublesome—received a *lettre de cachet* directly from the king informing them that they would be confined to the *Maison Royale*. There was no trial nor any opportunity to appeal. Conditions at Charenton were squalid, and restraints such as shackles, chains and lockups were commonly employed. Revolutionaries closed down the asylum in 1794, but it reopened two years later as *La Maison de Charenton* (no longer *Royale*), now under the auspices of the civil government.

Antoine Bayle made one of the great discoveries in the history of psychiatry while working at Charenton, yet the asylum is best known for its notorious patient, Donatien Alphonse François, Marquis de Sade, who was incarcerated at Charenton four years prior to Bayle's arrival. Sade was a wealthy nobleman who lived a tumultuous life. Best known as an author, he wrote novels, philosophical essays and plays, each of which was in some measure revolutionary, libertarian, violent and pornographic. Although most of these works wound up either burnt or banned, our contemporary word 'sadism' speaks to the Marquis' lasting influence.

First imprisoned in 1763 for mistreating prostitutes, Sade eventually spent a total of thirty-two years (excluding short periods of freedom) in a variety of prisons and insane asylums. His tenure at Charenton began after he published two particularly outrageous works, *Justine* and *Juliette.* Napoleon ordered his arrest, and Sade, faced with the prospect of long-term imprisonment, agreed to a declaration of insanity. Also, as part of the agreement, Sade's family committed to paying his *pension* (room and board) at Charenton. He remained at Charenton for twelve years. During most of that time, he lived fairly comfortably with his long-time female companion. He also had an intimate relationship with a chambermaid—14 years old when it began—that continued almost to his death.

As for Antoine Bayle, he arrived at Charenton as a medical intern. Going to Charenton immediately after his medical schooling was a curious decision, given that he had no experience in psychiatry. He may have needed a job, any job, but he may also have had a plan. Bayle's uncle and Bayle's professor in Paris were both scientifically inclined physicians. Contrary to the opinion of many other physicians, they believed that autopsies held the key to understanding diseases. As testament to that conviction, the uncle, who specialized in tuberculosis, performed 900 post-mortem dissections throughout his career, all at a single Parisian hospital. It must surely have crossed Antoine's mind that something might be learned of madness by examining the brains of deceased patients.

Human dissections were already an essential part of medical training in England, and interest in the procedure was spreading rapidly across Europe. Since the methods for preserving bodies after death were woefully inadequate, the supply fell well short of the demand. The situation became so dire that a black market in cadavers arose, based on grave robbing and body snatching. There were even reports of murders being committed for the purpose of obtaining autopsy material. In France as in England, the best source for bodies was at hospitals and asylums, *but only for insiders.* Having correctly sized up the situation, Antoine Bayle began doing dissections almost immediately upon arriving at Charenton.

Bayle took up his position at Charenton in 1818 at the age of nineteen years. He soon became aware of strained relations between its director,

Antoine Bayle

François-Simonet de Coulmiers, and its chief physician, Antoine Royer-Collard. De Coulmiers was a former priest in the Catholic church with no medical training. He saw madness as basically a psychological problem. He had little interest in brain abnormalities or physical treatments, renounced all forms of restraint, and practiced moral therapy. Somewhat as Pinel had done in Paris, De Coulmiers encouraged artistic expression in the form of theatre, and he found a willing participant in the Marquis de Sade, who promptly wrote several new plays and staged them within the walls of the asylum. Sade's fellow patients performed the parts, while other patients and invited guests watched.

Royer-Collard was entirely different. Having recently completed his medical training in Paris, he wanted to install a modern, medically oriented regime at Charenton. Given their different priorities, it was inevitable that Royer-Collard and de Coulmiers would clash. A typical dispute concerned how much information they would enter into patient records. Should the records contain a complete history of the patient's illness, his social and financial status, the effects of different treatments, and details pertaining to family members—as Royer-Collard demanded—or should they contain little more than the patient's name, birthdate and diagnosis—as de Coulmiers preferred? In essence, it was a power struggle between a lay administrator and his chief medical officer. A sheet of paper found in the institution's archive suggests what was at stake. It contains Royer-Collard's notes for a letter intended for François-Simonet de Coulmiers, but evidently never delivered. The following passage is telling,

> It is to me and not to you that the patients are entrusted for everything concerning their malady and its treatment ... As for you, you are charged with furnishing [them] with food, bedding, laundry and blankets, with insuring that the measures ... prescribed by the chief physician are executed.[20]

More concerning for Antoine Bayle was the disagreement between de Coulmiers and Royer-Collard in regard to autopsies. True to their backgrounds, de Coulmiers opposed them on moral grounds, while Royer-Collard saw them as potentially useful. Fortunately for Bayle, the line of his command came from the doctor, not the administrator. So, taking comfort in Royer-Collard's encouragement, he proceeded with his plan.

Never having worked at a psychiatric institution prior to Charenton, Bayle could hardly believe some of the patients. But could anyone, really, believe a man who insists that he is Napoleon Bonaparte (unless, of course, he actually *is* Napoleon)? At Charenton there were several Napoleons. You may wonder what transpired when two or more of these patients, all identifying as Napoleon, met in the courtyard. For an answer, you could turn to a study conducted at Michigan's Ypsilanti State Hospital in the 1950s, where a similar situation existed. There, three men all claimed to be Jesus Christ. A psychologist, eager to see how what would happen, arranged for the men to live together. The researcher watched and listened for two years before concluding that none of the men had changed his heartfelt identity.

Patients with demonstrably false beliefs about themselves often imagine that they are amazing characters, so-called delusions of grandeur. Antoine Bayle found a conspicuous cluster of patients at Charenton with delusions of this type. These patients claimed extraordinary social powers and outrageous wealth. And, in addition to the striking evidence of mental derangement, they had physical problems. They had difficulty in speaking, their gaits were unsteady, and they were prone to emotional extremes. Doctors noticed a progression of symptoms. In the beginning, the symptoms were primarily physical and manifested as a partial paralysis. Later, the psychological symptoms worsened and became manifested with delusions, restlessness and sometimes uncontrollable violence. In the final stage, the patients

---

[20] Jan Ellen Goldstein (1987), p. 116, note 173. See suggested readings.

were almost totally paralyzed and demented. They could no longer walk or speak intelligibly. It was this group of late-stage patients that Bayle chose to study.

Fortunately for us, Bayle kept notes on every one of his 1453 patients. At one point, he divided the lot into patients who had, or did not have, the symptoms described above. Among women, 25 of 606 patients (4%) fit the profile, whereas among men it was 189 of 847 patients (22%). Males were clearly more at risk. There was not yet a name for the syndrome, so Bayle called it *aliénation ambitieuse avec paralysie incomplète*, or ambitious alienation with partial paralysis. To unpack this, we need to understand that *aliénation* meant insanity in nineteenth century France. Patients were seen as alienated from normal society. The qualification 'ambitious' was meant to imply the severity of the illness. And, by joining insanity *with* partial paralysis, Bayle emphasized the fact that the two features occur concurrently. This last point put Bayle at odds with other psychiatrists, who thought there was a progression from partial paralysis to insanity. Later, the illness came to be known by other names, for reasons to be explained.

Although Bayle had no preconceived idea about what he would find in the brain, he was determined to look. He probably had not heard about Johann Christian Reil's method for hardening the brain, and even if he had, he himself lacked the technical wherewithal to prepare slices for microscopic examination. Consequently, he relied solely on gross examinations (pun intended). Ideally, he would have performed all the autopsies immediately after death, but it wasn't always possible. He could tell by the color of the corpse how long it had been lying unattended. If ashen-colored, it was fresh; if blue at the hands and feet, it was at least twelve hours old. Longer periods brought first a green tint, later black. Bodies begin to decompose immediately after death due bacterial consumption. The process produces vast amounts of hydrogen sulfide and methane gases which rapidly inflate the stomach. Eventually, the stomach wall ruptures, and the gases spread into the thighs and across the chest. The tongue protrudes, dripping lung fluids. The eyes bulge and pop out of their sockets. And everywhere, the horrible, putrid odor of a decaying body. Bayle may have used alcohol or mercury to slow the petrification process, but more likely he simply put up with it. Unable to look at the delicate nervous elements *inside* the brain—because they quickly turned to mush—he focused on what he could see just *outside* the brain, that is, in the brain's coverings.

One of the first autopsies was done on the body of a lemonade seller named Claude-Francois L. From Bayle's notes we know that Claude-Francois 'had drunk excessively and indulged immoderately in the pleasures of venery [sexual indulgence]." When first observed at Charenton, "He is the Emperor Napoleon, he has immense wealth; forty thousand barrels of gold ... Ordinarily calm, he is sometimes extremely excited, and even violent if he is opposed. He speaks with great difficulty and walks with a staggering gait. He does not sleep; he eats well, and his legs are slightly edematous [swollen with water].' A few months later, 'There is a general paleness and flaccidity; sensations are obtuse, and no attention is paid to objects around him ... No matter what he is asked, he replies that he is the emperor, that his two sons are emperors, that they live at the Tuileries, that he has millions and still more millions and that his wife has three *croix d'honneur*.'[21]

Bayle used a sharp blade to cut him open. 'The body was extremely thin; the legs and feet were infiltrated, and there were scabs on various parts of the body.' Within the chest, however, 'all the organs are healthy.' Similarly, with the abdominal cavity, 'The gastric mucus membrane is thickened, rough and crying under the instrument [*criant sous l'instrument*]. Other organs are healthy.'

Bayle turned to the head. He shaved off the hair, then turned a trepan to cut a hole in the skull. He cut three holes, positioning each so as to form a triangle. Then he cut lines between the holes and lifted the triangular piece from the rest of the skull. Gazing into the gap, he saw not the brain per se, but a thick fibrous membrane, the dura mater (Latin, 'tough mother'). He peeled away the dura mater to expose another layer of connective tissue, this the arachnoid mater, a structure thinner and more delicate than the dura mater. It is named the 'arachnoid' in recognition of its resemblance to the wispy, thread-like arrangement of a spider web (scientific class, Arachnida). Bringing a lamp close to the cadaver, Bayle peered through the semi-transparent arachnoid mater to view the grey brain beneath. It was tightly wrapped in yet another membrane, the translucent pia mater ('tender mother'). Collectively, the three membranes—known as the meninges—protect the brain from injurious movements, aid in the dis-

---

[21] Quotations from Bayle's thesis, 'Recherches sur l'arachnitis chronique' (1822) are taken from the English translation found in Merrill Moore and H.C. Solomon, 'Contributions of Haslam, Bayle, and Esmarch and Jessen to the history of neurosyphilis.' *Archives of Neurology and Psychiatry* 32(4):804–839 (1934). Additional material is taken from Bayle's *Traité des maladies du cerveau et de ses membranes: maladies mentales* (1826).

tribution of cerebrospinal fluid and form a physical matrix that organizes the arrangement of blood vessels. The meninges are illustrated on the cover of this book. The dura mater is draped over the man's eyes; the arachnoid membrane is shown adhering to the right cerebral hemisphere (left side of the image); the transparent pia mater clings to the exposed brain on the left cerebral hemisphere (right side of the image).

Bayle described in detail what he saw during the dissection of Claude-Francois L.'s head. 'A slight serosity [serum-like fluid] is present between the two layers of the arachnoid ... The cerebral arachnoid at the base of the brain is healthy; that of the convexity and of the inner surface of the [cerebral] hemispheres is opaque, whitish in some places and in other places keeping part of its transparency, thickened very firm, and easy to remove from the surface of the cerebrum ... The pia mater is very red, injected, and infiltrated, with a great quantity of serous fluid.'

Bayle examined the head of another deceased patient, Jean-Francois M., who had been a sculptor. Prior to his death he was 'subject to attacks of abundant and periodic bloody flux that, since the [therapeutic] application of leeches, had been stopped for some time and had not reappeared.' However, at a certain point in his life, 'his intellectual faculties grew deranged in a rapid manner, and sometime later his elation diminished. There followed an exclusive and ambitious *délire* [delirium]; he had fifteen thousand pounds of income; the gigantic projects he was going to carry out were going to bring him millions ... he was going to build a château finer than the Tuileries and the Louvre.' Later, 'He has six billions of money, two hundred ships; he has just bought Italy and is considering taking possession of Asia. He is the best artist in Europe.' Later still, 'He staggered so in his gait that he could hardly stand up; he gritted his teeth frequently; his excretions were involuntary; speech was extremely slow and faltering.' And in the final month of his life, 'There was no sign of any voluntary act. He could not get up at all, or even sit up. His extremities hung limp from his trunk, and occasionally they would have trembling involuntary motions.'

The autopsy findings for Jean-Francois M. were similar to those for Claude-Francois L., that is, nothing unusual in the chest or abdomen but clear pathology in the cerebral membranes. The arachnoid mater had an 'abundance' of serous fluid, and 'more than eight ounces of serous fluid was found at the base of the skull or coming out of the spinal cord.' The brain's ventricles were likewise filled with fluid, swollen to 'a third larger than in the ordinary condition.' And, 'the arachnoid that covers them is thickened in a remarkable manner ...'

Bayle described six cases in a thesis published in 1822 and another fifteen cases in 1826. Every case consisted of the same dominant features: grandiose delusions, worsening paralysis and inflammation of the arachnoid membrane. It was a unique combination involving both clinical symptoms and pathology. Understandably, Bayle felt justified in elevating the disorder from a syndrome (*aliénation ambiteuse avec paralysie incomplète*) to a disease. He called the new disease chronic arachnitis. Never before had anyone linked a mental illness to a specific brain-related pathology.

Long after Bayle's death, modern medical researchers scoured the old medical literature for symptoms comparable to chronic arachnitis. Finding nothing exactly like it before Bayle's time, they concluded that Bayle had discovered a newly emerging disease. True or not, Bayle was the first to describe and name it. After he died, chronic arachnitis spread rapidly and became, in the nineteenth century, one the world's most prevalent diseases. It was especially common among middle-aged men. At any one time, in any given asylum, as many as one-third of all male patients had the disease. The symptoms remained the same, but not the name. English physicians called it 'progressive (or general) paralysis of the insane.' In Germany, it was 'dementia paralytica', and in America, 'general paresis'. French doctors had no less than nineteen different terms for the same condition. The name confusion ended when Bayle's chronic arachnitis was identified as the late-stage manifestation of untreated syphilis. Thereafter, the condition was diagnosed as neurosyphilis. In 1905, researchers found that syphilis—and thus neurosyphilis—is caused by a bacterium, *Treponema pallidum.*

You might think that Bayle's history-making discovery would earn him a promotion, but that is not what happened. When Antoine Royer-Collard died, Bayle lost his protector at Charenton. Royer-Collard's position was filled by Jean-Etienne Esquirol, a former student of Philippe Pinel who was already a rising star on the French psychiatry scene. Like Pinel, he supported asylum reforms, but he also followed Pinel in focusing on patient symptoms rather than any underlying mechanisms. Speculations about anatomical pathologies were pointless, he maintained, because doctors do not need to know the cause of an illness in order to treat it. 'For the cure of madness,' he declared, 'it is no more necessary to be familiar with its nature than it is necessary to be familiar with the nature of pain to successfully employ pain relievers and sedatives.'[22] Esquirol was so put off by Bayle's

---

[22] Jean-Étienne Dominique Esquirol, *Des Maladies Mentales Considérées sous les Rapports Médical, Hygiénique et médico-légal.* Paris: J.-B Bailliere (1838). Quote in vol.1, p. 114.

studies of brain pathology that he refused to renew his contract. Moreover, due to Esquirol's considerable influence within medical circles, Bayle was unable to find work at any other asylum. As a result, he spent the rest of his life struggling as an independent, non-specialist physician. To supplement his meager income, he wrote textbooks and provided bibliographic services to the Faculty of Medicine in Paris.

Sixty years after Bayle's initial observations, an English doctor published a comprehensive treatise on general paralysis of the insane.[23] The work was dedicated to Antoine Bayle. In case after case, the author detailed his patients' profligate spending and extravagant enterprises. Twenty pages were devoted to descriptions of the inflamed arachnoid membrane, and a further twenty-six pages discussed abnormalities in cerebral blood vessels. Later still, near the end of the nineteenth century, two German psychiatrists finally examined the microscopic appearance of nerve cells in patients who had died of Bayle's illness. Using hardened post-mortem brain slices, they found numerous distortions of size and shape. One member of this duo was Franz Nissl, who pioneered the use of colored dyes for examining nerve cells. Nissl's collaborator was Alois Alzheimer, best known for describing a type of dementia. Nissl and Alzheimer belonged to a new wave of psychiatrists who spent as much time in the laboratory as in the wards. Working together, the two friends reported their findings in a five-hundred-page publication which left no doubt about the sorry state of the brain in patients with progressive paralysis of the insane.

Perspective

Antoine Bayle not only described a new disease, he also demonstrated a new way of diagnosing mental illnesses. Rather than relying on ambiguous mental symptoms, chronic arachnitis was reliably diagnosed from physical evidence—albeit not in a way that could benefit either doctor or patient. For the first time, *physical* signs held as much weight as psychological symptoms. He didn't say that the mental symptoms were *caused* by inflammation of the cerebral membranes, but he proved a close relationship. By noting the presence of brain pathology even in the early stages of the illness—when there were no lesions in either the stomach or the intestines—he shot down the idea that psychological disturbances arise only secondarily from lesions in those visceral organs. Moreover, in case after case, he reported that paral-

---

[23] Wm. Julius Mickle, *General Paralysis of the Insane.* London: H.K. Lewis (1880).

ysis, mental disturbance and inflammation on the surface of the brain all worsened in step.

Psychiatrists throughout Europe awoke to the possibility that brain correlates of psychiatric illnesses other than progressive paralysis of the insane might be found. Initially controversial, the idea was gradually adopted. Fifty years after Bayle's dissertation, a German physician by the name of Wilhelm Griesinger famously declared, in a widely circulated article, that 'mental illnesses are really brain illnesses.' Another German psychiatrist, Emil Kraepelin, used progressive paralysis of the insane as the model upon which he built his concept of schizophrenia (initially named *dementia praecox*).

Suggested readings

Edward M. Brown, 'French psychiatry's initial reception of Bayle's discovery of general paresis of the insane.' *Bulletin of the History of Medicine* 68:235–253 (1994).

Jan Ellen Goldstein, *Console and Classify: The French Psychiatric Profession in the Nineteenth Century*. Cambridge, UK: Cambridge University Press (1987).

3 Swollen ventricles

Antoine Bayle's discovery of inflamed arachnoid membranes opened the door to biological explanations of mental illness, but only slightly because the arachnoid membranes are not actually *in* the brain. Psychiatrists were understandably more interested in what was happening in the brain itself, where the mind resides. Following upon Alois Alzheimer and Franz Nissl's report of brain abnormalities in progressive paralysis of the insane, the search was on for abnormalities in other mental disorders. Attentions turned to *dementia praecox*—now called schizophrenia—the most prevalent and most striking of the psychotic disorders. Schizophrenia is a multi-faceted disorder featuring hallucinations (usually auditory), delusions (more often of the paranoid variety than of the grandiose variety), disorganized thought, loss of motivation and social withdrawal.

Emil Kraepelin, the German psychiatrist who first identified *dementia praecox*, was initially sceptical about brain science. Only in the final edition of his textbook, completed near the end of his life in 1919, did Kraepelin devote eleven pages to a description of 'morbid anatomy'.[24] Much of Kraepelin's anatomical summary is based on the work of Alois Alzheimer, who had published his first paper on *dementia praecox* while working in Frankfort. Recognizing his talents, Kraepelin persuaded Alzheimer to move to Heidelberg, where Kraepelin had established a small research group. Later, they both moved to a newly built psychiatric hospital in Munich. It was in Munich that Alzheimer found 'severe and widespread disease' in the cerebral cortex of patients with *dementia praecox*. What mostly caught his attention were changes in the small nerve cells occupying the superficial layers. 'The nuclei are very much swollen, the nuclear membrane greatly wrinkled, the body of the cell considerably shrunk with a tendency to disintegration.' There were also accumulations of fat, 'amoeboid hyperplasia' of glia cells, a thinning of nerve fibers, and a 'diffuse loss of cortical cells.' Franz Nissl, also a member of Kraepelin's research team, reported similar changes.

---

[24] Emil Kraepelin, *Dementia Praecox and Paraphrenia*, trans. Mary Barclay. Edinburgh: E.& S. Livingstone (1919).

Like any good scientist with data in hand, Kraepelin offered a detailed interpretation of these anatomical findings. He focused on damage to the small nerve cells of cortical layers 2 and 3 (there are six layers in total). He assumed that these neurons transform sensory information into abstract concepts. Any loss of these cells, therefore, would necessarily destroy the 'permanent foundations of the psychic life', and lead to the characteristic disruption of 'inner harmony' seen in *dementia praecox*. Although there may be some broad truth in Kraepelin's interpretation, subsequent research poured cold water on its specific claims.

Because Kraepelin was Europe's most esteemed psychiatrist, his assertions encouraged further studies of neural pathology. Sadly however, very little of that research stood the test of time. By the late 1950s most of Alzheimer's work and that of his contemporaries it had been discredited, and schizophrenia become the 'graveyard of neuropathologists.' Reviewing the history of the field in 1968, one author wrote,

> Brain tissue changes have been described in schizophrenia, but controls have been inadequate and findings have been inconclusive or conflicting ... All the reported microscopic abnormalities (in the brains of schizophrenia) have been challenged as non-specific ... attributed to misjudgment of the limits of normal variation, misinterpretation of artifacts, or the uncritical attribution of special significance to casual, coincidental findings.'[25]

One big problem with early neuroanatomical studies was their use of post-mortem specimens. As previously noted, the brain immediately degrades once it is deprived of oxygen. Although invisible to the naked eye, cellular changes are inevitable. To avoid mistaking the resulting damage for pathology caused by disease, the schizophrenia brains should have been compared with 'normal' brains, but that was not done. Hence, the frequent 'misinterpretation of artifacts' mentioned above. Not until the afternoon of November 8, 1895 did anyone think of examining an intact, living brain.

We are indebted to Wilhelm Röntgen, a professor of physics at the University of Würzburg in Germany, for enabling us to look inside our bodies. He did so only after overcoming significant obstacles. The original source of his problems was an incident in high school where he allegedly circulated a caricature of one of his teachers. Whether true or not, Röntgen was expelled

---

[25] Peter C. Rosenbaum, 'Metabolic, physiological, anatomic, and genetic studies in the schizophrenias: A review and analysis.' *The Journal of Nervous and Mental Disease* 146:103–126 (1968), p. 111.

from school and denied a diploma. At the time, he was living in Holland, but after the incident he was blocked from attending any university in that country. Fortunately, he was able to continue his education in Zurich, and after establishing his own laboratory at Würzburg, he began experimenting with vacuum tubes.

European physicists were fascinated with vacuum tubes, which were simply glass tubes that had been vacuumed under high pressure to remove air. The tubes were usually fitted with a pair of metal electrodes. If an electrical current was passed from one electrode to the other—thus through the vacuum—the glass near the positive electrode, the anode, turned a greenish color. Physicists attributed the phenomenon to the emission of an invisible something from the negative, or cathode, electrode. They named those things 'cathode rays', and they were eventually found to be electrons traveling from the cathode to the anode.

On the historic day, Röntgen was working with one of these tubes when he noticed a piece of paper lying about one meter away. This particular paper had been coated with a fluorescent paint that made it sensitive to light. To prevent the paper from being affected by cathode rays, he covered the tube with black cardboard prior to the experiment. Nevertheless, as soon as he switched on the electrical current, he noticed a faint green glow on the sensitive paper. The room was pitch black and Röntgen saw no light leaking through the cardboard, yet something—again that word—had travelled from the vacuum to the fluorescent paper. When later asked by a journalist what went through his mind at that moment, he replied, 'I did not think. I investigated ... I assumed the effect must have come from the tube ... I tried it successfully at greater and greater distances, even at two meters. It seemed a new kind of invisible light ... clearly something new, something unrecorded [up until then].'[26] Not knowing what they were, he called them X-rays. Unlike cathode rays, which consist of charged electrons, X-rays are massless, pure electromagnetic radiation. They differ from visible light, radio waves and microwaves only in wavelength. The wavelengths of X-rays are shorter than those of any light that can be detected by the human eye.

Röntgen went on to tell the journalist that 'having discovered the existence of a new kind of rays, I of course began to investigate what they would do.' He set up a fluorescent screen and placed his hand between it and the radiating tube. Turning to the screen, he saw each of his finger

---

[26] H.J.W. Dam, 'The new marvel in photography.' *McClure's Magazine*, VI (5), 1896, p. 413.

bones surrounded by reddish flesh. He replaced the fluorescent screen with a photograph plate and took pictures of various X-rayed objects. He kept silent about all of this for six weeks before sending off a manuscript to a scientific journal and an X-ray photograph of his wife's hand to friends. Anna's finger bones were starkly evident, as was the large bulge surrounding the middle segment of her left hand—her wedding ring.

Physicians took an immediate interest in X-rays, and it wasn't long before they began exploring their possible uses. Most soft tissues showed up poorly, but bones and air-filled structures, including the lungs, were well defined. Initial results for the brain were disappointing, because even large tumors cast only a vague shadow. Doctors detected tumors by observing the displacement of brain ventricles, but the ventricles were themselves indistinct. Walter Dandy, a neurosurgeon at Johns Hopkins University in Baltimore, Maryland, found X-rays helpful in only six percent of cases when looking for tumors.

The brain has four ventricles, all located deep in the brain. The specialized cells that line the interior walls of the two lateral ventricles secrete cerebrospinal fluid. From there the fluid circulates through channels to the unpaired third and fourth ventricles. It then goes into the space beneath the arachnoid membrane. While searching for ways to improve X-ray contrast for his neurological work, Dandy learned of the fact that gas in the abdominal cavity sometimes casts X-ray 'shadows' on the stomach and intestines. The presence of air darkens the area around the organs and effectively outlines them. Dandy reasoned that if he could replace the cerebrospinal fluid with air, he would create contrast sufficient for him to clearly see the ventricles. He began, in 1918, with children suspected of hydrocephalus, a dangerous condition in which the ventricles become engorged with cere-

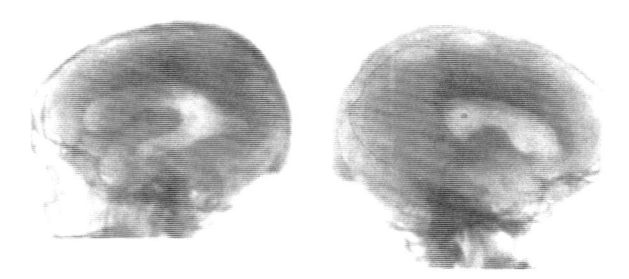

Ventriculograms showing normal ventricle (left) and ventricle compressed by a tumor (right). [W. Dandy, 1920]

brospinal fluid. First, he drilled a burr hole into the skull, then he pushed a hypodermic needle straight into one of the lateral ventricles. He withdrew all the cerebrospinal fluid—as much as one third of a liter—and replaced it with the same volume of air.

The images that Dandy obtained with the procedure allowed him to see tumors and blockages in and around the ventricular system. Catching these problems in their early stages made it possible to operate before the tumors became life-threatening. On the downside, patients experienced severe headaches, nausea and vomiting for many days afterwards; there were also a few deaths.

One year after inventing this procedure, Dandy came up with a better way of achieving the same result. Rather than inserting a needle into the ventricles, Dandy withdrew cerebrospinal fluid from the sub-arachnoid space. Since the arachnoid membrane, as well as the space beneath it, extends all the way down to the end of the spinal cord, and even a bit further, he inserted his needle between two of the lower vertebrae on the patient's backside. Physicians had been drawing cerebrospinal fluid in this manner for decades, but they only took small samples. Dandy took as much as he could. Since different parts of the ventricular system are oriented in different directions, Dandy had to tilt the body at various angles to drain all the fluid—surely an unpleasant experience for the patient.

Dandy's setup is shown in the illustration on the following page. The patient is bent slightly forward to allow the needle to be inserted. His head, and the device for generating X-rays, are both hidden behind the large fluorescent screen. An arrangement of tubes allows the doctor to switch between draining cerebrospinal fluid and injecting air, while a beaker collects the drained fluid.

All things considered, Dandy's new method—named pneumoencephalography (air-brain-imaging)—was easy to perform, reasonably safe and capable of producing decent results. Indeed, pneumoencephalography was the method of choice for imaging living brains up until the introduction of computer assisted imaging in the 1970s. Dandy's patients still suffered headaches and vomiting, but at least they did not have to worry about a hole in the skull.

Up until 1927, brain pneumoencephalography was used primarily for detecting tumors. We do not know what led a pair of German doctors, Walter Jacobi and Herbert Winkler, to X-ray mental patients. Did they think that they would see traces of insanity in these fuzzy images? Not likely, because there had been no reports of large lesions or significant degeneration in post-

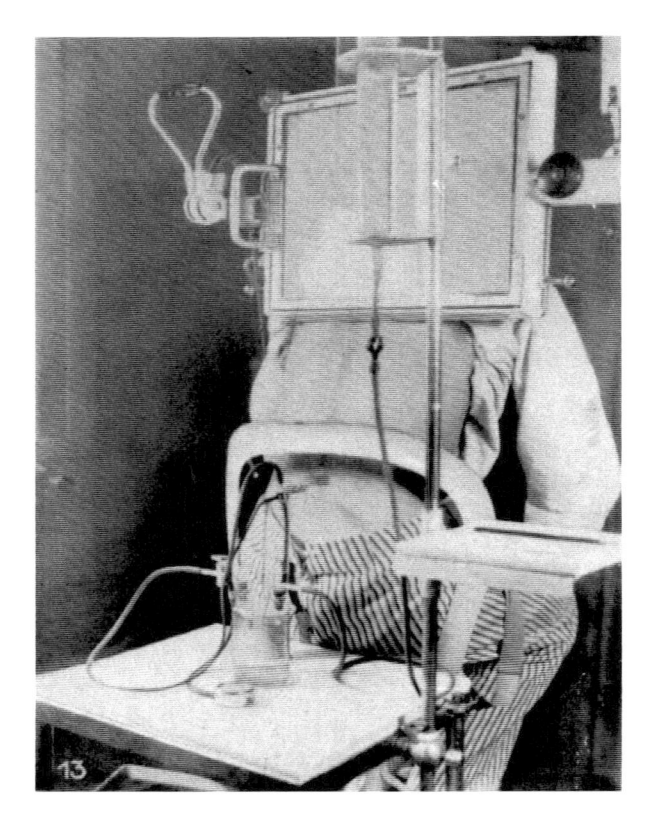

Setup for pneumoencephalography [O. Schiersmann, Leipzig, 1942]

mortem studies. On the other hand, Jacobi and Winkler must have read in Dandy's papers that ventricular sizes varied considerably from patient to patient. While the extremely large ventricles were tied to imposing tumors or blocked channels, the smaller variations were unexplained. Only a leap of imagination could have linked these fluid-filled cavities to schizophrenia, but Jacobi or Winkler had an idea and they set out to test it.

Jacobi and Winkler seized upon an opportunity made possible by the availability of captive subjects for an experiment that was inherently dangerous. Jacobi, the senior author of the study, was a professor of psychiatry in Jena and head of the Thuringia state mental hospital. Although laws were in place requiring doctors to inform patients of the nature of the experiment and obtain their consent, in practice the regulations were often overlooked. Consequently asylums, including the one in Jena, provided a plentiful supply of subjects, willing or not.

Rather than selecting patients at random, Jacobi and Winkler wisely decided to focus on schizophrenia. For unknown reasons, they withdrew cerebrospinal fluid not from the sub-arachnoid space but from the cisterna magna, which is a fluid collecting area tucked in behind the cerebellum. They accessed the cisterna magna by inserting a long needle into the skin just beneath a prominent bump at the back of the head. If they had pressed the needle too deeply they could have triggered respiratory failure and death, but apparently they avoided any such incidents. Nevertheless, the patients sweated and choked throughout the procedure.

Jacobi and Winkler's initial findings came from nineteen male patients. Every patient had been diagnosed with schizophrenia and each was subtyped as either paranoid, catatonic or hebephrenic (the latter with disorganized or bizarre behaviors). Since there were no healthy persons in the sample, nor any patient with an illness other than schizophrenia, there was no control group. Each case was individually described and documented with X-ray photographs, but no measurements were reported.

Case number six was a 49-year-old male with mild paranoid schizophrenia. Jacobi and Winkler describe him as exhibiting 'irritability with violent arousal, speech disability, impaired ideas, physical sensations.' Four X-rays were taken, each from a different perspective. The patient's eyeglasses can

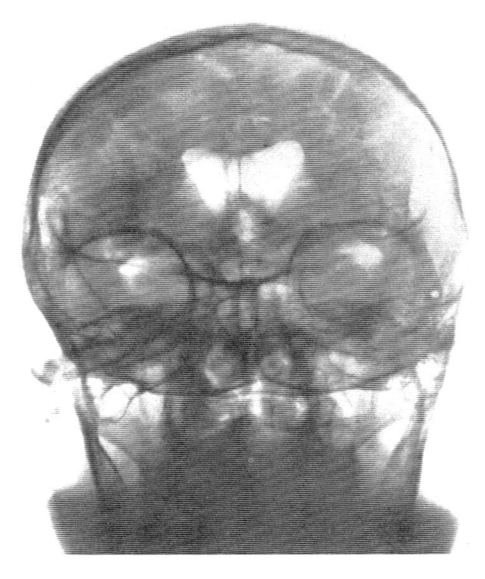

Case number 6 from Jacobi and Winkler, 1927. Note asymmetry of left-right ventricles.

be seen in the frontal view. Centered above the eyeglasses are the lightly shaded lateral ventricles. Commenting on the case, the authors write, 'Left hemisphere larger than the right. Lateral ventricle moderately dilated, left slightly more than the right. Likewise, expansion of the third ventricle. Further downwards, the fourth ventricle is also larger than normal. Slight ventricular migration to the left.' Diagnosis: 'Hydrocephalus internus [literally, water in the brain], moderate grade.'[27]

It turned out that eighteen of the nineteen patients had hydrocephalus. This is a significant result, because hydrocephalus is ordinarily rare. For the first time, psychiatrists had evidence of a brain abnormality correlating with mental illness. Jacobi and Winkler wrote that 'the question of whether the results arise in the course of the disease or whether they are to be interpreted in the context of some abnormal development can hardly be answered.'[28] In other words, were the enlarged ventricles present *before* the onset of schizophrenia or only afterwards? They did not comment on how enlarged ventricles might possibly relate to schizophrenia which is, after all, an illness affecting thought and behavior, not cerebrospinal fluid. An answer to that question came much later.

Immediately following Jacobi and Winkler's breakthrough, several investigators replicated the basic finding. Other studies attempted to go beyond the original finding by examining whether the size of the ventricular enlargement correlates with the severity of symptoms or the duration of the illness; these studies yielded inconsistent results. Also, when individuals were X-rayed on multiple occasions, some studies found that the ventricles grew in step with mental deterioration, whereas other studies reported no correspondence. So, the uncertainties created by Jacobi and Winkler's original study persisted. Only after the invention of the CT scanner did the doubts disappear. CT scanning—short for computed tomography—creates a 3-dimensional virtual brain.

The very first CT scanner went into action on October 1, 1971, for the purpose of examining a suspected brain tumor. The patient's head was covered with a large rubber cap filled with water. Scanning took nine days. Afterwards, a computer needed two and a half hours to process the data. Another two hours were needed to print the first image, a picture measuring just 80 pixels by 80 pixels. Today, scanning and processing are done in minutes, and single images typically measure 1024 pixels by 1024 pixels.

---

[27] W. Jacobi and H. Winkler, 'Encephalographische Studien an chronisch Schizophrenen.' *Archiv für Psychiatrie und Nervenkrankheiten* 81:299–332 (1927), p. 311.
[28] Ibid, p. 331.

The company that made the first CT scanner greatly underestimated the commercial potential, hoping to sell, at best, twenty-five machines worldwide.

The X-rays used in modern CT scanning are fundamentally unchanged from those used by Jacobi and Winkler, but everything else about the devices is different. For example, early radiologists had to rotate their patients in a stepwise manner, taking separate exposures at each angle. Only in this way could they view the brain from a variety of geometric perspectives. Even so, the procedure did not work well, because objects in the foreground blocked the view of objects in the background, and vice versa. By contrast, in modern CT scanning the X-ray emitter is rotated, not the patient. At each position, the machine takes multiple X-ray 'slices' as it moves through the brain. As many as several hundred slices are taken at a single angle of rotation. The slices are very thin (about 1 mm thick), so there is hardly any superimposition and the images are sharp. Once slices have been taken from all necessary angles, the computer goes to work. It combines all the captured images to create a brain that is *virtually* transparent. Physicians can now view any part of the brain from any angle.

Although the computations rely on complex mathematics, even the earliest CT scanners were up to the job. Remarkably, the man who built the first CT scanner, and who worked out the necessary mathematics, had little formal education beyond age sixteen. Godfrey Hounsfield was an Englishman who first learned about radio and electronics while serving in the Royal Air Force during World War II. Later, after attended a technical college, he got a job designing computers. Upon completing his first major project, Hounsfield was 'given the opportunity to go away quietly and think of other areas of research which I thought might be fruitful.'[29] It was then that he came up with the idea of a CT scanner. Hounsfield's employer was a company called Electrical and Musical Industries (EMI). It just so happened that EMI held the exclusive rights to music written by the Beatles. They also owned the legendary Abbey Road Studios where the Beatles recorded their hits. From both sources, EMI earned gobs of money, which probably explains why Hounsfield's employer gave him the freedom to 'think of research that might be fruitful.'

Doctor Eve Johnstone was making preparations for her study long before her new EMI CT scanner arrived at the Clinical Research Centre in Harrow, England. She and her colleagues in psychiatry were naturally skeptical about Jacobi and Winkler's work. They worried about the murkiness of

---

[29] Quotations from Hounsfield's Nobel Prize biographical sketch (1979).

Eve Johnstone [Julia Bland, BJPsych Bulletin 41(4), 2017]

the pictures, the lack of measurements and the absence of a healthy control group, so they were anxious to replicate Jacobi and Winkler's findings using modern techniques. For subjects, they selected a group of male schizophrenia patients residing at a local mental hospital. In addition, as a control group, Dr. Johnstone recruited a group of 'normal males' from her hospital's non-professional staff. Since it is not necessary to drain the cerebrospinal fluid for a CT scan, people happily volunteered. The volunteer group was matched as closely as possible to the patient group in terms of sex, age and occupation, thereby providing some assurance that any detected difference in brain anatomy would be due to the patients' illness rather than some other attribute.

Johnstone and her colleagues printed photographs of the slice images taken from an angle 'parallel to the orbitomeatal line,'[30] this being the best angle for viewing the ventricles. The size of each ventricle was measured by rolling a planimeter around the circumference of the cavity; measurements were made on every slice that showed the same ventricle. To avoid investigator bias, the person making the measurements did not know whether the image came from a patient or from one of the normal volun-

---

[30] The orbitomeatal line runs from the eye to the ear.

teers. After all the calculations had been completed, and the identities of all the subjects revealed, it was found that ventricular sizes were considerably larger in schizophrenia patients than in normal volunteers. Only one of eight volunteers had a ventricular size greater than the smallest size seen in seventeen schizophrenia patients. The investigators also found that 'within the group of schizophrenic patients, increased ventricular size was highly significantly related to indices of cognitive impairment.'[31] In other words, the worse the cognitive impairment, the larger the ventricles. Johnstone and colleagues' landmark study was published in the prestigious medical journal, *The Lancet*.

Not only did Johnstone et al.'s work confirm Jacobi and Winkler's discovery from fifty years earlier, it came at a propitious time during the so-called anti-psychiatry movement. Several vocal psychiatrists allied with some equally outspoken academics were arguing that there is no such thing as a mental *illness*. There are only unusual behaviors and non-functional social conventions. The CT-scan proved them wrong. During a recent interview, Eve Johnstone describes how she felt about her breakthrough investigation,

> I felt it had to be that this [schizophrenia] was a disease, but I couldn't prove it ... and then the non-invasive method of CT scanning came in. I was lucky. Before that people had to do pneumoencephalography (injecting air into the ventricles and X-raying them, resulting in terrible headaches and worse), so there were no controls because of the dangers of the technique.[32]

One might reasonably ask whether the treatments given schizophrenia patients affect ventricular size. Johnstone found that neither electroconvulsive shocks nor insulin-induced comas factored into their results. Moreover, despite the fact that most of Dr. Johnstone's patients had been given antipsychotic medications, the ventricles in those who received drugs were no larger than the ventricles than in patients who had no drugs.

Even though large ventricles correlate robustly with schizophrenia, it is not possible to diagnose someone by measuring their ventricles, because not everyone with the psychological symptoms of schizophrenia has large ventricles, and conversely, some people have large ventricles but no schizophrenia.

---

[31] E.C. Johnstone et al., 'Cerebral ventricular size and cognitive impairment in chronic schizophrenia.' *The Lancet* 308(7992):924–926 (1976), p. 924.

[32] Julia Bland, 'Scottish independence: the view of psychiatry from Edinburgh.' *BJPsych Bulletin* 41 (4), 234–236 (2017), p.235.

The latter fact was overlooked—intentionally or otherwise—by the defense lawyers for John Hinckley, the man who shot President Ronald Reagan. They argued that Hinkley was not responsible for the act because he had enlarged ventricles and therefore schizophrenia. The judge tossed out the argument but nonetheless upheld the insanity defense.

Perspective

No one could have predicted that the first brain abnormality to be associated with a mental disorder would be swollen ventricles. The discovery raised the question, how, exactly, do swollen ventricles relate to schizophrenia? Jacobi and Winkler were unable to say 'whether the results arise in the course of the disease or whether they are to be interpreted in the context of some abnormal development.' Almost 50 years later, when Johnstone and colleagues confirmed their findings, they repeated almost verbatim—but now in English—the earlier question, "The question obviously arises as to whether increased ventricular size is a consequence of the pathological process or whether increased ventricular size may in some way predispose to a severe and cognitively incapacitating form of the disease."[33] Put differently, are swollen ventricles the *cause* or the *consequence* of schizophrenia?

The enlarged ventricles could not themselves be responsible for schizophrenia because they lack nerve cells. Nor could they be simply 'predisposing' for the illness because, if that were true, ventricle sizes would not change over time, whereas in fact they do. The ventricles grower larger with age in both schizophrenia patients and in normal, healthy individuals, but the rate of growth is approximately three to four times greater in patients than in non-patients.[34]

If it were true that swollen ventricles are a consequence that arises only 'in the course of the disease', that would not be interesting if were due to the patients' lifestyle or medications. For example, schizophrenia patients tend to smoke excessively, and they typically get little exercise. If swollen ventricles were just an accidental *correlate* of schizophrenia, they could not be used as the basis for either preventing the illness or improving treatments.

Emil Kraepelin saw schizophrenia as a premature variety of dementia—*dementia praecox*—and he understood dementia as a degenerative dis-

---

[33] E.C. Johnstone et al. (1976), p.926.

[34] Matthew J. Kempton et al., 'Progressive lateral ventricular enlargement in schizophrenia: A meta-analysis of longitudinal MRI studies.' *Schizophrenia Research* 120:54–62 (2010).

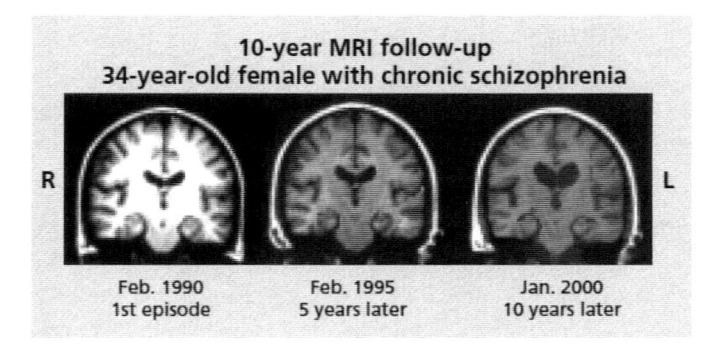

Progressive expansion of lateral ventricles (center, black) [Lynn E. DeLisi et al., Dialogues in Clinical Neuroscience 8, 2006]

ease. It isn't clear whether he was thinking of psychological degeneration or neural degeneration, but we know that he never *saw* neural degeneration. The idea of neural degeneration was still hanging in the air—together with the significance of swollen ventricles—when Eve Johnstone decided to test it.[35] She reasoned that maybe the ventricles had expanded to fill space left vacant by dead or dying nerve cells (neurons). Using the same CT scanning machine and the same patients as in her initial study, she made measurements of brain size in her schizophrenia patients and compared the results with measurements taken from healthy individuals. The data reported in this follow-up study are equivocal, because the methods were crude. Still, it was a start in the right direction.

Later research, discussed in Chapter 12, used MRI machines and found clear evidence for the loss of brain tissue in schizophrenia brains. Whole nerve cells aren't shrinking or dying, only the slender extensions known as dendrites are dying. While each dendrite is tiny, there are billions of them, and they hold the synapses where individual neurons communicate with one another. Therefore, the loss of dendrites could account for many features of schizophrenia.

Jacobi and Winkler discovered the first biomarker for schizophrenia, but swollen ventricles are by no means the only biomarker for schizophrenia. Nor is schizophrenia the only mental illness with biomarkers. We will encounter more biomarkers in later chapters.

---

[35] E.C. Johnstone et al., 'The dementia of dementia praecox.' *Acta Psychiatrica Scandinavica* 57:305–324 (1978).

Suggested readings

Lynn E. DeLisi et al., 'Understanding structural brain changes in schizophrenia.' *Dialogues in Clinical Neuroscience* 8:71–78 (2006).

Anne Harrington, *Mind Fixers: Psychiatry's Troubled Search for the Biology of Mental Illness.* New York: W.W. Norton (2019).

4 The dog that drank from a glass

Late in the nineteenth century, a young woman from a prominent Viennese family walked into her doctor's office concerned about a persistent cough, loss of appetite and crossed eyes. The physician, Dr. Josef Breuer, was a highly respected general practitioner. Earlier in his career, he had researched how nerves control the amount of air that we take into our lungs. The patient was Bertha Pappenheim, twenty-one years old at the time of her first consultation with Dr. Breuer. According to Breuer, 'She was markedly intelligent, with an astonishingly quick grasp of things and a penetrating intuition.' Although 'bubbling over with intellectual vitality,' Bertha evidently 'led an extremely monotonous existence in her puritanically-minded family.' To compensate, one might suppose, 'she embellished her life ... by indulging in systematic day-dreaming.'[36]

Bertha Pappenheim's father had a serious medical condition, and it was after she become his primary caretaker that Bertha's own symptoms worsened. The more she attended to his numerous needs, the more tired she grew, and the more concerning became her physical disabilities. Whereas she had previously been 'energetic, tenacious and persistent,' she was now beset with frequent headaches (on the left side) and partial paralysis in her arms and legs. She also felt as though the walls of her room were tumbling down all around her. Despite his wide experience, Breuer did not know how to treat this patient. All he could think of doing was give her choral hydrate, a sedative drug that comes with a strong, nauseating odor.

Five months after Bertha Pappenheim first began seeing Breuer, her beloved father died. This led to a further deterioration in her health. The problems with her vision worsened in a troublesome manner. Presented with a bundle of flowers, she saw only one. She didn't recognize friends and associates because their faces looked waxed. There were also striking changes in her speech and in her understanding of the languages spoken to her. Prior to her illness, she conversed comfortably in German, English,

---

[36] Josef Breuer and Sigmund Freud, *Studies on Hysteria*, translated by James Strachey and included in the *Standard Edition of the Complete Psychological Works of Sigmund Freud*. London: Hogarth Press (1895, 1955). Quotations pertaining to Bertha Pappenheim are from this source.

Josef Breuer and Bertha Pappenheim [Gamma-Rapho via Getty Images/API]

French and Italian. Now, she spoke only English. When people used German words—those of her native tongue—she behaved as though she did not understand. And whereas she had earlier eaten very little, she now stopped eating altogether. Breuer, who visited Bertha Pappenheim almost daily, had to personally place food in her mouth. He was gravely concerned and uncertain how to proceed.

Breuer thought it might be a brain problem, 'a tubercle in the left *fossa Sylvii* with a slowly expanding chronic meningitis.' On the other hand, the nervous character of her coughing and the hallucinations suggested a psychological cause. Breuer, in his written account of the case describes two very different states of mind. At times, she would seem relatively normal, although anxious and somewhat depressed (melancholic). At other times, she rapidly switched to an alternative state characterized by hallucinations and 'naughty' behaviors. Her hallucinations featured dead heads, skeletons and black snakes in her hair. As for the naughty behavior, it consisted of throwing cushions, tearing buttons from her bedclothes and the like. What happened next was not just a breakthrough in the case, it was a revolution in the treatment of mental illness.

Bertha had gotten herself into a daily rhythm. Afternoons, she'd become drowsy and enter into a kind of hypnotic state, which she described as being 'in the clouds.' While up there, she would sometimes give voice to the hallucinations that had haunted her during the day. Afterwards—back on earth—she'd be calm and cheerful. Evidently, by recalling details of the hallucinations and making them vivid in her mind, she got them to disappear—at least temporarily. In telling others about this experience, she would speak of her 'talking cure' or 'chimney sweeping'. Once Dr. Breuer realized what was happening, he encouraged Bertha to tell him about her hallucinations, or simply talk to him about what was troubling her. On some occasions, he used hypnosis to loosen her memory and lessen her anxiety. These tactics apparently worked, because the bad memories vanished. Breuer spoke of it as 'catharsis', from a Greek word meaning purification or cleansing. Aristotle used the word to describe what happens to theatre goers while watching an exceptionally dramatic performance.

One particular episode of chimney sweeping proved especially significant, more so even for future generations of psychiatrists than for either Josef Breuer or Bertha Pappenheim. It occurred during a summer of extreme heat. Although suffering badly from thirst, Bertha, for no obvious reason, found it impossible to drink. As soon as her lips touched the glass of water, she pushed it away. This behavior continued for about six weeks, during which time she satisfied her thirst by eating fruits. Then one day, during hypnosis,

> she grumbled about her English lady-companion whom she did not care for, and went on to describe, with every sign of disgust, how she had once gone into that lady's room and how her little dog—horrid creature!—had drunk [water] out of a glass. The patient said nothing, as she wanted to be polite. After giving further energetic expression to the anger she had held back, she asked for something to drink, drank a large quantity of water without any difficulty and woke from her hypnosis with the glass at her lips; and thereupon the disturbance vanished, never to return.

Sigmund Freud's creative mind would later turn this minor incident into a major theory and a popular therapeutic method. We will come to that, but first, the conclusion of Bertha Pappenheim's story. Sometime after the dog hallucination, Bertha Pappenheim was sent to a private clinic on Lake Constance in Switzerland, a tranquil spot on the northern flank of the Alp mountains. While there, she acquired a severe facial pain and became reliant on heavy doses of chloral hydrate and morphine. She also experienced multiple relapses of a psychological kind, including recurrent mental 'absences' and long periods during which she could not speak German. Nevertheless, she got better. After her release from the sanatorium, Bertha returned to Vienna where she remained healthy while working on behalf of feminist and Jewish causes.

To understand how the dog in Bertha's dream transformed psychiatry in the twentieth century, we need to look at how Sigmund Freud became involved in her case. Freud was born in Moravia, but he moved with his family to Vienna at a young age. After excelling as a student in gymnasium[37], he studied medicine, but he was drawn more to science and philosophy than conventional medicine. Not surprising, therefore, that he began his professional life in a research laboratory. Working sequentially under several supervisors over a span of six years, Freud occupied himself with various biology projects. First, he studied eel gonads. Seeking to confirm the long-held belief that eels are hermaphrodites, he dissected nearly four hundred specimens. In the end, he reached the disappointing conclusion that it was impossible to tell whether, in fact, they were hermaphrodites.[38] Next, as part of a project designed to clarify the evolution of the nervous system, he conducted neuroanatomical research on a primitive fish. In the course of this work, he discovered previously unknown neural elements in the spinal cord, and he invented new chemical methods for preparing tissues for microscopic examination. This work, conducted in the Physiological Institute at the University of Vienna, was supervised by Ernst Brücke, a distinguished professor who became a father figure for Freud.

In November of 1882, Freud was working at the Vienna General Hospital as a junior medical doctor and part-time researcher. The prominent neuroanatomist, Theodor Meynert, was his supervisor. After work, Freud sometimes dropped by to visit his friend, Josef Breuer. Their frank conversations ranged from intellectual give-and-take to professional gossip. On several such occasions—after Bertha Pappenheim had been sent to the Swiss sanatorium— Breuer spoke to Freud about his patient. Clearly, the case was still troubling him and, as Breuer revealed more and more details of Bertha's long illness, Freud grew increasingly interested. The men agreed that she suffered from hysteria, a widely discussed mental disorder at the time. However, what particularly intrigued Freud was her so-called talking cure. Years later, Freud and Breuer co-authored a book, *Studies on*

---

[37] In the German educational system, a gymnasium is a secondary school that emphasizes academic learning. Equivalent to the American prep school.

[38] European freshwater eels of the type studied by Freud, are hermaphrodites when young, but males or females as adults.

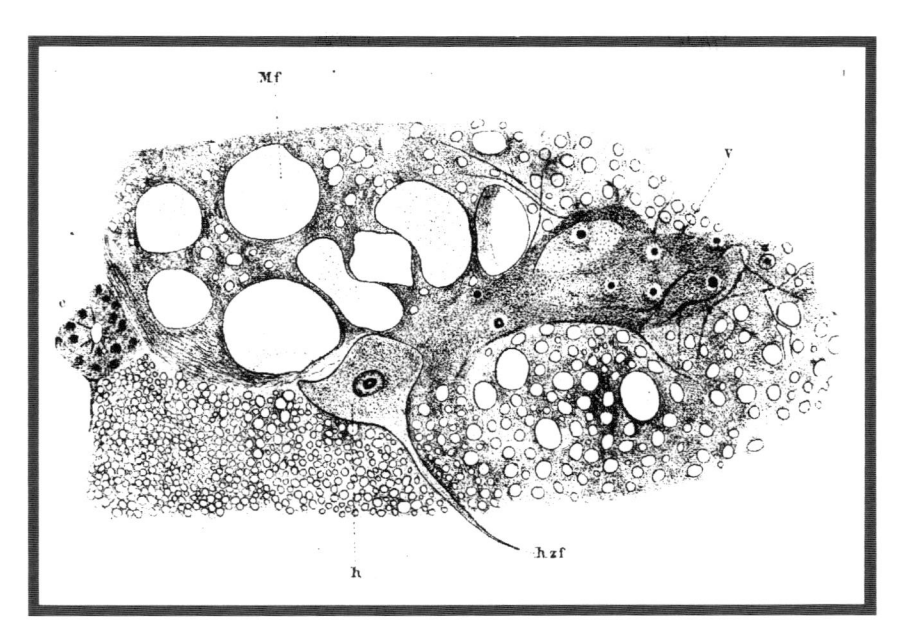

Freud's drawing of a neuron in the spinal cord of a lamprey larva (Ammocoete), 1887

Hysteria, that featured Bertha Pappenheim as its centerpiece, except the name Bertha Pappenheim appears nowhere in the book; she was replaced by the pseudo-named, Anna O. *Studies on Hysteria* was the foundation upon which the large edifice of psychoanalysis was subsequently built.

Hysteria is a most curious illness, or at least it was. After its removal from the *Diagnostic and Statistical Manual of Mental Disorders*, hysteria ceased to be *any* kind of illness. It was first recognized as a specific medical condition in the seventeenth century. Vaguely defined and broadly applied, it was a catchall diagnosis for unusual behaviors that could not be explained by any single physical condition. Passionate outbursts, accompanied by heavy sobbing, uncoordinated limb movements, and twitching were characteristic. Doctors felt that the disorder was more common among women than men, so they named it hysteria, from the Greek word for uterus. In Freud's time, doctors assumed that patients had an underlying mental problem that 'converted' to observable behavioral problems—but how that happened was a mystery.

The leading authority on hysteria in the late nineteenth century was the physician Jean-Martin Charcot who worked at the Salpêtrière hospital in Paris. Apart from his studies on hysteria, Charcot is known for pioneering

Sigmund Freud, 1914 [Max Halberstadt]

work on multiple sclerosis, Parkinson's disease and other neurological disorders. Charcot's success brought him international fame and many international visitors, including Sigmund Freud who had broadened his interests and was seeking new opportunities. Freud travelled to Paris on an academic leave three years after he and Josef Breuer had discussed Martha Pappenheim's case. Charcot dazzled Freud with his knowledge and charisma. Freud was particularly impressed by Charcot's claim that hypnosis can be used to cure hysterics. Charcot famously demonstrated his hypnotic technique before enthralled audiences comprised of physicians and other notables.

Josef Breuer was also familiar with Charcot's work, and even before Freud's trip to Paris, Breuer had tried hypnosis with Bertha Pappenheim. However, when Breuer and Freud got around to writing about their case (10 years after the Parisian visit), they downplayed the value of hypnosis as a therapeutic technique. Contrary to Charcot's claim, Breuer found that not all of his hysteric patients could be hypnotized. Moreover, he and Freud

La Leçon Clinique du Dr. Charcot painted by André Brouillet, 1887

had effectively treated two cases—Miss Lucy R. and Fraulein Elisabeth v. R.— without using hypnosis, not even the self-administered type employed by Bertha Pappenheim. It was enough to get the women to talk freely. Bertha's talking cure had proven better than Charcot's hypnosis.

Freud and Breuer wrote in their book that Bertha's conscious recall of the horrible dog and the water glass was the key for unlocking her mental block. They noted that 'a number of extremely obstinate whims were similarly removed after she described the experiences which had given rise to them.' After further elaborations of the procedure, Bertha Pappenheim's talking cure became Freud's method of free association, the central element in his treatment of psychological problems.

Inside Freud's residence at 19 Berggasse Street, Vienna, one room was especially designed as a consulting room for patients. Along one wall stood an oddly shaped 'analytic couch', upon which the patient—or 'analysand'—laid. Covered with a Persian rug and piled high with pillows, the couch was outfitted for maximum comfort. Freud also placed an additional rug at the foot of the bed, should the patient need it. The room was otherwise filled with sculptures, photographs of friends, various antiquities that Freud had collected over the years, and more oriental rugs. Freud

Freud's consulting room, 1938 [Edmund Engelmann; Sigmund Freud Museum]

especially liked artifacts created by the ancient Mediterranean civilizations of Rome, Egypt and Greece. The cultural trappings created an atmosphere conducive to unfettered talk.

Freud listened attentively as the patient recited his or her troubles. Gradually, in the course of successive appointments, he employed increasingly targeted tactics, coaxing the patient toward free association. He wanted his patients to speak about their worst fears, their most anguished experiences, but he found that they preferred to talk about everything *except* emotionally laden events. It was as though they *had* no hurtful memories. Bertha Pappenheim, for example, initially ignored—had 'forgotten'—her memory of the dog and the water glass. Freud saw his job as helping the patient discover that which he, Freud, knew must exist. He likened the method to 'excavating a buried city.' Later, he realized that painful memories are not buried by accident, but rather by mental mechanisms whose job it is to hide from consciousness all disturbing memories. In the language of psychoanalysis, the mind 'represses' such memories. Talking helps to uncover the hurtful memories, and thus relieves the patient of his or her psychological burden.

One naturally asks where memories go when repressed. Where is the place of burial? The obvious answer: if they can no longer be accessed by the conscious mind, they must be in the unconscious. That is where they lie hidden until excavated by free association. Bertha's memory of the dog experience was dispatched to the unconscious, and if we believe Freud, it shared the space with repressed memories of a sexual nature, because these too can be traumatic. Sex played an important part in Freud's later theories, but in *Studies on Hysteria* he noted that Bertha was 'sexually astonishingly undeveloped', and he had very little to say about sex in that book.

Freud did not discover the unconscious mind, nor did he invent it. Philosophers before him had made similar proposals. The difference is, Freud made a big thing of it. He imagined the unconscious crowded not only with repressed memories but also with instinctual drives (Freud's id) and moral principles (Freud's superego). While some people deny that there is any such thing as the unconscious, others have shown it, in illustrations, lying beneath the conscious mind.

Imagine a young man, whom we will call Freddie, enjoying a picnic with his mother in a forested park.[39] She hugs him and plants a kiss on his neck. Surprised, Freddie experiences a mix of feelings, one of which is the unmistakable sense of erotic pleasure. Quite naturally, the incident, and especially his reaction, leaves Freddie shaken and disturbed. One week later, he is talking with a friend who, in the course of conversation, enquires about his mother. Then, a short while later, the men discuss a certain style of oil painting. Freddie starts describing the work of a local artist but draws a blank around the painter's name. No matter how hard he tries, he cannot recall that name, which happens to be Jonathan Wood. What is the matter? Why can't Freddie remember the artist's name?

A Freudian would interpret Freddie's memory lapse in terms of psychological repression. In the moments immediately after his shamed reaction to the kiss, Freddie buried the experience in the unconscious, and later, when searching for the artist's name, his conscious mind did not allow him to remember, because it recognized an association between the name (Jonathan *Wood*) and the incident with his mother *in the forest.*

The story presents a version of Freud's famous Oedipus complex. According to an ancient Greek myth, the tragic hero, Oedipus, wound up marrying his mother following a series of unfortunate events. Freud invented a psychological condition based on a reading of the myth. He believed that boys unconsciously want to have sex with their mothers. In some cases, he

---

[39] This fictional story is based on a real incident experienced by Freud himself, as described in *The Psychopathology of Everyday Life,* chapter 1. See suggested readings.

claimed, such muted thoughts continue into adulthood and cause troublesome psychological conflicts.

Perspective

Everyone agrees that Sigmund Freud was unusually creative and productive, a genius according to some. Beginning with Bertha Pappenheim (aka Anna O.) and ending with a massive amount of writing, Sigmund Freud constructed psychoanalysis. Its popularity grew steadily until reaching a zenith of popularity in the mid-1960s. One third of American psychiatrists received psychoanalytic training during that time, and two thirds said that they had adopted at least some of Freud's ideas. Following widespread publicity in newspapers, magazines, radio and television, everyone—not just doctors and patients—was talking about psychoanalysis. As a result, the American public tended to equate psychoanalysis with the whole of psychiatry.

A decade later psychoanalysis was in precipitous decline in America and elsewhere, due in part to the arrival of effective medications for common depression (Prozac) and mild anxiety (Librium). Also, psychoanalysis faced competition from alternative forms of psychotherapy, including cognitive therapy and cognitive-behavioral psychotherapy. While the alternatives incorporated some elements of Freud's complex theory—including the unconscious—they rejected its emphasis on sexual matters. Group therapy, couples therapy and family therapy also drew potential patients away from psychoanalysis.

Freud's enduring contribution to psychiatry was his discovery of psychotherapy. Throughout the ages, ordinary conversations have helped troubled individuals, but Freud realized that *certain kinds* of talking are more effective than others. He took Bertha Pappenheim's talking cure and built it up to become psychoanalysis. In doing so, he created psychotherapy as a professional service. All subsequent forms of psychotherapy grew from the model of psychoanalysis and, collectively, they have assisted millions of people. That is Freud's remarkable legacy.

Freud's theoretical concepts merit less praise because they raise serious questions about their validity. Is repression real? Does the unconscious exist? The Oedipus complex, the id, the superego—which experiments prove their existence? As a matter of fact, there are no such experiments. Moreover, it is hard to imagine *any* way to either prove or disprove this stuff. There is simply no experiment, nor any observation, that will allow these ideas to pass the test of reality. Freud thought himself a scientist, but in truth he was a philosopher. He *discovered* psychotherapy, but he *speculated* about the nature of mind.

Suggested readings

Sigmund Freud, *The Psychopathology of Everyday Life.* New York: Penguin Classics (1901, 2003).

Peter Gay, *Freud: A Life for our Time.* New York: W.W. Norton (1998).

Calvin S. Hall, *A Primer of Freudian Psychology.* New York: Penguin Putnam (1954, 1999).

5 Twins have their day

Members of a family tend to look alike: the son looks like his father, the sister looks like her brother. Likewise, mental illness runs in families: the grandmother had bipolar disorder, the grandson has bipolar disorder. We call it heredity. As early as the fourth century B.C., the wise Hippocrates pondered how it could happen. 'The seed,' he wrote, 'comes from all parts of the body, healthy seed from healthy parts, diseased seed from diseased parts.'[40] When all the various seeds unite in the embryo, they create a complete body that resembles the parents. Since the offspring may be born of 'diseased seed from diseased parts,' diseases carried by one or both parents are passed on to the children. Hippocrates's ideas influenced the so-called preformationists of the late seventeenth century. Their explanation was simpler, yet all the more fantastic, for they believed that the entire form of the unborn adult is already present in the sperm or egg.

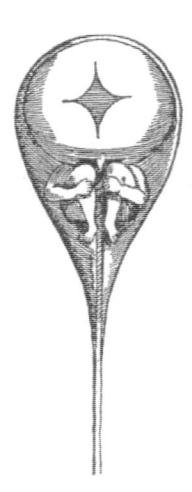

Preformation, a human homunculus inside a sperm [Nicolaas Hartsoeker, 1695]

---

[40] Hippocrates, *Airs Waters Places*, part 14.

While the similarity of physical features across generations was plainly visible to all ancients, it may not have been obvious that family similarities also extend to behaviors. Since there were no written histories of family life, patterns of behavior could have gone unnoticed. Even psychological traits are heritable, but these too could have been missed, because mental life is complex and infinitely variable. And, while it is true that most mental illnesses are at least partially inherited, none is so strongly tied to genetics that the same illness invariably appears in every generation. These considerations complicated and delayed the realization that heredity plays a strong role in the genesis of mental illness.

Political cartoon mocking a minister with a large nose [Honoré Daumier, 1833]

Asylums started recording information about patients in the eighteenth century, but the earliest surviving documents show only admissions, deaths and discharges. Over time, the data became more fulsome and included case histories. Doctors took what patient information they had to categorize cases according to probable cause. The conclusions they drew from these data were discussed by William Black in his book published in 1789.[41]

---

[41] William Black, *Comparative View of the Mortality of the Human Species at All Ages; and of the Diseases and Casualties by Which They are Destroyed or Annoyed.* London: C. Dilly (1788), pp. 249–250.

With regard to certain of these proposals, Black wrote, 'Most of the proximate causes assigned in authors [sic] for madness, are mere hypotheses; and of no active use to the community or to medicine.' He refused to believe one author who had written that insanity at Bethlem—in one particular year—was caused entirely by financial losses 'in the South-Sea scheme.' Determined to prove this man wrong, Black 'took the trouble' to investigate for himself records kept at the same hospital. In a sample that contained 'nearly one third of the whole patients during fifteen years,' Black found the leading cause to be 'misfortunes, troubles, disappointments and grief (206 cases), followed by family and hereditary (115 cases), fever (110 cases) and religion and methodism (90 cases). As for revolutions of the seasons and effects of the moon, these had 'no conspicuous effects.'

Other analyses, conducted elsewhere, further implicated family and heredity as the leading causes of insanity. A report from the York Retreat in England stated that parental illnesses caused insanity in 70 patients, while indirect ancestors were responsible in 143 cases. Overall, heredity—either direct or indirect—was the presumed cause of illness in 51 percent of cases at York. Doctors and asylum directors throughout Europe and North America welcomed such reports, because they were feeling pressure from the rising tide of patients. Coming to grips with the cause of mental illness was seen as an essential first step in dealing with the problem.

Asylum populations further exploded in the second half of the nineteenth century. Reports spoke of astonishingly high rates of insanity. In Scotland, one study found that one of every 390 citizens was insane. Topping that, a Norwegian investigator named Ludvig Dahl compiled census data from dozens of individual parishes, counting a total of 5,071 insane persons (including 'idiots'), or one in every 293 citizens. These startling statistics drove people to look deeper into the phenomenon of heredity, it being the likely cause. Dahl, for example, created what was probably the first pedigree chart, or family tree. His chart showed relationships among five generations of a single family, complete with the mental status of every individual. Fourteen of the 27 family members in recent generations were identified as insane (including 'idiots').

When heredity became a hot topic among European intellectuals, it was inevitable that two of England's most prominent scientists would get involved. Charles Darwin, of course, knew all about heredity because it was central to his theory of evolution. But it was also, for him, a personal issue because he and his wife had the same grandfather, Josiah Wedgwood, the maker of fine pottery. In other words, Charles Darwin and Emma Wedgewood were first cousins. Soon after the marriage, Darwin became aware of reports describing deformation, disease and mental defects in children born of closely related parents. Anxious about what might happen with his own children, Darwin sought reassurance from statistics. To this end, he prevailed upon a friend who happened to be a member of parliament, pleading with him to get a question on cousin marriages inserted into the census. That effort failed (parliament did not insert the question), leaving Charles and Emma in the dark on the issue as their family grew to include ten children. Three of the children died before the age of eleven, three others never had any children of their own, while the remaining four boys had successful careers. Despite suggestions to the contrary, it is impossible to say what effect, if any, inbreeding had on the lives of these children.

Charles Darwin with eldest child, William Francis Galton

The second English scientist fascinated by heredity was Charles Darwin's half-cousin, Francis Galton. Whereas Darwin will forever be known as the father of evolutionary biology, Galton's legacy is more mixed. He thought himself a genius, and he probably was. Wikipedia's summary of his expertise tells it all: statistician, polymath, sociologist, psychologist, anthropologist, eugenicist, tropical explorer, geographer, inventor, meteorologist, proto-geneticist and psychometrician. Galton came to the study of heredity late in life, after reading Darwin's monumental work, *The Origin of Species*, published in 1859. After conducting research into heredity, Galton became an advocate of eugenics, the social program that aims to improve human populations through selective breeding. His association with the discredited eugenics movement tarnished his name, but one cannot deny his contributions to the vexing problem of how, and in what measure, human traits are inherited.

Darwin and Galton briefly collaborated in an attempt to prove Darwin's theory of heredity. It began around 1868 when Darwin wrote to a correspondent, 'I wish I had known of these views of Hippocrates before I had published, for they seem almost identical with mine—merely a change of terms—and an application of them to classes of facts necessarily unknown to the old philosopher.' The change of terms refers to Darwin's preference for the word 'pangenesis', meaning genesis in the whole body, while the application of new facts refers to recent discoveries in regard to plant and animal cells. Darwin proposed that every part of the body emits a small particle, called a 'gemmule'. For reproduction, all the gemmules—from everywhere in the body—collect in the sperm or egg. Each gemmule carries the unique configuration of the associated body part, *including* any changes that may have occurred during the life of the individual. Darwin also had thoughts on what happens to traits as they pass from one generation to the next. He believed that the child receives a blended copy of the mother's traits and the father's traits. For example, if the mother has red hair and the father black hair, the child will have brown hair. His critics were quick to point out that the assumption could not be correct, since blending would eliminate all distinctive traits, in which case Darwin's own theory of evolution—based on the selection of beneficial traits—would be falsified. Anyway, Francis Galton agreed to test Darwin's idea by conducting a series of blood transfusion experiments with pigmented rabbits. Unfortunately for both geniuses, the results provided absolutely no support for Darwin's blending idea.

While happy to help Darwin test his theory, Galton himself was less interested in biology than statistics. He saw statistics as the means by which one could predict future events based on past events. More particularly, he thought that he could calculate the probabilities of a person acquiring certain traits, whether physical or mental. As a first step, Galton formulated what he called the Law of Ancestral Heredity, whereby 'the two parents contribute between them on the average one-half, or 0.5 of the total heritage of the offspring; the four grandparents, one-quarter, or (0.5)2; the eight great-grandparents, one-eighth, or (0.5)3, and so on.'[42] To test the

---

[42] Francis Galton, 'The average contribution of each several ancestor [sic] to the total heritage of the offspring.' *Proceedings of the Royal Society of London* 61:401–413 (1897), p. 402.

propositions, Galton's well-to-do collaborators collected mounds of family history data and constructed numerous family pedigrees. Elementary applications of Galton's law seemed to bear out the predictions, so Galton added correlation and other mathematical tools to increase the utility of hereditary studies. One of the first products of these advanced methods was Galton's study of the inheritance of genius, his own included of course. Later, he investigated the inheritance of insanity and criminality. But it was his studies of feeble-mindedness (idiocy) that had the greatest impact. Government ministers had encouraged the work, hoping to stem the flow of patients into their increasingly crowded mental asylums. When the data suggested a strong pattern of inheritance in feeble-mindedness, Galton argued that it was time for a program of selective human reproduction. More on this in the Perspective section at the end of the chapter.

As Galton was promoting eugenics in London, biologists in Germany were updating Darwin's theory of pangenesis. Abandoning the notion of gemmules, they argued for predispositions (*Anlagen*) which, they said, determine individual traits. Present in the embryo, the *Anlagen* were supposedly responsible not only for physical traits, but also for mental traits such as 'temperament, education, favorite pursuits, social intercourse, morality and religiosity'.[43] And crucially, psychiatrists believed that a specific type of *Anlage* was responsible for mental illness. There was much discussion about how, exactly, an *Anlage* could act to increase the risk for mental illness. Read today, these treatises resemble modern genetics, except it was never clear whether the Germans thought of *Anlagen* as abstract essences or physical particles. Gregor Mendel's experiments with edible peas sharpened the debate.

Mendel grew up on the family farm where he worked as a gardener and beekeeper. Poor and seeking educational opportunities, he joined St. Thomas's Abbey in the town of Brno, now part of the Czech Republic. While training to be a priest, he found time on his hands. So, encouraged by elders who knew of his farming background, he began studying the inheritance of traits in peas. In the years between 1856 and 1863, he planted tens of thousands of plants on land within the abbey grounds. In numerous individual experiments, he fertilized one true-breeding variety with pollen from a second true-breeding variety and then observed what type of plants emerged in succeeding generations. From this work came Mendel's 'law of dominance', which contrasts so-called dominant trains with so-called recessive traits. Yellow seed color, for example, is a dominant trait. Therefore,

---

[43] Theodore M. Porter (2018), p. 76. See suggested readings.

when Mendel crossed a yellow-seed plant with a green-seed plant, *all* first generation plants had yellow seeds. Green seed color, on the other hand, is a recessive trait, so *none* of the first-generation plants had green seeds, but one-quarter of the second-generation plants had green seeds. Note that the crossing of a yellow-seed variety and a green-seed variety never resulted in blended offspring, that is, there were no seeds of a yellow-green type.

Mendel's experiments with the humble pea plant dealt Darwin's idea of blended inheritance a fatal blow while simultaneously boosting the idea of discrete factors in heredity. The Germans called them *Anlagen,* Mendel called them elementen, and we now call them genes. Despite the great importance of Mendel's work, it was not immediately recognized as such. Mendel announced his results at two meetings of the local natural history society in 1865, but only about forty people attended, and apparently none understood their significance. His work lay fallow until rediscovered at the turn of the century. By that time, chromosomes had been discovered, and soon the *Anlagen*, the elementen and the genes all found homes in chromosomes. No longer did anyone doubt that they were real physical things.

Gregor Mendel (left) and Ernst Rüdin

As Mendel's work became widely known, researchers in various fields considered potential applications, and psychiatrists were no less interested than cattle breeders and agriculturalists. The psychiatric community at the time was busy identifying and defining the different kinds of mental illness. Rather than simply madness, there was now a long and rapidly growing list of seemingly unique disorders. So, with the insertion of genetics into the discussion, researchers began to ask, Are there specific genes for specific mental illnesses? And, if so, are the genes of the dominant type or the recessive type?

A Swiss-German psychiatrist was the first to take up the challenge. Ernst Rüdin had always been interested in the social consequences of mental illness, much more so than in treatments. Above all, he hoped to find a way of preventing mental illness. Early in his career, he expressed a 'strong urge... to wipe out illness at its roots, in particular to prevent insanity.' This would appear to be a laudable goal, but regrettably, it was an attitude that wound up leading Rüdin into some dark areas of professional misconduct. We will learn more about these failings below, but first, his research. It began with what we would today call epidemiology, and from there it progressed to something like modern genetics.

When Rüdin examined admission records from the psychiatric hospital in Munich, he found a surprising number of families in which two or more individuals had been diagnosed with schizophrenia. To better understand the evidence, he initiated a large detailed investigation of the affected families. Contrary to the practice of earlier researchers, who had assumed that the hospital records were complete and accurate, Rüdin sought to confirm and elaborate them. He gathered as much information as possible, not only on the patients themselves but on the patients' families. In addition to interviewing family members, he spoke with attending physicians and received comments from teachers and school officials. It was a lot of work, but it provided him with an unprecedented amount of reliable data. He also collaborated with some of Germany's most knowledgeable statisticians to calculate the probability of a child developing schizophrenia based on the history of illness in the family. Due to the size of the study and the care with which it was conducted, psychiatrists and other professionals eagerly awaited the results.

The question foremost on everyone's mind was whether schizophrenia is inherited as a dominant gene or a recessive gene. To answer that question, Rüdin focused on the patient's immediate family. He found relevant information on 755 schizophrenia patients, 2,732 siblings and most of the parents. If schizophrenia were a dominant Mendelian trait, every child with schizophrenia should have had at least one parent with schizophrenia, but Rüdin did not find that to be the case. Alternatively, if schizophrenia were a recessive trait, 25 percent of the siblings should have had schizophrenia, but again, the data did not fit the model. Rather than 25 percent, the data indicated that only 5 percent of the siblings had schizophrenia. Desperate to prove the relevance of Mendel's laws, Rüdin considered that two genes acting together might account for the illness. But even after applying appropriate analyses, he still had no straightforward evidence for either dominant genes or recessive genes. The numbers simply weren't there.

Although Rüdin failed to relate the inheritance of mental illness to the inheritance of pea plant colors, he did confirm the general relevance of heredity. Moreover, his statistics on the risks of developing either schizophrenia or bipolar disorder match up well with modern values. His research showed that a child with one schizophrenic parent had a 10 percent risk of developing schizophrenia, and a child with one bipolar parent had a 32 percent risk of developing bipolar disorder. By comparison, the modern values are 13 percent and 15 to 20 percent respectively. His views on the causes of mental illness also align with current opinion in that he did not say that heredity explains everything; life experiences are also important.

Children get genes from their parents, but the parents also provide a home environment complete with all its physical, emotional and psychological peculiarities. That environment may be impoverished, it may contain germs, and the mother and father may fight. Any of these factors, and countless others, could account for mental illness even in the absence of hereditary factors. Rüdin realized that a common environment could also explain family patterns of illness, such as when multiple siblings acquire schizophrenia. Most probably however, as Rüdin and most of his contemporaries understood, mental illness is caused by a combination of hereditary factors *and* environmental factors. Rüdin understood this and so did Francis Galton. The problem, as Galton famously put it, lay in separating 'nature from nurture'.[44]

While grappling with the dilemma of heredity versus environment, scientists discovered that twin pairs provide a near-perfect means of resolving the issue. As with any set of siblings, the contribution of the environment is similar for both twins, because both grow up in the same home. Therefore, *if genes contribute nothing* to the risk of illness—if all that matters is the environment—then we would expect that if one twin gets a particular illness, the other twin will get it too. Let's call this a 'double-hit', meaning that both twins have the illness. Importantly, in the scenario just described, both twins will become ill regardless of whether they are identical or fraternal. However, *if genes do matter*, then much depends on whether the twins

---

[44] In modern usage, genetics has replaced nature, and nurture is now environment. The environment is understood to include personal experiences, social interactions and physical situations.

are identical (100 percent shared genes) or fraternal (50 percent shared genes). In the case of identical twins, we'd still expect double-hits, but for fraternal twins, we'd expect many more single-hits because, while the environments remain the same, the risky genes might be in just one of the twins. By applying appropriate mathematics to the rates of double-hits and single-hits in identical twins versus fraternal twins, it is possible to tease out the relative contributions of heredity and environment. It can be done for a specific mental illness or, indeed, for any trait. As of 2015, the twin method had been used to determine the relative contributions of nature and nurture in 17,804 different human traits.[45]

Back in Victorian England, Francis Galton was constantly on the lookout for new ways of testing his hereditary models. Naturally enough, he was the first person to use twins in a study of nature versus nurture. What is surprising, though, is that he completely missed the point of using twins, and he misinterpreted the results. He set out to see how life histories affect, or fail to affect, physical appearances, personality and handwriting. To this end, he studied 'similar' twins growing up in different environments and 'dissimilar' twins growing up in the same environment. He found that some, but not all, of the similar pairs became less similar when their environments changed. Confusing yes, and inconclusive too. At least the results for the dissimilar twins were more conclusive. Of them, he wrote, 'I have not a single case in which my correspondents [his research collaborators] speak of originally dissimilar characters having become more assimilated though identity of nurture.' Then came his illogical interpretation, 'There is no escape from the conclusion that nature prevails enormously over nurture.'[46]

Apart from the poor design and the false conclusion, we cannot fault Galton for having failed to compare actual identical twins with actual fraternal twins—instead of 'similar' and 'dissimilar' twins—for the simple reason that he did not know the extent of their differences. He only knew that some pairs looked more similar than others. It would be another half century before biologists discovered that identical twins come from a single sperm fertilizing a single egg, whereas fraternal twins come from two separate sperm fertilizing two separate eggs. Even then, researchers continued for some time to rely on surface appearances for distinguishing the two types. It was not until the introduction of DNA analyses that people came to

---

[45] Tinca J.C. Polderman et al., 'Meta-analysis of the heritability of human traits based on fifty years of twin studies,' *Nature Genetics* 47:702–709 (2015).

[46] Francis Galton, 'The history of twins, as a criterion of the relative powers of nature and nurture.' *Fraser's Magazine*, November 1875. Quotes on pp. 575, 576.

understand the deeper meaning of identical versus fraternal when speaking of twins. Ever since, twin studies routinely confirm the twin type by examining DNA.

Twin studies began in earnest in the early 1920s. First came a study by a German ophthalmologist named Walter Jablonski.[47] He wanted to know if refraction and astigmatism arise from a hereditary disposition or from environmental exposures. Using what is now considered to be the 'classical' twin method, he measured corneal refractions and degrees of astigmatism in pairs of identical twin pairs and compared the differences to those found in pairs of fraternal twin pairs. After finding smaller differences in the identical pairs than in the fraternal pairs, he concluded that genetics are chiefly responsible for determining eye shapes. Shortly afterwards, a German dermatologist conducted a similar study in regard to birthmarks (naevi). As with the visual markers used by Walter Jablonski, the dermatologist found that the number of birthmarks on an individual is more similar in pairs of identical twins than in pairs of non-identical twins. In the same year, the American psychologist Curtis Merriman used an unconventional, nonclassical, method for his investigation of intelligence. After challenging his subjects with a battery of four tests, he found that the scores correlated 98 percent in pairs of identical twins, implying a strong genetic basis, but he did not test any fraternal twins. Modern studies put the correlation for identical adult twins at around 80 percent, and around 60 percent for fraternal twins.

So, what do twin studies say about mental illness? The first studies were conducted by members of Ernst Rüdin's group in Munich, one of whom, Hans Luxenburger, searched through hospital records at twelve Bavarian mental institutions.[48] From a total of 16,382 patients with twin siblings, Luxenburger found 32 twin pairs in which at least one twin was diagnosed with schizophrenia. The sample size is too small for reliable statistics, but the results are nonetheless striking. In 19 identical pairs, there were 11 cases in which both twins had schizophrenia. By contrast, in *none* of the 13 pairs of fraternal twins did both twins have schizophrenia. Luxenberger also looked at twins with an 'affective' illness (primarily mania and depression), with similar results. Still, he was disappointed, because he expected

---

[47] Shiao Hui M. Liew et al., 'The first "classical" twin study? Analysis of refractive error using monozygotic and dizygotic twins published in 1922.' *Twin Research and Human Genetics* 8(3):198–200 (2005).

[48] The research of Hans Luxenburger and other twin study pioneers is described in I.I. Gottesman (1991). See Suggesting Readings.

that the identical twins would have *exactly* the same medical histories and symptoms, and that was not the case. Leaving aside Luxenberger's regrets, and despite the caveat concerning sample sizes, his results have turned out to be very much in line with modern twin studies.

Franz Kallmann was another psychiatrist working in Rüdin's department. Fearing for his safety in a climate of rising antisemitism, he fled to the United States in 1936. Once settled in New York, he looked for twins in records of the state's psychiatric institutions. He came up with nearly 600 twin pairs in which at least one member had schizophrenia. Like Luxenburger before him, he found many more double-hits in identical twins than in fraternal twins. Because his patient sample was larger than Luxenburger's, and because he was by then an American, his study was seen—in America—as more credible. Also in Rüdin's department during the mid-1930s was Eliot Slater, an ambitious young psychiatrist visiting from London, England. After returning home, he and a colleague conducted a large twin study at the Maudsley Hospital. They tracked several types of psychiatric conditions in addition to schizophrenia and affective disorders. Once again, the conclusion was inescapable: mental illness has a strong hereditary component.

Scientists weren't satisfied with descriptors like a 'strong hereditary component.' They wanted to know the exact percentage that could be attributed to heredity. The answer came in the 1960s with the invention of a quantitative method for just that purpose. Heritability is a technical term that quantifies the proportion of risk that can be explained by genetic variation; the remaining proportion is attributed to the environment.[49] Of the several ways of calculating heritability, the easiest is by means of a well-conducted twin study. In its simplest form, the method involves subtracting the rate of double-hits in fraternal pairs (both twins have the illness) from the rate of double-hits in identical pairs and multiplying the result by two.[50] For example, if 80 percent of identical twin pairs are double-hits, while fraternal twins have only 60 percent double-hits, the heritability is 2 x 20, or 40, meaning that 40 percent of the risk is attributed to hereditary factors, 60 percent to environmental factors.

---

[49] More precisely, heritability estimates *the proportion of risk variability that is attributed to genetics.*

[50] Methods of estimating heritability are controversial. For a technical review of the issues, see P.M. Visscher, W.G. Hill and N.R. Wray, 'Heritability in the genomics era—concepts and misconceptions.' *Nature Reviews Genetics* 9: 255–266 (2008).

The chart below shows heritability estimates for several common psychiatric disorders.[51]

Mental Illness	Heritability (Range)
Autism	64 %–91 %
Bipolar disorder	73 %–93 %
Major depressive disorder	41 %–49 %
Schizophrenia	73 %–90 %

The chance that someone will become ill with one of these disorders depends largely on the DNA that he or she inherits. With the exception of depression, inherited factors matter far more than any environmental influence, and that includes family interactions. Note that the chart shows heritability values expressed in ranges rather than single values. Part of the variability is due to the inevitable small sample sizes in twin studies, which make for imperfect statistics. Besides that, the method is sensitive to where the study is conducted. Different locations have different environments, thus yielding different heritability estimates.

A final point about heritability. It measures the relative roles of heredity and environment within a specific population at a particular time. It does *not* explain the cause or causes of illness, either in a population or in any individual. Insights into specific genetic and environmental causes are certainly desirable, but unfortunately, extremely difficult to acquire. Scientists use the word 'complex' when speaking of mental illnesses and other illnesses like cancer, diabetes and heart disease. It means that there is no simple cause—not a single gene, not two genes, three or even dozens of genes; neither a germ nor a poison. For most complex illnesses, hundreds of genes and a similar number of environmental factors likely contribute. Furthermore, interactions occur between genes, between environmental factors, and between genes and the environment. Much work remains to be done before we reach a deep scientific understanding of the causes of complex illnesses.

---

[51] Estimates from R. Uher, 'Gene-environment interactions in severe mental illness.' *Frontiers in Psychiatry* 5:48 (2014); K.S. Kendler et al., 'The genetic epidemiology of treated major depression in Sweden.' *American Journal of Psychiatry* 175 (11):1137–1144 (2018); B. Tick et al., 'Heritability of autism spectrum disorders: A meta-analysis of twin studies.' *Journal of Child Psychology and Psychiatry* 57(5):585–595 (2016).

Perspective

Scientific studies of heredity, especially twin studies, help us identify the sources of mental illness. It is no longer acceptable to say that it is God's will, possession by the devil or moral failure. No, it all comes down to heredity and the environment. Ignorance of this fact breeds stigma and blaming the victim, whereas twin studies contribute to realistic, non-judgemental attitudes.[52]

However, there is a dark side to research on hereditary, namely its use in justifying unethical theories and practices. These unfortunate applications did not spring exclusively from studies of mental illness, but persons with mental illness have been especially affected. Therefore, any perspective on discoveries in this field must include consideration of their multiple consequences.[53]

It all started in the late nineteenth century, as the implications of Charles Darwin's work sank in. Darwin filled his famous book, *On the Origin of Species*, with striking examples of animal species changing over time. He described how natural selection acts to increase biological fitness, defined as the ability to survive and reproduce. Species lacking suitable traits suffer from neglect in the selection process, so they degenerate and go extinct. Some contemporaries of Darwin started thinking about the possibility of largescale changes in human societies—not in terms of increased fitness, but rather as a possible example of *decreased* fitness.

Commentators connected rising crime rates and rising admissions at mental asylums with a trend toward moral degeneration. Left unimpeded, they said, moral degeneration would be the ruin of mankind. One of the loudest voices spreading alarm belonged to Benedict Morel, a psychiatrist working in Rouen, France. His patients came from poor families, and many drank excessive amounts of alcohol. He imagined a pattern of degeneration sweeping through human societies, passing from one generation to the next and worsening in each successive generation. Thus, family members in the first generation might be alcoholic, feeble-minded and depraved, in the second generation they would have epilepsy or hysteria, in the third generation insanity, and so on until our species went extinct. The idea of moral degen-

---

[52] For more on the stigmatization of mental illness, see Ronald Chase, *The Physical Basis of Mental Illness*. Philadelphia, PA: Routledge (2012).

[53] Eugenics and degeneration theory are fully examined in Philippa Levine's book (2017). See suggested readings.

eration became a popular theory of mental illness in Europe and America, favored by psychiatrists as well as the general public.

Degeneration theory eventually died for lack of evidence, but not before it nurtured an equally dismal theory, also based on hereditary principles. Francis Galton was an instigator and one of its most forceful promoters. As a complement to Darwin's theory of natural selection, Galton proposed a program of 'rational selection', in which society would reduce the number of degenerate citizens, while simultaneously increasing the number of gifted citizens. In 1883, he coined the word eugenics, from the Greek words *eu*, meaning good, and *genes*, meaning born. The eugenicists encouraged reproduction by 'high-quality' persons through offers of financial rewards and other incentives. At the same time, they sought to limit reproduction in families marked by intellectual or physical 'defects'. They wanted to prohibit marriages between 'low-quality' individuals, either through the mandatory use of contraception and abortion or other means. And, most controversially, they advocated sterilization for persons judged unfit (in the Darwinian sense).

The first forced sterilizations were done in the United States, but the worst violations were committed in Nazi Germany where, in 1933, a law for 'the prevention of hereditarily diseased offspring' effectively legalized 300,000 forced sterilizations. It targeted individuals identified as congenitally blind, feebleminded or insane. The sterilization program was followed by a murderous policy of involuntary euthanasia—named *Aktion T4*— that claimed another 300,000 victims, mostly mental patients and people with physical disabilities. These killings happened *before* the opening of concentration camps, and Jews were not singled out. The eugenicists thought they were building a better, healthier Germany. Others had a broader vision which was not just about illness and disability, but also race. Theirs was a plan for 'racial hygiene'.

An unsettling detail in this sordid history is the fact that Ernst Rüdin, the psychiatrist who conducted groundbreaking research into the hereditary origins of mental illness, was an early and ardent supporter of racial hygiene. In 1936, he assured Adolph Hitler that 'the results [of his research] will contribute to providing an ever-firmer basis for the further expansion and realization of your racial hygiene program in the German Volk.'[54] Persuaded by Rüdin's commitment, Hitler rewarded him with funding for an additional 48 secretaries and 12 more scientists. Eliot Slater and Franz Kallmann—both

---

[54] Matthias M. Weber, 'Ernst Rüdin, 1874–1952: A German psychiatrist and geneticist.' *American Journal of Medical Genetics* 67:323–331 (1996), p. 328.

of whom worked in Rudin's department on twin research—also flirted with eugenics. Hermann Siemens, the dermatologist who hit upon the correct design for twin studies, became a Nazi and a promoter of racial hygiene. And, in Chapter 7 we will see that Hans Asperger's contributions to psychiatry were similarly tainted by collaboration with the Nazis. These were all complex men, stalwart in science yet misled in morals.

Suggested readings

Irving I. Gottesman, *Schizophrenia Genesis.* New York: W.H. Freeman (1991).

Philippa Levine, *Eugenics: A Very Short Introduction.* Oxford, UK: Oxford University Press (2nd ed., 2017).

Theodore M. Porter, *Genetics in the Madhouse.* Princeton, NJ: Princeton University Press (2018).

6 A disruption at 1q42.1

Confirming a role for heredity in mental illness was a great starter, but harder tasks lay ahead. Many scientifically minded psychiatrists thought that the mechanism of hereditary transmission would be quickly ascertained after Georg Mendel discovered dominant and recessive genes, but Ernst Rüdin proved them wrong. Later, just when DNA was about to be discovered—on the early morning of November 1, 1952 to be exact—a big bang was heard on a small Pacific island.

Only a few American weapon experts were there to watch the first detonation of a hydrogen bomb (H-bomb, fusion bomb, thermonuclear bomb). Dubbed 'Mike', the bomb was almost 500 times more powerful than the bomb that devastated the Japanese city of Nagasaki a few years earlier. Not to be outdone by Mike, the Soviet Union quickly conducted its own thermonuclear weapon test, and on March 1, 1954, the United States completely destroyed a pristine Pacific atoll named Bikini. These explosions not only wreaked havoc on the ground, they also sent vast amounts of radioactive dust into the air. The radioactive fallout from the Bikini blast alone contaminated an area of 7,000 square miles. Because radiation of the type present in that dust damages cellular DNA, it didn't take long for doctors to realize the risk to human health, especially if there was to be more testing, let alone thermonuclear warfare.

As a precaution, the Medical Research Council of the United Kingdom established a research group in Scotland. They named it the Clinical Effects of Radiation Unit and charged it with analyzing the blood of newborn babies. The unit faithfully carried out its job, not stopping until it had obtained 10,000 samples. In addition to biochemical testing, the researchers put blood cells under a microscope to examine chromosomes, the small, wiggly packages of DNA present in all human cells. It is not possible to identify gene mutations with this method, but it is relatively easy to see chromosomal abnormalities. Humans have 24 different chromosomes (including the two sex chromosomes, X and Y). Each one can be uniquely identified by its characteristic size and shape. After staining, it is also pos-

Human chromosomes [National Human Genome Research Institute, USA]

sible to see light and dark areas, called bands, that are also distinctive for each chromosome.

A related project took blood samples from boys detained at institutions for juvenile delinquents; the Brits called them borstals. One of these samples came under scrutiny after it was found to contain a chromosomal abnormality. The sample in question was provided by a 'physically normal' 18-year old who had been diagnosed with 'adolescent conduct disorder'. Tests on members of the boy's family revealed similar chromosomal abnormalities in the father, the paternal grandfather and other individuals scattered across four generations. This was the beginning of a tortuous path that eventually led to the identification of gene mutations contributing to mental illness.[55]

We pause here to understand in more detail the nature of the abnormalities seen in the Scottish family. As mentioned, chromosomes have light and dark bands. They are so distinctive and so consistent that any deviation from the normal pattern can be immediately recognized by a trained observer. In cells of the borstal boy, experts saw a band on chromosome 1 that is ordinarily found on chromosome 11, and another band on chromosome 11 that had evidently moved from chromosome 1. Events such as these, where two chunks of DNA trade places across two chromosomes, are called balanced translocations. If the translocation occurs in a sperm cell or an ovum, it will be present in every cell of the newborn child, and it

---

[55] Patricia A. Jacobs et al., 'Studies on a family with three cytogenetic markers.' *Annals of Human Genetics* 33:325–336 (1970).

will be passed on through successive generations, but not in every individual. Chromosomal translations are fairly common, appearing about once in every 500 newborns. Usually they cause no harm, and indeed, it was said at the time that everyone in the Scottish family was healthy. Except, of course, for the 18-year-old, who was a juvenile delinquent.

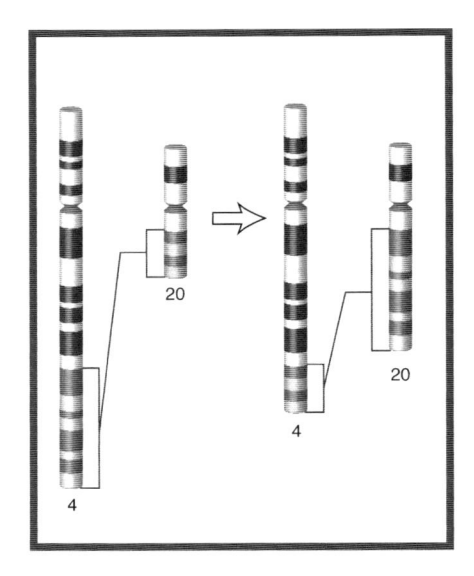

Schematic illustration of translocation, here involving chromosomes 4 and 20 [Human Genome Research Institute, USA]

Twenty years after the initial report, scientists in Edinburgh began to suspect that, actually, all was not well within the family. Their concerns surfaced after learning of a paper read at a meeting of the American Society of Human Genetics. Scientists at the meeting reported on an American family in which five members had a chromosomal translocation, and all five were ill with 'an affective disorder'. The report rang a bell with the Edinburgh investigators, causing them to question the now decades-old assessment of mental health in the Scottish family. They decided to track down as many family members as they could, update all the medical histories and re-examine all the chromosomes. For the medical histories, they scrutinized relevant hospital records, notes taken by family doctors and pharmaceutical prescriptions. They conducted in-person interviews with family members and their caregivers. And, when warranted in a particular case, a psychiatrist made a specific diagnosis. All of this was done by one group of researchers, while a second group re-examined the chromosomes.

To reduce the chance that an assessment of chromosomal damage might be biased by an earlier assessment of mental illness—or vice versa—each research group worked independently of the other.

By the time the research started, nineteen members of the four-generation family had died. It was not possible to examine chromosomes in the deceased, but it proved relatively easy to update pertinent medical information. Altogether, researchers managed to assess a total of 77 family members for both mental health and chromosomal damage. It is important to note that researchers did not expect that every person in the pedigree would have a translocation. When just one parent has this type of abnormality, only half of the children inherit it and, as it turned out, 34 of the 77 family members had the translocation—pretty close to 50 percent. Knowing who had the translocation and who did not, the researchers could now match up the chromosome data with the psychological assessments.

The results, announced in the U.K.'s most prestigious medical journal, were striking.[56] The main finding was that 16 of the 34 persons *with the translocation* had a psychiatric diagnosis (nearly 50%), compared to only 5 of 43 persons *with no translation* (12 percent). When the investigators split the mental disorders into serious conditions (schizophrenia, major depression, suicide) and minor conditions (anxiety, minor depression, alcoholism), they found that individuals carrying the chromosomal translocation had a mix of serious disorders and minor disorders, whereas individuals with no translation had only minor issues, if any.

These numbers clearly indicate an association between the chromosomal abnormality and mental illness. The study authors closed their groundbreaking article with a typically British—and scientific—understatement, 'The findings together point to ... a promising area to examine for a gene or series of genes predisposing to some cases of major mental illness.'

Since the translocations in the Scottish family were balanced—with chromosomes 1 and 11 exchanging bits of their DNA—the sought-after 'gene or series of genes' could have been on either chromosome 1 or chromosome 11. However, after further analysis, it was determined that the translocated band on chromosome 11 contained no gene at all, whereas the translocated band on chromosome 1 had two genes.[57] Biologists have a scheme for nam-

---

[56] David St. Clair et al., 'Association within a family of a balanced autosomal translocation with major mental illness.' *The Lancet* 336:13–16 (1990).

[57] Only about one percent of human DNA contains genes that code for, or make, protein. Other DNA sequences, known as non-coding genes or non-coding DNA, do not make protein but regulate the activity of protein-coding genes. The translocated band on chromosome 11 is one such DNA sequence.

ing chromosomal bands according to their locations. The band on which the two genes were found is 1q42.1, referring to the long arm q of chromosome 1 (rather than the short arm p), region number 4, band number 2, sub-band 1.

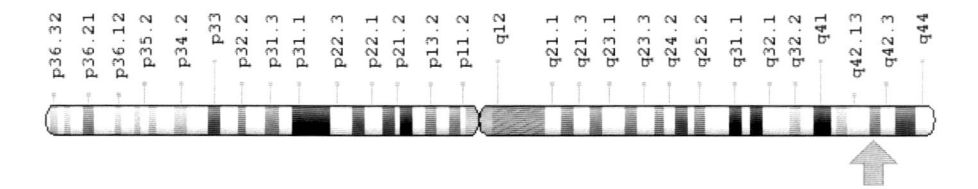

Location (arrow) of *DISC* genes on short arm q of chromosome 1 [National Library of Medicine, USA]

The next step involved drilling down to learn what, exactly, was the problem with the genes located at 1q42.1. Surprisingly, they found no mutation in either gene, meaning no change in the DNA code. However, they did find that the genes were shorter than normal. Somehow, part of the DNA got discarded during translocation. Just as biologists name chromosomal bands, geneticists name genes, with the discoverer assuming the responsibility. In this case, the two genes were named Disrupted-in-Schizophrenia 1 and Disrupted-in-Schizophrenia 2, abbreviated as *DISC1* and *DISC2*. It may seem like an odd choice, given that schizophrenia was just one of several mental illnesses identified in the Scottish family, but schizophrenia, with its frequently bizarre behaviors and poor prognosis, has long been emblematic of severe mental illnesses. In the years since their discovery, *DISC1* and *DISC2* have been the subjects of more than 17,000 research articles.

In 2001, psychiatrists conducted yet another study of the Scottish family.[58] There were more interviews with doctors and family members, more case notes, and better adherence to up-to-date diagnostic criteria. The investigators summarized their results in the form of a family tree, shown on the next page. Due to deaths, slightly fewer family members were available for assessments this time around, but nonetheless, the results were much the same. Of the 29 family members *with a translocation*, 1 had bipolar disorder, 7 had schizophrenia and 10 had major depression, whereas none

---

[58] D.H.R. Blackwood et al., 'Schizophrenia and affective disorders—cosegregation with a translocation at chromosome 1q42 that directly disrupts brain-expressed genes: clinical and P300 findings in a family.' *American Journal of Human Genetics* 69:428–433 (2001).

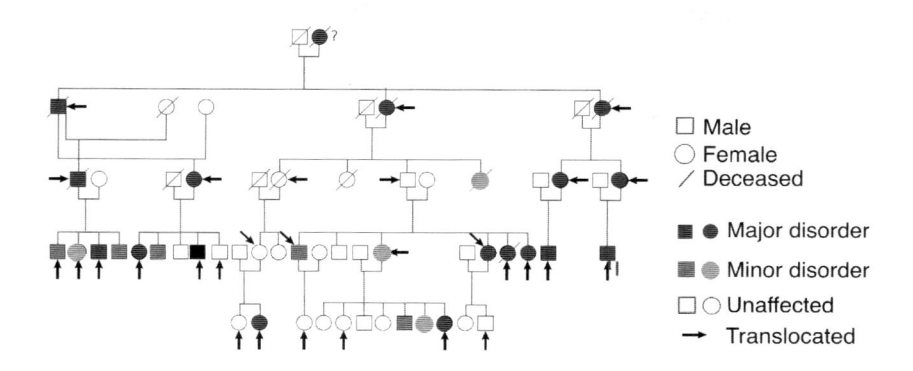

Family pedigree. Each row is a separate generation. [modified from Blackwood et al., 2001]

of the 38 family members *without a translocation* had a major psychiatric illness. Three investigations in thirty-one years confirmed a strong association between disrupted *DISC genes* and major psychiatric illness. Since the methods ramped up each time, so too did confidence in the results.

Something interesting is obviously happening with *DISC1* and *DISC2*, but exactly how the anomalies relate to mental illness is a question that remains open to this day. One thing is clear, however. It cannot be that disruption of these genes is enough to cause mental illness, because many individuals who have the disruptions remain healthy. Rather than causing an illness, the disruption seems to raise the *risk* of illness. Something else must contribute to the risk, either additional gene defects or life experiences or both.

Most genes make proteins, but a few do not, and *DISC2* belongs in the latter category. Therefore, and without going into details, suffice it to say that researchers have largely ignored *DISC2* in their efforts to understand the 1q42.1 translocation.[59] The focus turned to the protein made by *DISC1*. Some proteins promote chemical reactions, others act as messengers or signal receptors, while still others transport, store or pump biochemicals. The name of the protein made by the *DISC1* gene is—naturally enough—DISC1.[60] What, then, is the function of DISC1? It is a crucial question, because knowing what a protein does provides clues to its role in creating illness. That knowledge, in turn, helps us design better treatments

---

[59] See note 3.

[60] Biologists write *DISC1*, in italics, when referring to the gene. They write DISC1, no italics, when referring to the protein made by the gene.

and possibly even prevent an illness from developing in the first place. Although methods exist for discovering protein functions, they do not always deliver as promised, and that has been the case for the DISC1 protein.

The human body contains approximately 20,000 different proteins, yet functions are known for less than half that number. The chemical structure of the protein, by itself, is rarely sufficient for inferring function, so researchers have come up with experimental methods of discovery. If the protein of interest is also present in mice, the 'knockout' experiment can be used. Researchers employ molecular tricks to disable (knockout) the gene that makes the protein, then they look to see what happens to the experimental animal or more commonly, its offspring. If something doesn't look right or doesn't work right in the absence of the protein, scientists can usually track down the precise function. However, when there are no obvious effects, or the animal dies as was the case with *DISC1* knockouts, researchers turn to other strategies.

Most proteins accomplish their tasks by interacting with other proteins. Therefore, if you can identify the partner proteins, and you know the function of one or more of the partner proteins, the function of your mystery protein is likely similar. Researchers found thirty-four protein partners of DISC1.[61] Fortunately, the function of most of these interacting proteins was already known. In one way or another, they all pertain to synapses, those tiny structures situated at the points of contact between neurons. Each interacting protein is involved with either the construction of synapses, their participation in early brain development or their modifiability. Given the important functions of synapses, it is easy to imagine how a disrupted gene—in this case *DISC1*—could mess up synapses, which in turn could produce the signs and symptoms of mental illness. Easy to imagine, but difficult to prove, and so far, none of the possible scenarios has been validated.[62]

Inconclusive though they were, researchers saw enough in the protein interaction results to designate *DISC1* as a 'candidate gene' for schizophrenia, meaning that it was a gene that *might* be responsible for schizophrenia. Dozens more genes were later nominated, but *DISC1* was the first. Genes gained candidate status based on various criteria. Some, such as *DISC1*,

---

[61] L. M. Camargo et al., 'Disrupted in schizophrenia 1 interactome: evidence for the close connectivity of risk genes and a potential synaptic basis for schizophrenia.' *Molecular Psychiatry* 12:74–86 (2006).

[62] Akira Sawa, '*DISC1* and its protein interactomes for mental function.' *Biological Psychiatry* 85:283–284 (2019).

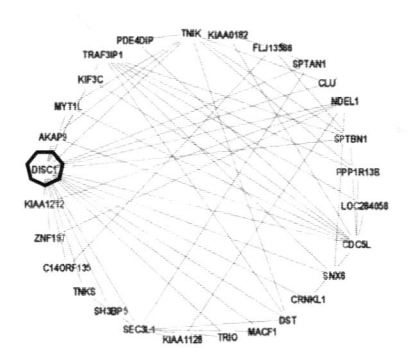

DISC1 protein interactome [Camargo et al., 2006]

were nominated based on their involvement with synapses. Others qualified because they make proteins involved with dopamine or serotonin, two neurotransmitters targeted by antipsychotic medications. A few were chosen based on their roles in neurodevelopment or immune functions. The protein products of these candidate genes had fetching names like brain-derived neurotrophic factor, v-akt murine thymona viral oncogene homolog 1, dystrobrevin binding protein 1, and glutamate receptor metabotropic 2.

Interest in candidate genes increased following reports that one or another of the candidate genes was more frequently mutated in schizophrenia patients than in healthy individuals. Intriguing, but not necessarily meaningful, because mutations are actually quite common, even in perfectly healthy people. Mutations are defined as changes in the sequence of DNA 'letters' that comprise the genetic code. Every cell in every human has about 3.3 billion DNA letters strung out on its chromosomes. Letter changes (mutations) occur at unpredictable spots throughout the genome, and most of them are harmless. They are so common that roughly one in every thousand DNA letters differs between any two individuals. Another way to look at this is to think of each person having 4–5 million genetic variants.[63] Considering these kinds of numbers, it is entirely possible to get misleading results *purely by chance* when testing for gene mutations.

Now, take a moment to think about coins instead of DNA letters. Imagine that you have a coin that you suspect is unbalanced. Ordinarily, if you flipped a perfectly good coin ten times, you would expect it to come up

---

[63] Strictly speaking, the *process* that creates genetic variation is called mutation. However, in popular usage 'mutation' refers to the *thing* itself, the genetic variant. In this book the terms mutation and variation are used interchangeably.

heads five times and tails five times. However, if the suspicious coin now comes up with six heads and four tails, would you be convinced that the suspicious coin is indeed unbalanced? Of course not. Any good scientist would say that it proves nothing. More flips are required—many more. Genetic researchers *did* test many patients and at least as many healthy controls before announcing an association between a candidate gene and schizophrenia. Nevertheless, subsequent research showed that they didn't test enough.

Ultimately, *DISC1*, along with all other candidate genes, fell victim to 'false positive' results due to inadequate sample sizes—something like tossing a coin ten times rather than a thousand times. The inadequacy of those early studies became apparent after the introduction of a new method of genetic analysis, called the genome-wide association study, or GWAS. Rather than testing one candidate gene after another in separate analyses, the GWAS scans across the entire genome searching for *any* variation that can be associated with a specific human trait. First used to study the risk of heart attacks, it has since been applied to many medical conditions including diabetes, hypertension, age-related macular degeneration and, of course, mental illness.

The largest GWAS for schizophrenia, so far, enrolled 37,000 patients and 113,000 healthy controls.[64] Unfortunately, when the results came in they showed the candidate genes performing poorly. Not a single one—not even *DISC1*—was found to be mutated more often in patients than in healthy persons. On a more positive note, the study found 108 places in the genome in which a single-letter variation of the DNA code was associated with schizophrenia.[65] Scientists hoped to link these variations to some essential brain mechanism, but that proved difficult because only a few of the variant sites lie within genes that code for proteins. Instead, they lie within the noncoding genes mentioned above, those that make molecules for controlling the activity of protein-coding genes. The control mechanisms are complex, so the ultimate effect of the mutations remains obscure. Anyway, the entire set of 108 mutations explains only a small fraction of the heritability of schizophrenia. Even if a child carried all 108 mutations (highly unlikely),

---

[64] Schizophrenia Working Group of the Psychiatric Genomics Consortium, 'Biological insights from 108 schizophrenia-associated genetic loci.' *Nature* 511(7510):421–427 (2014).

[65] The technical name for a site-specific variation in the DNA code is 'single-nucleotide polymorphism', abbreviated SNP.

his or her chance of developing schizophrenia would be only about three percent greater than if he or she had none of the mutations.

DISC1 had one last chance. As powerful as GWASs are, they do not actually examine the entire genome. Each GWAS probes the DNA at only few million positions. The only way to check every individual DNA letter—all 3.3 billion—is to read the whole genome letter by letter. Whole genome sequencing was first accomplished in 2001, with one human subject. Two groups accomplished the feat, one financed by the United States government, the other by private interests. The publicly funded project required eleven years of work at a cost of $3,000,000. The privately funded project went more quickly because it piggy-backed on techniques and data from the government project, so it cost a mere $300,000. Currently, the cost is about $1,000, and it can be done in little more than one hour. Unfortunately for those who had championed the significance of *DISC1*, whole genome sequencing has not detected an association between any variation of *DISC1* and schizophrenia. It has detected a few genetic anomalies that associate with schizophrenia, but no single letter mutations additional to the 108 previously reported.

Perspective

This chapter began with family heredity, moved on to chromosomes, then genes, proteins, and finally DNA letters. It is a familiar pattern in science, going from big things to smaller and smaller things. Known as reductionism, it describes a hierarchy of explanation. Heredity explains human traits, chromosomes explain heredity, genes make proteins that function in the brain and, finally, tiny changes in DNA circle back to explain mental illness. History has repeated shown that reductionism yields satisfying answers to difficult questions.

The structure of DNA, discovered in 1954, was thought to be the key that would open a world of wonder for scientific psychiatry. With understandable enthusiasm, investigators approached a Scottish family as though it were the spring from which would gush molecular explanations for human misery. Unfortunately, the outcome turned out to be less fulfilling than had been hoped. Today, we no longer imagine that a single gene mutation—even one hundred different mutations—is responsible for any major mental illness. *DISC1* went from being the poster child of psychiatric genetics to the fall guy.

In the previous chapter, we learned how twin studies enable scientists to quantify the relative importance of heredity and the environment. For example, we know that schizophrenia is about 80 percent heritable. Even so—and researchers hate to admit this—only about 25 percent of that heritability is explained by the results from all genome-wide association and DNA sequencing studies. Nor is there any single genetic variant that we know to be present in every case of schizophrenia. This huge difference between estimated heritability and known genetic factors, has been dubbed the problem of 'missing heritability'. It is a problem that plagues not only schizophrenia research, but also research into other mental illness and, in fact, all complex illnesses (cancer, diabetes, heart disease).

Some specialists argue that the heritability estimates are inflated by flawed calculations. Others point to shortcomings in the interpretation of genetic research data or the failure to take into account such things as replicated genes, gene-by-gene interactions, gene-by-environment interactions and inherited effects not mediated by DNA (epigenetics). Perhaps the missing heritability lies in molecular variants not yet detected due to inadequate sample sizes (think coin tossing). Schizophrenia may not depend on a mere 108 variants, but on several hundred or even several thousands of variants, each of which, alone, accounts for just a tiny fraction of risk. If so, we might be able to find them, but only if we tested hundreds of thousands of patients. Alternatively, there are hints of extremely rare variants which individually increase risk quite substantially, but again, very large patient samples are needed to detect them.

Finally, one has to bear in mind that genetic research usually seeks to identify variants that associate with a particular mental illness. But what is a 'particular mental illness'? Schizophrenia, especially, is notoriously difficult to define and diagnose. As we will see in chapter 15, people are losing confidence in the traditional definitions of mental illnesses. If researchers rely on definitions that are fundamentally flawed, then the whole study of heritability is likewise flawed.

Psychiatric genetics is neither dead nor useless. It is at an impasse, halted by incredible complexity and a data-rich fog. Hopefully, with time and continued research, the fog will clear. We will then move on to early interventions and precisely targeted therapeutics.

Suggested readings

Siddhartha Mukherjee, *The Gene: An Intimate History.* New York: Scribner (2016).

Patrick F. Sullivan, 'Questions about *DISC1* as a genetic risk factor for schizophrenia.' *Molecular Psychiatry* 18:1050–1052 (2013).

7 A new disorder twice discovered

While it may be true that histories are written by winners, it is equally true that no writer knows the whole story, and some first-person witnesses know more than they wish to divulge. To get the true story, the full story, one must read several versions. Such is the case with the discovery of autism, about which there are competing claims. Initially, at least in North American, it was assumed that autism was discovered in 1943 by the American psychiatrist Leo Kanner who described 'early infant autism'. German historians, however, told the story of a young Austrian doctor named Hans Asperger who had already spoken of 'autistic psychopathy' as early as 1938. In the midst of the controversy, a bombshell landed, forcing a re-examination of claims and an affirmation of ethical priorities.

Kanner was born in Austria, lived with his family in Berlin, then resettled in the United States, where he established a child psychiatric clinic at Johns Hopkins University in Baltimore. A photograph of Kanner appears to validate contemporary descriptions of him as warm and sympathetic. He spoke English with a heavy Germanic accent that matched the American stereotype of a psychiatrist, even though that stereotype was based on the voice of Sigmund Freud, and Kanner himself was not a psychoanalyst. Kanner's textbook on child psychiatry was the first ever published in English (1935), a language that he mastered doing *New York Times* crossword puzzles.

One day Kanner received a long letter from a man living in Forest, Mississippi (population 3,000). It came from Oliver Tripplet, father of five-year old Donald Tripplet who had been living at an institution during the previous two years. The institution was neither a mental hospital nor any other type of hospital, but rather a place advertised as providing protection against infection by tuberculous. Donald's parents thought it a convenient location for Donald's safekeeping, but his mother, Mary, may also have been acting on her belief that her son was 'hopelessly insane'.[66] Oliver's characterization was more concrete, and heavily detailed in his letter. He wrote that the

---

[66] Quotations pertaining to Donald Tripplet are from John Donvan and Caren Zucker, 'Autism's first child.' *The Atlantic*, October 2010.

Leo Kanner [National Library of Medicine, USA]

boy had withdrawn 'into his shell' with the intention of 'living within himself.' He seemed 'perfectly oblivious to everything about him,' and acted as though his parents were simply part of the landscape. Donald had 'a mania for spinning blocks and pans and other round objects.' He was fascinated by numbers, pictures of United States presidents and letters of the alphabet. Other things—such as milk, swings and tricycles—he intensely disliked. He talked very little, but endlessly repeated the words 'business', 'chrysanthemum' and 'trumpet vine'. Any change of routine or interruption of his mental state triggered a temper tantrum.

Oliver also mentioned several of Donald's unusual mental skills. By the age of two, for example, he was able to recite by heart the 23rd Psalm and had memorized 25 questions and answers from the Presbyterian catechism. In Oliver's opinion, Donald seemed to be 'always thinking and thinking.' He was 'happiest when left alone.'

Oliver's letter so intrigued Dr. Kanner that he invited the entire family to come see him at his Baltimore office. Once in the room, Donald went straight to the wooden blocks 'without paying the least attention to the persons present.' Kanner further recalled that Donald remained completely indifferent to him throughout the visit, regarding him as though he were simply 'the desk, the bookshelf, or the filing cabinet.'

Kanner's curiosity about Donald led him to retain Donald at his clinic for two weeks. After Donald returned home, Mary kept Kanner informed of her son's behavior by supplying him with further details of Donald's strange behaviors. Four years passed. Kanner remained baffled, the Tripplets remained frustrated. At one point, Kanner confessed to Mary, 'Nobody realizes more than I do myself that at no time have you or your husband been given a clear-cut and unequivocal ... diagnostic term.' The reason, he explained, was that he was seeing, 'for the first time a condition which has not hitherto been described by psychiatric or any other literature.' Finally, in a letter to Donald and Mary dated September 1942, Kanner wrote 'I have now accumulated a series of eight other cases which are very much like Don's.' Moreover, he had a diagnosis—a new condition that he was calling 'autistic disturbance of affective contact' (affective refers to moods and feelings). He later renamed the condition 'early infantile autism'.

In the following year, an article published in *The Nervous Child*, introduced the journal's professional readers to the new diagnostic category.[67] Kanner began, 'There have come to our attention a number of children whose condition differs so markedly and uniquely from anything reported so far, that each case merits ... a detailed consideration of its fascinating peculiarities.' Although Kanner' definition of autism drew from his personal observations of eleven children, five pages were devoted to a discussion of Donald Tripplet. Kanner emphasized Donald's preoccupation with objects, his strong desire for maintaining consistent routines, and his limited language. Even more striking, however, was the paucity of the child's social interactions, especially those calling for emotional expression. It is significant that Kanner pointedly distinguished autism from mental retardation and schizophrenia, two conditions with which he was well acquainted. He noted that contrary to schizophrenia, no child had hallucinations, and contrary to mental retardation, several of his autistic children had exceptional memories or cognitive skills.

People often wonder what happens to autistic children when they become adults. The question bubbled up in the minds of two journalists who realized that Donald Tripplet was still alive in 2010.[68] Tracking him down in his hometown of Forest, Mississippi, they found Donald— seventy-seven years old—playing golf. He had worked in a bank and traveled extensively by car. He still had unusual traits such as assigning a unique number to every person he met, but overall he was leading a fairly normal life.

While Leo Kanner was discovering autism in America, Hans Asperger was doing the same in Austria at the University of Vienna. Asperger was

---

[67] Leo Kanner, 'Autistic disturbances of affective contact.' *The Nervous Child* 2:217–250 (1943). Although Kanner's article became a classic of the psychiatric literature, the journal itself folded a few years later.

[68] J. Donvan and C. Zucker (2010).

Donald Tripplet, age 82 years [Ylevental]

the director of a clinic with a history of innovative practices. Its name, the Curative Education Clinic, was taken from the name of its most successful innovation, *Heilpädagogik*, translating as 'curative education'. Conceived by an earlier director of the clinic, *Heilpädagogik* combined education, psychological theory and scientific methodologies in a comprehensive therapeutic strategy. In keeping with the concept, the physical space at the clinic was made to look home-like, and the nursing staff made every effort to engage the kids in a sympathetic manner. They told the children stories, sang with them and mounted theatrical productions for their entertainment. It was a novel and compassionate form of child psychiatry, at least in the early years of Asperger's directorship. After that, not so much.

A recent biography characterizes Hans Asperger as 'a courteous, old-fashioned gentleman.'[69] In his childhood, he read many books, mastered several languages and took long hikes in the mountains. But those who knew him say that he was socially awkward and had few friends. In the beginning of his administration at the Curative Education Clinic, Asperger kept a low profile. Clinicians at the time were reluctant to designate any child as either 'normal' or 'abnormal', and few children were tagged with a specific diagnosis. Asperger generally adhered to the prevailing view. He wrote that 'there are as many approaches as there are different personalities. It is impossible to establish a rigid set of criteria for a diagnosis.'[70]

---

[69] Adam Feinstein (2010), p. 10. See suggested readings.
[70] Edith Sheffer (2018), p. 81. See suggested readings.

Hans Asperger working with a boy in in the Curative Education Clinic, Vienna [Maria Asperger Felder]

In October of 1937, Asperger gave a lecture on 'The mentally abnormal child.' Although he spoke at length about socially challenged children, he expressed no need for a diagnostic label. One year later, however, he delivered another lecture on the same subject, and now he used the term autistic psychopathy in reference to those same children. Few people paid any notice to Asperger's announcement because he inserted it into a poorly attended lecture, and while the lecture was subsequently published in the *Viennese Clinical Weekly* (English translation), the readership of that newsletter was likewise small. Asperger continued to observe patients with a view to sharpening the new diagnosis, but meanwhile, he chose not to establish a 'rigid set of criteria'. Only in 1944, in his postdoctoral thesis (*Habilitation*), did he present a full description of autistic psychopathology together with diagnostic criteria. But again, the document was not widely circulated, because it was an academic paper written entirely in German.

Although Asperger claims in his thesis that he diagnosed autism after observing more than two hundred children, his presentation rests almost entirely on four case studies, all boys. One of these kids, Fritz, was sent to Asperger's clinic from his kindergarten, where he 'never tolerated or engaged with other children,' and even attacked them. Fritz 'never did what he was told. He did just what he wanted to, or the opposite.' Furthermore, he ate the most impossible things, including whole pencils and paper, in considerable quantities. Asperger's fascination led him to use exclamation marks: 'How odd is his use of eye contact! How odd is his voice, how odd his manner of speaking and his way of moving!'[71]

Harro, another boy featured in Asperger's thesis, was sent to the clinic after his school reported that his odd behaviors were disrupting the classroom. Asperger wrote that Harro was 'not as severely disturbed' as Fritz. Instead, 'the positive aspects of autism [were] more obvious: the independence in thought, experience and speech ... On the ward he remained a stranger. One would never see him join in a game with others. Most of the time, he sat in a corner buried in a book, oblivious to the noise or movement around him.'

Asperger called it autistic psychopathy, Kanner called it early infantile autism. Because they described different cases, the original publications sometimes give the impression that each author is writing about a different condition, but their definitions were fuzzy enough to cover a range of symptoms. Although both men mentioned difficulties in social communication and reduced emotional expression as core symptoms, they emphasized different things. Whereas Kanner noted poor speech, Asperger described the speech as more peculiar than deficient. Kanner wrote that the condition is present from birth ('inborn'), while Asperger saw it as a developmental disorder. Asperger's children have clumsy movements, Kanner's children do not. Above all, the doctors differed in their views on cognition. Asperger, far more often than Kanner, comments on his children's creativity, their 'rare maturity of artistic taste' and their intellects. He believed that many were capable of attending normal schools. On the whole, it seems that Asperger's children were less disabled than Kanner's. Asperger hardly mentions any girls in his thesis, and even today, psychiatrists diagnose fewer girls than boys with the high-functioning type of autism, now known as Asperger's syndrome.

History tends to acclaim those who come first, and neglect or downplay those who come later. So, who discovered autism? For sure, neither Asperger nor Kanner coined the term autism, because that term was already

---

[71] Quotations are taken from the English translation of Asperger's thesis. Included in *Autism and Asperger syndrome,* ed. Uta Frith. Cambridge, UK: Cambridge University Press (1991).

present in the German-language psychiatric literature. In 1910, the psychiatrist Eugen Bleuler wrote that *der autismus* (from the Greek *auto*, meaning self) is symptomatic of schizophrenia. In his words, 'We term autism the loss of contact with reality together with the relative and absolute predominance of an interior life.'[72] Thus, when first used, autism referred to a trait, a psychological type, but not *a diagnosable illness*. Outside of Germany, the Soviet child psychiatrist Grunya Efimovna Sukhareva described what was likely the same disorder in 1925, although nowhere in her publication did she speak of 'autism'.

For decades, the American psychiatric community—unaware of Asperger's writings—credited Kanner with the discovery. It is hard to imagine Americans reading Asperger's article in the *Viennese Clinical Weekly*, and Asperger's postdoctoral thesis was likewise ignored until translated by the husband of an autism specialist in 1981. American psychiatrists eventually learned of the overlapping content in Asperger's thesis and Kanner's *The Nervous Child* article, but that did not stop them from crediting Kanner with the discovery because his article appeared in print one year earlier than Asperger's thesis (1943 versus 1944).

That was how matters stood until Steve Silberman, a science writer with verve, uncovered certain facts about autism—some fascinating, others downright disturbing. Overall, his book invites readers to consider autism not as an illness but rather as a personality type, hence its title, *NeuroTribes*.[73] But it is his historical research that caught the attention of persons interested in the question, who discovered autism? Thanks to Silberman, we now know that some American psychiatrists, including Leo Kanner, were aware of Asperger's early work on autism and chose to ignore it. Kanner would have known about the work not because he was a regular reader of the *Viennese Clinical Weekly*, but because two of his close associates in Baltimore had previously worked with Asperger in Vienna. Georg Frankl was a doctor and diagnostician at the Curative Education Clinic, and Anni Weiss, a psychologist, also worked there. Sensing the rise of Nazi anti-Semitism, Frankl and Weiss emigrated to the United States. Before leaving Vienna, however, they published articles in professional journals about children with awkward social behaviors. Frankl wrote that they did not 'sense the atmosphere' and had a 'poor understanding of the emotional content of the spoken word.' Weiss, in her article, noted the unusual skills of

---

[72] Edward Shorter, *A Historical Dictionary of Psychiatry*. New York: Oxford University Press (2005).

[73] Steve Silberman (2016). See suggested readings.

some children, citing those who were 'calendar experts, jugglers of figures, and artists of mnemonics.'[74]

Clearly, professionals in the Curative Education Clinic were familiar with the set of behaviors that we now associate with autism. Moreover, they used the term 'autistic' in regard to those behaviors. Frankl, for example, stated in his article that certain of the children did not have 'extreme autism'. Unlike Asperger, who often expressed a disparaging attitude toward autistic children, Frankl and Weiss looked upon these same children with wonder and admiration. Significantly, Frankl and Weiss published their articles 10 years before Kanner announced *his* autistic disorder.

Why Kanner did not mention Asperger when he presented his case for a new diagnosis is anybody's guess. Possibly, he had read the transcript of Asperger's lecture, published in the *Viennese Clinical Weekly* (1938), but dismissed it as insufficient to serve as a precedent. Or, he might have assumed, from speaking with Frankl and Weiss, that specialists were already familiar with the symptoms of autism, but no one had yet put a name to it or declared autism a distinct disorder. He might have wished to keep quiet about Asperger in order to reserve for himself the honor of discovery. And finally, it is possible that Kanner knew about Asperger's priority, but chose to ignore it on account of other information obtained from Frankl and Weiss, information about Asperger that would shake the world of autism decades later. In particular, Frankl and Weiss might have explained why Asperger declared autism a new disorder in his 1938 lecture, when just a year earlier he had said that there was no need for a diagnostic label. To make the point, they would have told Kanner much more than he wished to hear.

We do not know what, exactly, Frankl and Weiss told Kanner about life in Vienna before they left, but they must surely have mentioned the morning of March 12, 1938, when tanks of the German Wehrmacht rolled down the street in front of the Curative Education Clinic. It was the day on which Nazi Germany annexed Austria (the *Anschluss*), and it was also the calendar day that fell almost exactly midway between the dates of Asperger's two lectures on autism. Far from an invasion resisted by defiant Austrians, the foreign troops encountered only cheering crowds and showers of fresh flowers. Acts of intimidation and violence toward Jews intensified. Six months later, on the night of November 9, 1938 (*Kristallnacht*), 95 synagogues were destroyed, and 6,547 Jews were arrested. Soon thereafter, German soldiers sent 3,700 Jews to the Dachau concentration camp. In the

---

[74] Quotes from E. Sheffer (2018), pp. 55, 57.

midst of all of this, hardcore Austrian Nazis emerged from their closets to assume important roles in government and medicine. The medical school, the university hospital and Asperger's clinic all got Nazi directors.

Eduard Pernkopf inaugurated as dean of the University of Vienna Medical School, April 26, 1938 [Austrian National Library]

The Nazi program of racial hygiene—mentioned in Chapter 5—was meant to remove from German society all residents not belonging to the mythical Aryan race, as well as all deviants and persons affected by hereditary medical conditions such as mental illness. According to the author Edith Sheffer, racial hygiene was implemented by means of a 'diagnosis regime' that validated repressive measures on the basis of medical diagnoses.[75] For this purpose, the Vienna Public Health Office compiled personal data on 767,000 individuals. Along with information pertaining to race, criminal record, and school performance, the files documented current and previous medical diagnoses. These data were used to justify deportations, incarcerations and killings. Sheffer believes that Asperger knew full well what the Nazis were up to, and that he created the autism diagnosis as a way of contributing to the program. If so, it would explain why Asperger announced the new diagnosis six months after the German tanks rolled into Vienna.

---

[75] E. Sheffer (2018), see suggested readings.

The extent of Asperger's involvement with the Nazis has come under intense scrutiny in recent years. In the beginning, commentators were willing to give Asperger the benefit of doubt. In 2010, one author refuted the claim that Asperger had 'affinities' with the Nazis, claiming instead that 'there seems to be no evidence of this whatsoever.'[76] But also in 2010, speakers at a symposium marking thirty years since Asperger's death hinted at darker facts, and soon afterwards, researchers descended upon Vienna looking for documents. What they found blew the story wide open.[77]

Close to Vienna, on sprawling grounds amidst soft landscape, lay the Steinhof Psychiatric Institute. It contained 34 attractive pavilions, nine of which were reserved for children. During the war years, more than 7,500 deaths occurred at Steinhof. Most of the victims were adults, but at least 789 children died in the complex named Spiegelgrund, and specifically in Pavilion number 15, the so-called 'death pavilion'. The vast majority of the deaths resulted from malnutrition, gross neglect and barbiturate overdosing. Asperger was consultant to a committee that sent children to Spiegelgrund, amongst which 35 children on a single day with instructions 'to be dispatched for Jekelius action.' Erwin Jekelius, a hardcore Nazi, was in charge at Spiegelgrund. Given that he had additional responsibilities that went far beyond Spiegelgrund (described below), the instructions amounted to murder. Asperger also sent nine other children directly to Spiegelgrund from his ward, and two of these children died there.

If ever a case were to be made for guilt by association, Asperger would be a prime example. Nothing speaks more loudly than the names of his three co-founders of the Vienna Society, all of whom were bona fide Nazis. Franz Hamburger was a powerful member of the party who advocated for the advancement of racial hygiene through sterilization, euthanasia, and medical experimentation. Max Gundel was a city councillor who arrested thousands of persons and helped to establish Vienna's child euthanasia program. The third co-founder was Erwin Jekelius. Even while serving as the first president of the Society for Curative Education, Jekelius was directing two euthanasia facilities. As part of his job in the latter capacity he personally supervised the deaths of 4,000 adults and 100 children. In plain terms, Jekelius was a mass murder, so bad that he nearly married Adolph Hitler's sister.

---

[76] A. Feinstein (2010), p. 15.

[77] Herwig Czech, 'Hans Asperger, national socialism, and "race hygiene" in Nazi-era Vienna.' *Molecular Autism* 9:29 (2018). https://doi.org/10.1186/s13229-018-0208-6.

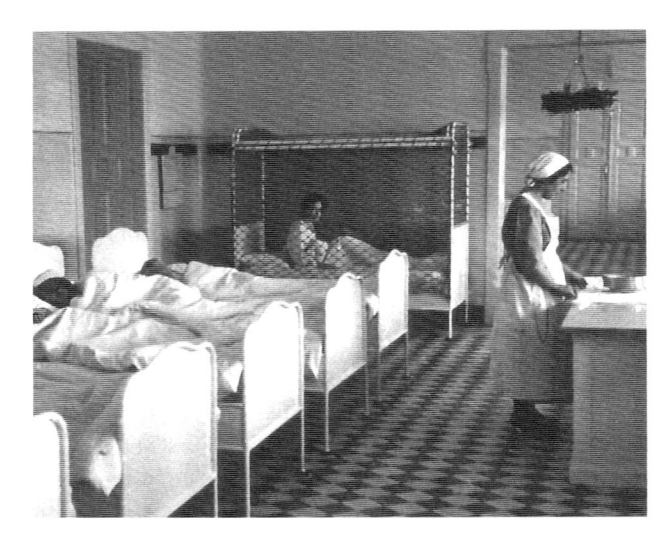

Ward in Am Spiegelgrund clinic, Vienna, 1940s [Documentation Centre of the Austrian Resistance]

Asperger left the Curative Education Clinic during World War II. He served briefly with German occupational forces in Croatia before resuming his work at the clinic after the war ended. In 1962, at age fifty-seven, he was appointed honorary Chairman of the prestigious Vienna Pediatric Clinic.

Despite all the damaging evidence, the exact nature of Asperger's involvement in Nazi activities remains uncertain. He did not join the National Socialist party, and he never admitted to knowingly committing the horrible crimes of which he has been accused. Since he would have put his career in jeopardy if he had *not* cooperated with the Nazis, one could say that autistic psychopathy was an invention born of necessity, and everything else flowed from the same imperative. Perhaps Asperger's own assessment comes closest to the truth. Speaking retrospectively in 1974, he said, 'The Nazi period came, and it was clear from my previous life, as with many "nationalists", that one went along with it.'

That said, we leave the final judgment to Edith Sheffer. Commenting upon the hundreds of documented deaths at Spiegelgrund, she writes,

> Asperger appears to have been involved in the transfer of at least forty-four children to Spiegelgrund ... Given that he served as a consultant to numerous city offices, and that the records are incomplete, the total number of children Asperger recommended for Spiegelgrund is likely higher ... These youths were

not simply statistics, however, nor an abstract set of symptoms. Asperger personally examined many of them, touching their bodies and talking to them face-to-face.[78]

Perspective

The tangled history of autism leaves unresolved issues. If we start with who discovered it, the nod must go to Asperger on account of his 1938 lecture and its subsequent, albeit obscure, publication. Whether Kanner knew of Asperger's precedence and if so, whether he intentionally ignored it, remains an open question. Nor should we forget Grunya Efimovna Sukhareva, who described something like autism in 1925—much earlier than either man—but chose not to name it. It is remarkable that all these discoveries occurred around the same time, in the second quarter of the twentieth century. Commenting on similar coincidences in his own field of mathematics, the Hungarian Farkas Bolyai noted that, 'When the time is ripe for certain things, these things appear in different places in the manner of violets coming to light in early spring.'

The near simultaneity of autism's dual discoveries begs another question, Is it really possible to 'discover' something that ordinary people would have known about for ages? After all, as Leo Kanner stated, autistic children possess 'fascinating peculiarities.' Surely, parents would have noticed, if not neighbors and employers. Unless, as Bolyai hinted at, the time may not have been ripe. That is to say, maybe autism had only just arisen as a new phenomenon. Or, maybe it took dedicated professionals working in a novel type of medical clinic—one specializing in pediatric psychiatry—to recognize the unique features of this extraordinary syndrome.

The British psychiatrist Lorna Wing spoke with Hans Asperger over tea at a London hospital shortly before his death in 1980. She said that 'Asperger firmly believed his was a separate syndrome, unrelated to Kanner's, although it had a lot of features in common.'[79] Social interactions are problematic in both types. However, language and intelligence remain relatively intact in Asperger's syndrome, whereas they are strongly degraded in Kanner's syndrome. Thus, Asperger's syndrome is generally seen as recognizing a distinct group of high functioning individuals who nonetheless retain the core social disability. Wing accepted Asperger's interpretation and promoted it, thereby giving recognition to what we now call Asperger

---

[78] E. Sheffer (2018), p. 147.
[79] Feinstein (2010), p. 10.

syndrome. The *International Classification of Diseases* retains Asperger syndrome as a subtype of autism spectrum disorder, but the latest edition of the *Diagnostic and Statistical Manual of Mental Disorders* (2013) merges Kanner's version and Asperger's version into a single disorder, 'autism spectrum disorder'. Some people embrace Asperger syndrome as confirmation of a distinct personality type. Others shun the term on account of its association with Hans Alzheimer and his repugnant activities during the Nazi era; these people prefer to speak only of the autistic spectrum.

Still others argue that autism should not be listed in any diagnostic manual, since it is neither a mental illness nor a mental disorder. Clearly, it is much less disabling than progressive paralysis of the insane or major depression or schizophrenia. And, children diagnosed with Asperger syndrome are—in some respects—*more* capable than so-called 'normal' children. Therefore, some persons with autism, and some of their supporters, prefer to view autism as a 'different way of being', not necessarily unhealthy and not necessarily disadvantaged.

Suggested readings

Uta Frith, *Autism: A Very Short Introduction.* Oxford, UK: Oxford University Press (2008).

Adam Feinstein, *A History of Autism: Conversations with the Pioneers.* Chichester, UK: Wiley-Blackwell (2010).

Edith Sheffer, *Asperger's Children.* New York: W. W. Norton (2018).

Steve Silberman, *NeuroTribes: The Legacy of Autism and The Future of Neurodiversity.* New York: Avery (2016).

8 How shocking it was

Strange though it may be, all our weightless mental experiences come from a three-pound, electro-chemical machine. This bizarre relationship between the physical and the mental allows for two fundamentally different treatment options in psychiatry. Psychotherapy (talk therapy) directly addresses the mental aspect without bothering with the physical brain. It works reasonably well for many minor illnesses, but not at all for conditions such as schizophrenia, bipolar disorder, major depression, and obsessive-compulsive disorder. For serious mental illness, psychiatry relies on treatments that target the electro-chemical machine. In this chapter, we look at discovered procedures for altering—in a beneficial way—the electrical side of brain activity.

Long before people thought about medical treatments for mental illness, they thought about what, exactly, the brain is made of and how it works. The fact that it works with electrical phenomena like voltages and currents escaped notice until late in the eighteenth century. Prior to that time, both popular opinion and scholarly authors held to Galen's view—dating from the second century—that nervous function relies on animal spirits bubbling within nerve fibers.

Against this background of imagined spirits, a celebrated discovery changed everything around the year 1780. Luigi Galvani, an Italian physician and biological researcher, was dissecting a frog. Galvani dissected many frogs, and exactly what transpired in the course of that particular dissection is lost in the fog of history, but two speculations survive. Either Galvani's wife touched an exposed nerve with a metal instrument, or Galvani himself was attaching a hook to the frog's leg. Whatever the action, it caused the leg to twitch. Galvani understood the significance of what he witnessed: the nerves—and the muscles—work by electricity! He proceeded to conduct experiments looking for the source of electricity within the animal, while his contemporary, Alessandro Volta, contended that the electrical current came from *outside* the frog. Volta invented the battery and lent his name to the standard measure of electromotive force, so it is fair to assume that he knew something about electricity.

One thing Volta knew was that when two dissimilar metals touch, they create an electrical charge, essentially a battery. He also understood that when you connect the two poles of a battery, you complete an electrical circuit that allows current to be drawn from the battery. Therefore, he surmised that Galvani created a kind of battery by attaching a hook made of one type of metal to a railing made of another type of metal. Alternatively, his wife used a probe composed of two dissimilar metals. The illustration combines both scenarios. It shows a hand holding an arc made of zinc (z) and copper (c), with the frog's body completing the circuit. Volta was right about the source of the current, but Galvani gets credit for discovering the electrical basis of nervous function.

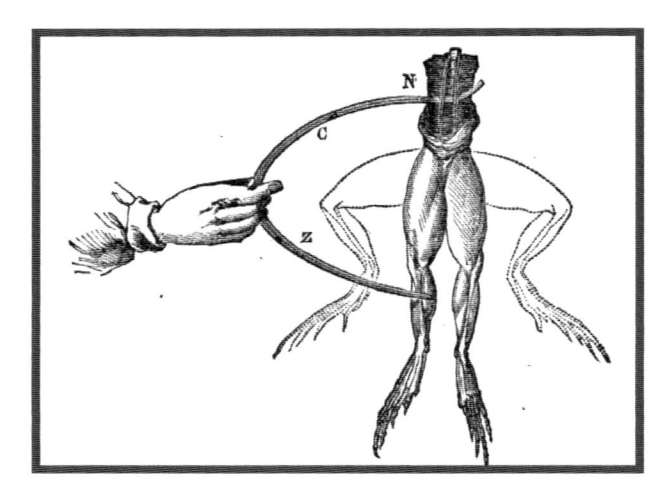

Luigi Galvani stimulates the frog's leg using a type of electrical battery

Galvani's discovery eventually led to treatments for mental illness based on electrical stimulation. But electrotherapy began long before Galvani. Even as early as 46 A.D., a Roman physician named Scribonius Largus was using it to relieve the pain of headaches and gout. He didn't have a battery, but he had a fish. Plato and Aristotle had earlier commented upon the electrical discharges produced by Torpedo fish (a type of ray), but evidently no one before Scribonius had exploited the discharges for medical purposes. He describes how he helped one patient,

> For any type of gout, a live black Torpedo should, when the pain begins, be placed under the feet. The patient must stand on a moist shore washed by the sea and he should stay like this

until his whole foot and leg up to the knee is numb. This takes away present pain and prevents pain from coming on if it has not already arisen. In this way, Anteros, a freedman of Tiberius was cured.[80]

Shocks from electric fish continued to be used for centuries, most commonly for numbing pain during birthings and surgeries. As late as 1777, just before Galvani's breakthrough research, an announcement in a London sheet advertised 'Torpedo eel' shocks for just two shillings sixpence.

The current produced by the Torpedo is of the 'direct' type, meaning that it flows constantly in the same direction, as opposed to the 'alternating' type used in most homes. Direct currents are also known as Galvanic currents, and it was Galvani's nephew, Giovanni Aldini, who conducted probably the first test of Galvanic currents in the treatment of a mental condition. Aldini was a professor of physics and very much involved in the Galvani-Volta debate. Although he protested Volta's interpretation of his uncle's experiments, he did not hesitate to use Volta's batteries in his own experimentation. He started by giving demonstrations with fresh human corpses. Performing before astonished audiences across Europe, he elicited muscle twitches from otherwise inert bodies.

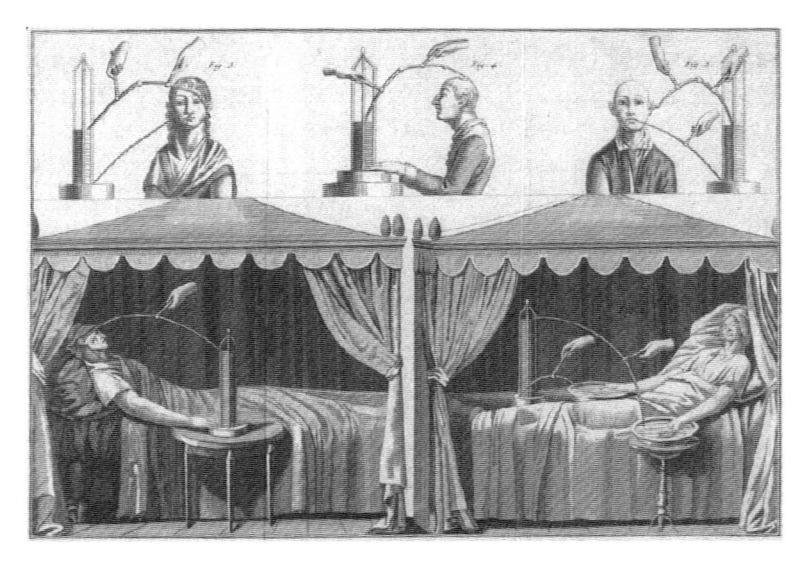

Giovanni Aldini's arrangements for treating depression and other illnesses

---

[80] P. Kellaway, 'The part played by electric fish in the early history of bioelectricity and electrotherapy.' *Bulletin of the History of Medicine* 20:112–137 (1946).

Even Philippe Pinel, chief of psychiatry at La Salpêtrière, took an interest in Aldini's work when he heard what Aldini had done with a 27-year-old farmer hospitalized in Bologna with depression. Aldini proceeded with caution when dealing with this man whose name was Lanzarini. He first passed a current through his own head, using a weaker voltage than applied to the corpses. The experiment made him lose sleep for 'several days,' but he was otherwise fine, so he set up Lanzarini with the man's hand resting on the bottom of a battery. The top of the battery was outfitted with a flexible metallic arm which Aldini placed on Lanzarini's moist head, thus allowing current to flow through the body. As anticipated, Lanzarini's mood improved in the following days, and Aldini hired him as a daytime domestic worker so that he could verify the change. Soon thereafter, Lanzarini was well enough to be released from hospital.

Interest in electrotherapy picked up in the mid-nineteenth century following theoretical breakthroughs. Professors and amateurs alike began experimenting with electrical devices of various sorts. The Serbian-born Nikola Tesla—whose name now appears on electric automobiles—was one such investigator. Another was Jacques Arsène d'Arsonval, an adventurous physician.[81] Both men entertained spectators with electrical 'tricks', such as igniting incandescent bulbs by touching them with their hands, even though they were not connected in any way to an electrical source.

One of the instruments invented at this time produced alternating currents (as opposed to direct currents), and Jacques Arsène d'Arsonval was anxious to test its therapeutic potential. He knew that when an alternating current runs through a wire coil (a solenoid), it induces a magnetic field. He also knew that if an object is placed *inside* the coil, a secondary current passes through the object. D'Arsonval called it 'autoconduction', today we call it electromagnetic induction. Acting on these principles, d'Arsonval asked his patients to sit inside a large cage constructed of coiled wire. With high frequency alternating currents (around 1 megahertz), the patient sensed a weak tingle in his or her body. In this manner, D'Arsonval treated 518 patients suffering from various disorders during the years 1894–1897. It was no small undertaking, since he gave each patient around 25 treatments, each one lasting 10–30 minutes. In total, D'Arsonval administered close to 13,000 electrical treatments. General effects included 'an increase in the secretions of all glands, easier elimination of the excreta and greater organic

---

[81] S. Reif-Acherman, 'Jacques Arsene d'Arsonval: his life and contributions to electrical instrumentation in physics and medicine. Part III: high-frequency experiences and the beginnings of diathermy.' *Proceedings of the IEEE* 105(2):394–404 (2017).

combustions.' The attending physicians reported 'progressive amelioration in the general health.' Chronic diseases, including arthritis 'in its various forms', rheumatism and diabetes were 'favourably affected' or 'very well influenced'. Disappointingly, however, patients with hysteria, neurasthenia and neuritis were 'not well influenced by high frequency currents.'[82]

Jacques Arsène d'Arsonval's setup for 'autoconduction'

Psychiatric patients waited another three decades before receiving a truly effective electrical treatment, and when it arrived it was entirely different from that which D'Arsonval had offered. There was, however, a connection to earlier research in that the new method was born, like Luigi Galvani, in Italy. Despite being unfairly maligned, electroconvulsive therapy (ECT) turned out to be one of the safest and most effective treatments for severe mental illness.

The first patient to be given electroconvulsive therapy was Enrico, an engineer from Milan who had been picked up by police while wandering around the railroad station in Rome hallucinating and speaking incoherently. The police took him to a psychiatric ward at the University of Rome where he was diagnosed with schizophrenia. Heading the unit was the highly regarded professor of psychiatry, Dr. Ugo Cerletti.

On the morning of April 11, 1938, Enrico lay on a hospital bed surrounded by Dr. Cerletti and several assistants. A nurse shaved his head and secured electrodes left and right on his temples (they looked like giant earphones). A

---

[82] G. Apostoli and G. Berlioz, 'The general therapeutic action of the alternating high frequency current.' *The British Medical Journal*, vol. 2, no. 1928:1717–1718 (1897).

second attendant placed a rubber bite guard into his mouth. In preparation for this moment, Cerletti's medical assistant, Lucio Bini, had visited a municipal slaughterhouse where pigs were numbed by electrical shock before being killed. Bini was responsible for building the device that would deliver the shock to Enrico, and he had gone to the slaughterhouse in search of a dosage that would be efficient but safe. Bini learned that a lethal dose for a pig is 400 volts, applied for one or two seconds. He calculated that a safe dose for humans would be 80 volts applied for one-quarter of a second. By comparison, when Galvani shocked his frog he used something like 0.5 volts.

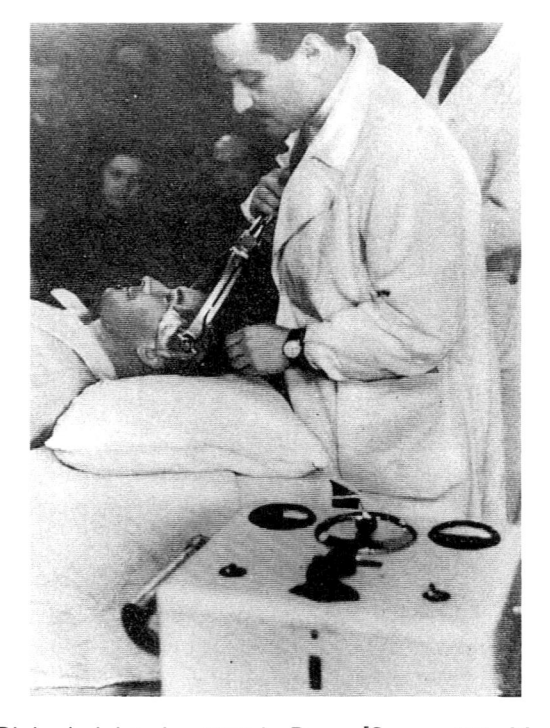

Lucio Bini administering ECT in Rome [Sapere 154, May 1941]

At 11:15, someone flipped a switch allowing electrical current to flow through Enrico's head. 'The patient showed an immediate contraction, a tonic spasm which involved all the muscles of his body; then, almost immediately, he relaxed and lay there without moving.'[83]

---

[83] Norman S. Endler, 'The origins of electroconvulsive therapy (ECT).' *Convulsive Therapy* 4(1):5–23 (1988), p. 14.

There are two eyewitness accounts of what happened next. According to one,[84] Enrico got two more electrical shocks on that first day, each at 80 volts but with progressively longer durations (1/4 second up to 3/4 second). After the final shock, Enrico sat up 'talking in his usual loose way' and walked quietly back to the ward. The second account[85] describes a different sequence of shocks and slightly different stimulus parameters (voltage and duration). Both accounts agree, however, about a subsequent treatment session that occurred either on April 11 or a few days later. This time, the voltage was raised from 80 volts to either 92 or 110 volts (depending on the account). The higher voltage produced a full blown 'grand mal' seizure.

> The patient's respiration was arrested, his face became pale and then took on a blue tinge, his jaws were clenched in trismus, as in lockjaw, the reflection of the cornea was lacking. I listened to his heart rate with a stethoscope and it continued to increase. [My colleague] counted the seconds since respiration arrest ...[86]

Gradually over the next ten minutes, the convulsions ended, and Enrico regained consciousness. His pulse returned to normal. Five minutes later, he was speaking, but remembering nothing. Similar to the previous occasion, Enrico walked back to the ward. As for the witness's own experience, 'We all breathed sighs of relief; it was not hot, but our foreheads were covered with sweat.' No wonder they were sweating. What they had done was unprecedented and dangerous. But it had been cautiously planned, and it was completed without serious harm.

Another eleven treatments were administered in the following weeks, during which time Enrico's symptoms receded. In mid-June, he was discharged from the hospital, evidently free of hallucinations and paranoia. It was written in hospital notes that he 'takes part eagerly and flawlessly in the routines of the clinic. Thought and memory unimpaired. He has full awareness of his former hallucinations ... He has been in correspondence with his family.'[87] He remained more or less well over the next couple of years, but later relapsed and was again admitted to a psychiatric hospital.

Physicians point to the high voltages used by Cerletti in the later treatments as the key to his success with Enrico. Indeed, the name of the treat-

---

[84] Ferdinando Accornero's account, translated by N. S. Endler (1988).

[85] Lucio Bini's notebook, translated by E. Bruno Magliocco, in *Convulsive Therapy* 11(4):260–261 (1995).

[86] Ferdinando Accornero in N. S. Endler (1988), p. 15.

[87] E. Shorter and D. Healy (2007), p. 42. See suggested reading.

ment incorporates its essential aspect, electro*convulsive* therapy. A convulsion is a violent involuntary muscle contraction, or a series of such contractions. Epileptic seizures often produce contractions, but they are not necessarily convulsive. Only the so-called grand mal seizures, such as those obtained by Cerletti and colleagues produce convulsions. They require very high levels of neuronal excitation and thus, strong shocks. Obviously, the psychological effects of ECT are due to the neuronal excitation rather than the muscular contractions, but no one has been able to explain why a massive excitation of neurons should relieve the symptoms of schizophrenia and depression.

Cerletti had a pretty good idea that ECT would work because, like any good scientist, he had been following what others were doing along similar lines. With the shine of psychoanalysis wearing thin, several psychiatrists had turned to 'somatic' therapies, that is, therapies of a physical nature. Cold baths, so popular in the previous century, and prolonged sleep (induced by barbiturate drugs), were familiar examples. Cerletti was particularly impressed with an innovative treatment for neurosyphilis pioneered by the Viennese doctor, Julius Wagner-Jauregg. He inoculated his patients with parasites of the type responsible for malaria. The patients developed a fever, but the neurosyphilis faded away, and he was able to treat the fever with quinine. For this, Wagner-Jauregg won the Nobel Prize in 1927.

A few years earlier, insulin was discovered, followed by the discovery of hypoglycemic shock, a potentially fatal condition caused by high levels of blood insulin. This discovery set in motion a series of unlikely events that eventually resulted in Cerletti's ECT experiment with Enrico, for the symptoms of hypoglycemia (low blood sugar) include loss of consciousness and seizures.

The story line connecting hypoglycemia, convulsions and psychiatric treatment begins with Dr. Manfred Sakel. After finishing medical school in Vienna, Sakel took a job in Berlin where he mainly treated heroin addicts. At the time, insulin was being used to treat a variety of illnesses, and Sakel was giving it to his addicts. A Canadian doctor who knew Sakel in Berlin later recalled how Sakel discovered the key ingredient in shock therapy, 'Once, one of [Sakel's] addicts who was also schizophrenic, accidentally slipped into a hypoglycemic coma [from too much insulin]. Sakel was scared but brought him out of the coma quickly with an injection of glucose. To his amazement, the patient showed a considerable improvement of his schizophrenic symptoms.' Sakel was so struck by the patient's psychological improvement that he decided to pursue insulin coma therapy as a treatment for schizophrenia. Asked years later what he thought of Sakel's insulin therapy for schizophrenia, Heinz Lehmann remarked, '[It was] a shock to the brain and the whole organism—like banging a watch on the table to make it go again when it stopped ... It was very risky, cumbersome and messy ... But it was the first and only game in town then.' [88]

With the Nazis about to seize power in Germany, Sakel, a Jew, moved to Vienna. From there, he reported remarkable results with insulin therapy. In a group of 58 patients recently diagnosed with schizophrenia, 86 percent had either a full recovery or a remission. Even patients with chronic schizophrenia experienced remissions in about half the cases. Sakel's choice of Vienna as a safe haven proved to be a mistake—as other Jewish psychiatrists were to learn—but he was able to escape to New York where he enjoyed fame and fortune. The fortune came from doing insulin coma treatments, the fame from his claim of having discovered electroconvulsive therapy. That claim, however, did not go unchallenged.

Once it became clear that only seizures strong enough to trigger convulsions would be effective in the treatment of schizophrenia, controversy arose over whether, in fact, convulsions had been part of Sakel's insulin treatments. Often, with low doses of insulin, a patient will experience a coma, but no seizure. Later in life, Sakel said that all of his patients had seizures, but he contradicted himself in other statements, stating that he avoided seizures because they were harmful. Thus, differing views on the significance of Sakel's insulin therapies in the runup to electroconvulsive therapy. Nonetheless, Cerletti knew of Sakel's work, and he considered using insulin before deciding on ECT instead.

Insulin therapy became electroconvulsive therapy thanks to the curiosity of a resolute investigator named Ladislaus Meduna. After graduating from a medical school in his native Hungary, Meduna spent the early part of his professional life as a laboratory researcher examining post-mortem brain tissues. Later, he obtained small pieces of brain that had been removed by surgeons when operating on epilepsy patients. Scanning the tissues under a microscope, he thought he saw differences between the brains of epileptic patients and those of schizophrenic patients. Specifically, he found more glia cells in the former group than in the latter group.[89] That got him thinking about an antagonism between epilepsy and schizophrenia. Searching the

---

[88] Interview with Heinz Lehmann in David Healy, *The Psychopharmacologists*. London, CRC Press (2001). Quotes on pp. 166, 167.

[89] Glia cells are non-neuronal cells in the brain. Although not directly involved in information processing, they serve important supportive functions.

medical literature for relevant information, he found an article in which the author remarked on 'the surprising rarity of a patient with epilepsy later developing schizophrenia.' Similarly, a group of doctors in Heidelberg reported that only around twenty schizophrenia patients from a total of six thousand in their hospital had ever had a convulsion. One more doctor, from an asylum in Switzerland, wrote that whenever a patient had both schizophrenia and epilepsy, the two alternated, with schizophrenia symptoms appearing only after the seizures had subsided or disappeared.[90]

Encouraged by these reports, Meduna formulated a scientific hypothesis, namely that brain seizures prevent, and might possibly relieve, schizophrenia. He set out to test the idea. It is not clear whether he was aware of Sakel's insulin studies at this time. In any case, while looking for a substance that would induce seizures in schizophrenia patients, he ran into a doctor at a conference who suggested camphor. Evidently camphor had been given to insane patients in the eighteenth century, also on the theory that epilepsy and madness are mutually exclusive. After first testing the safety of camphor on guinea pigs, Meduna was ready for a human trial.

Ladislas Meduna (left) and Ugo Cerletti, 1955 [Herbert L. Jackman]

---

[90] Modern evidence indicates no antagonism between schizophrenia and epilepsy. On the contrary, some evidence suggests a shared risk.

The carefully chosen first patient was a man with severe catatonia, an illness related to schizophrenia. During the previous four years, he 'never moved, never ate, never took care of his bodily needs and had to be tube-fed.'[91] Waiting before the injection, Meduna was extremely anxious, but afterwards he felt that he had achieved the desired effect, 'a classical epileptic attack that lasted 60 seconds.' Meduna recalls that 'when the attack was over and the patient recovered his consciousness, my legs suddenly gave out. My body began to tremble, a profuse sweat drenched me, and, as I later heard, my face was ashen gray.' Disappointment followed the melodrama when it became apparent that the patient's mental condition had not improved. He was given additional doses of camphor on subsequent days, and two days after the fifth injection, 'for the first time in four years he got out of his bed, began to talk, requested breakfast, dressed himself without any help, was interested in everything around him ... and asked how long he had been in the hospital.' In the following weeks, the patient experienced several rounds of relapse and camphor treatments, until one night he escaped from the hospital. Arriving at his home, he discovered a rascal living with his wife. He beat up both the man and his wife and remained in good psychological health for the next five years. Meanwhile, Meduna switched from camphor to the drug Metrazol, because Metrazol acted more quickly.

The lesson Ugo Cerletti learned from the combined results of insulin therapy and Metrazol therapy was that both worked by producing brain convulsions. On the flip side, both methods had shortcomings. There were reports of late-occurring seizures and pulmonary tuberculosis after Metrazol therapy, and hepatitis after insulin therapy. Besides, there were deaths. Subjectively, with both treatment protocols patients suffered an awful anticipation as their brain cells revved up before triggering convulsions. By contrast, ECT produced a concussion instantly and the side-effects were minimal; plus, there were no deaths.

Two important changes in the ECT procedure have been introduced since Cerletti's time. First, the patient is now anaesthetized before delivery of the electrical shock, and second, a muscle relaxing drug is used to minimize contractions of body and limbs. A series of 9–12 treatments is generally recommended, administered over a period of several weeks. Although patients often report short-term memory impairments, the procedure is otherwise safe. It causes no brain damage and no enduring memory loss. Although

---

[91] Quotes relating to Meduna's first patient are from part two of Meduna's autobiography. *Convulsive Therapy* 1(2):121–135 (1985).

initially developed for schizophrenia, ECT is now used mostly in cases of drug-resistant major depression, where 50–80 percent of patients experience a remission. Less frequently, ECT is used in the treatment of drug-resistant schizophrenia and catatonia.

Physicians wondered if it might be possible to achieve similar results with less shock. Rather than convulsing the entire brain, maybe they could convulse only certain areas. Or do without convulsions altogether, and gently stimulate neurons instead. Physics provides a few options. The most efficient method requires that electrodes be inserted into the brain. Although available today as a medical procedure, it has obvious drawbacks. Attaching electrodes to the surface of the brain is hardly more appealing because, while the brain has no sensors with which to 'feel' electricity, the scalp does have sensors and it is easily burnt. To get around these problems, Jacques D'Arsonval and others of his generation used electromagnetic induction, but the currents generated within their cage-like contraptions were too weak to affect brain functions. Silvanus P. Thompson, a physics professor at the City and Guilds Technical College in England, devised a simpler technique. Placing his head between two large magnets, he saw phosphenes (flickering lights) but reported no psychological effects.

It was not until the 1980s that someone finally figured out how to deliver focused electrical currents into the brain without burning the scalp. The problem was solved not by a psychiatrist but by doctors caring for patients with multiple sclerosis. In order to assess the condition of the patients' nerves, the neurologists needed to stimulate the nerves. The standard procedure had the doctor place electrodes on an arm or leg. He or she then passed electrical currents through the skin to the nerves beneath. For biophysical reasons, the smallest nerves require the largest electrical currents, and when these nerves needed to be tested, the examinations were painful. Anthony Barker was working as a medical physicist at the Royal Hallamshire Hospital in Sheffield, UK when he decided to tackle the problem.[92]

Barker's solution involved a magnetically induced current like that used by Jacques d'Arsonval and Silvanus P. Thompson. He replaced d'Arsonval's cage and Thompson's bulky magnets with a small, moveable instrument that generated extremely brief current pulses, each one approximately one-tenth of a millisecond in duration. When used for the evaluation of multiple sclerosis patients, Barker's magnetic stimulator was positioned beside the

---

[92] A.T. Barker and R. Jalinous, 'Non-invasive magnetic stimulation of human motor cortex.' *The Lancet*, May 11: 1106–1107 (1985).

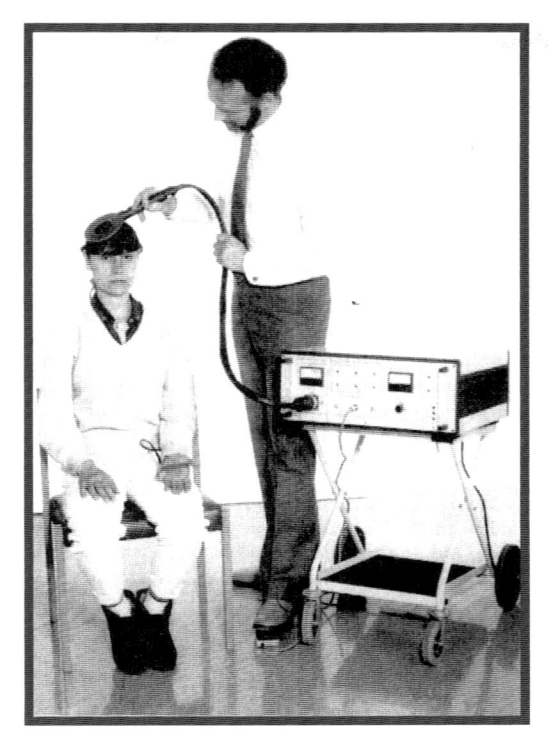

Anthony Barker demonstrating the first clinical magnetic stimulator [Handbook of Transcranial Magnetic Stimulation, 2002]

upper arm. The nerve's response to stimulation was registered by a second device placed on the lower arm.

Neurologists then realized that Barker's device was perfectly suited for stimulating the brain, that is, it could be used for transcranial magnetic stimulation, or TMS. The first application of TMS was in the evaluation of patients with Parkinson's disease. For this, doctors placed the stimulator on the top of the head, directly above the motor portion of the cerebral cortex. Surprisingly, some patients tested in this manner began to feel happier after the procedure, or at least less depressed. It was surprising because, while transcranial magnetic stimulation is like ECT in that it sends an electrical current through the brain, magnetic stimulation causes no convulsions. Thus, given the prospect of a safer, more gentle treatment for depression, teams of psychiatrists in multiple countries began to experiment.

The first trial, in Germany, involved two depressed patients who had failed to respond to treatments with 'amitriptyline, fluvoxamine, maprotiline and doxepine ... in combination with promethazine, thioridazine, haloperidol, flupentixol, lorazepam, additive light therapy and sleep deprivation during a period of more than four months.'[93] It was reported that TMS exerted a 'slight' beneficial effect in one patient but no noticeable effect in the second patient. Next, a group in Israel wrote that TMS produced a 'mild' effect in four of ten depressed patients. Other investigators, not involved in these initial studies, were encouraged by the fact that at least no harm had been done. They suggested that future trials should target the frontal lobes, since research had shown that the frontal lobes are involved in depression. They also called attention to a curious finding noted by doctors using ECT in depressed patients, namely that the treatment was most effective when directed toward the left side of the brain.

As the pace of research into the possible use of TMS heated up, Dr. Mark George led the effort at the National Institute for Mental Health (NIMH) in the United States. He had earlier discovered that a particular part of the frontal lobe, the prefrontal region, is strongly implicated in depression, so he targeted the left prefrontal cortex. Cautiously, he began by treating just three patients. Encouraged by the results, he recruited more patients for a trial that would utilize—for the first time—a placebo control.[94] Seven patients received TMS for 20 minutes, 5 days a week for 2 weeks. The TMS treatments were followed by 2 weeks of placebo, or sham stimulation, during which the magnetic coil was rotated so that it was incapable of stimulating the brain. Since the sham stimulation tingled the scalp in the same manner as the TMS stimulation, patients never knew whether they were getting real TMS or sham TMS. Another five patients received the same TMS and sham treatments, but in reverse order. Once a week, the patients were tested for depression. And, just as the patients were 'blind' to the type of stimulation (TMS or sham), so too were the psychiatrists blind to the type of stimulation the patients were getting when they were tested for depression. The results were compelling. The average depression score *decreased* by 5.25 points during the TMS phase but *increased* by 3.33 points during the sham phase. Mark George's double-blind experiment proved that TMS can reduce the symptoms of depression.

---

[93] G. Hoflich et al, 'Application of transcranial magnetic stimulation for treatment of drug-resistant major depression – a report of two cases.' *Human Psychopharmacology* 8:361–365 (1993).

[94] M.S. George et al., 'Mood improvement following daily left prefrontal repetitive transcranial magnetic stimulation in patients with depression: A placebo-controlled crossover trial.' *American Journal of Psychiatry* 154:1742–1756 (1997).

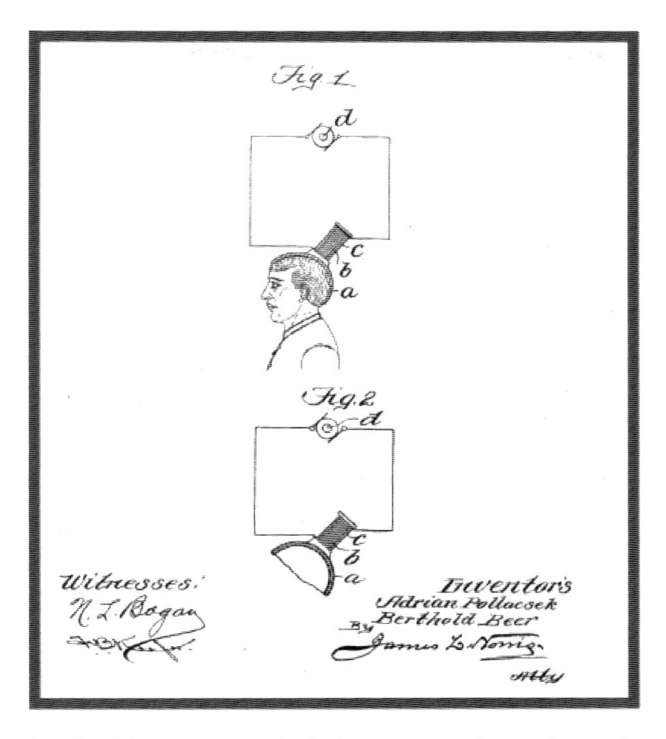

Patent application for 'electromagnetic device to treat depression and neuroses,' 1903 [Courtesy Dr. Mark S. George]

George's supervisor at NIMH suggested that he apply for a patent to secure his claim on the new therapy, but they had to shelve the plan after learning of a prior patent application for a similar treatment procedure. Evidently, two physicians working around the block from Sigmund Freud in Vienna had already obtained a United States patent in 1902 for 'a therapeutical apparatus comprising a magnetic body adapted to be placed adjacent to the diseased portion of a patient, and means for transmitting vibrations to said magnetic body through an alternating current of electricity.'

Despite Mark George's breakthrough experiment, TMS remained controversial—even heretical—in the minds of some psychiatrists. Sensitive to this fact, George's boss forbade him from speaking to the press about the work, claiming that it would 'sully the name of the NIH.'[95] George was eventually fired, and his former lab lost most of its funding, but George continued elsewhere and was honored for his pioneering work.

---

[95] Personal communication, Mark S. George (2019).

Perspective

Electroconvulsive therapy and transcranial magnetic stimulation are widely used today for medication-resistant mental disorders. TMS is generally offered to patients with mild depressive symptoms, while ECT is reserved for more severe cases of depression and, as originally intended, for schizophrenia. TMS requires more treatments over a longer period of time than ECT. Some patients that do not respond to TMS respond to ECT, and vice versa.

In the early days— up to 1950—ECT was known as electro*shock* therapy, or EST. It was a poor choice of words because it suggested a procedure that was dangerous and inhumane. Later, public opinion turned against ECT after release of the film version of Ken Kesey's novel, *One Flew Over the Cuckoo's Nest* (1975). The medical historians Edward Shorter and David Healy explain why the film was so damaging,

> The problem is that ECT lends itself beautifully to cinematic dramatization. There is the gurney, the weird music as the electro-therapist reaches for the button, the searing electrical storm as the patient's body writhes from the electric shock, the hollowed features and lifeless eyes afterward. No movie has ever depicted ECT administered with a muscle relaxant or an anesthetic.[96]

Regulatory agencies around the world have certified ECT for medical purposes, and the techniques for delivering it are constantly being modified for optimal safety and effectiveness. Regardless, some people say that ECT causes long-lasting cognitive problems. Others are turned off by misinformation relating to outdated practices. For these reasons, patients and families contemplating ECT need to be well informed and weigh inevitable risks against likely benefits. Scientists and doctors, on the other hand, must accept certain theoretical and practical limitations of electrotherapy. So far as ECT is concerned, it is a crude procedure with no established mechanism of action. TMS, on the other hand, is limited by physical factors that prevent it from targeting structures deep within the brain and make it unsuitable for selective stimulation of small areas. A newer method, deep brain stimulation, is meant to overcome both of these limitations, but the idea of leaving wires implanted in the brain is a non-starter for most people.

The brain may rely on electricity, but it is a delicate, highly complex organ constituted of tiny biological structures. In contrast, the electrother-

---

[96] E. Shorter and D. Healy (2007), p. 150. See Suggested Reading.

apies discussed in this chapter are blunt instruments that operate over large, ill-defined areas. It is a matter of concern that no psychiatrist or brain scientist is able to say exactly what happens in the brain during treatment with either ECT or TMS. They cannot even say whether the ultimate physiological effect is excitation or inhibition. Nevertheless, for some patients, ECT and TMS are the best options.

Suggested reading

Edward Shorter and David Healy, *Shock Therapy: A History of Electroconvulsive Treatment in Mental Illness.* Toronto: University of Toronto Press (2007).

9 Lithium: the first drug that worked

The discovery of effective drugs for mental illness ranks among the great successes of modern medicine. The first such drug, lithium, was found to be effective against mania in 1949. Soon after, in 1951, came chlorpromazine for schizophrenia and imipramine for depression. The so-called 'golden era' of psychopharmacology closed in 1955 with the discovery of benzodiazepine for anxiety.

Popular accounts often depict the treatment of mental patients in byegone days as either barbaric or absent, but that is not entirely fair. There were treatments, and not all were harsh. A few were actually kindly, as we saw in chapter 1. Some treatments reduced symptoms—usually by putting the patient to sleep— but none had lasting effects. Mostly, it was the agitated, disruptive patients who got treated. Hippocrates had recommended giving the powdered roots of hellebore plants, and even as late as the early nineteenth century, hellebore was still being used in some hospitals. It is a nasty substance that burns in the mouth and makes you vomit. When alcoholic drinks became widely available in the mid-nineteenth century, they quickly replaced hellebore. In Munich, for example, patients were allowed up to three and one-half liters of beer per day, even more if authorized by the patient's family. Highly agitated patients were given morphine or potassium bromide, the latter a cheap and effective drug but dangerous if taken too often. Most popular among physicians, however, was the synthetic compound, chloral hydrate. Although it has a strong calming effect, it is addictive, toxic and expensive. Asylum doctors also used two compounds obtained from plants belonging to the nightshade family, principally hyoscyamine and hyoscine, both of which were cheap to purchase. None of the drugs mentioned here were antipsychotic or anti-depressive. They were indiscriminate with regard to specific mental disorders, effective only because they put the patients to sleep.

Apart from drugs, the standard nineteenth century treatment was baths, sometimes hot, sometimes cold. Philippe Pinel, in Paris, is said to have preferred 'surprise' baths, whereas Emil Kraepelin, in Heidelberg, believed in long baths. One of Kraepelin's female patients was kept in a bath for three consecutive days. Forced bed stays were ordered for mildly agitated patients, usually in conjunction with sedation. More troublesome were the agitated patients. If they could not be quieted with sedatives, they were physically constrained by straight-jackets, hand cuffs and leg cuffs. They might also be locked into jail-like rooms.

Whereas sedatives, water baths and the like were somewhat useful, what psychiatrists really needed was drugs tailored to specific conditions. Their hopes were raised by advances made in general medicine, where doctors were finding cures for diseases by targeting the germs that cause the disease. One such advancement was announced in 1882 during a meeting of the German Physiological Society in Berlin. It was a small gathering of top-notch scientists including the physician Robert Koch who had brought with him a collection of microscope slides. On each of his slides, Koch had smeared a bit of lung tissue taken from an animal that had died of tuberculosis. As each man took his turn at the microscope (there were no women), none was surprised to see grey tubercles, because they were recognized as signatures of the disease. What did come as a surprise, were the worm-like profiles of the bacterium, *Mycobacterium tuberculosis*, made visible by Koch's new staining technique. Right there, with their own eyes, they were looking at the cause of tuberculosis. Following upon the discovery, Paul Ehrlich, Koch's student and collaborator, reasoned that a specific cause called for a specific cure, a 'magic bullet' to kill the pathogen. He and Koch tried but failed with a drug for tuberculosis, but he later succeeded with a drug for syphilis, the first synthetic medication against an infectious disease.

In psychiatry, the search for a magic bullet, or a cure of any kind, was compounded by the ill-defined nature of the target. At the beginning of the nineteenth century, none of the major disorders—mania, melancholia, dementia and idiocy—was seen as an actual illness equivalent to tuberculous and syphilis. That perception gradually changed, however, as psychiatry became accepted as a legitimate medical speciality. It happened in the final decades of the nineteenth century, and mostly in Germany. Emil Kraepelin was one of the leading voices in the campaign to modernise psychiatry. He believed that mental illnesses are very much like physical illnesses. Each one, he said, can be accurately diagnosed by reference to specific signs and symptoms, each has its own biological cause, and each can be cured—in principle—by using the proper physical agent. But belief was one thing, proof something else. With no psychiatric pharmacology yet in sight, Kraepelin tried other cures. As one example, he injected patients with extracts of testes on the theory that schizophrenia is caused by a toxin affecting the sexual organs. When none of the patients improved, he terminated the experiment.

Sigmund Freud bought none of this. Since he didn't go for the disease concept in psychiatry, he had no use for biological explanations or chemical cures (despite his background in biological research). He and Kraepelin agreed to disagree about these things, but psychiatrists elsewhere tended to take sides. John Cade, Director of the Bundoora Repatriation Mental Hospital in the state of Victoria, Australia, was an exception. He chose the middle ground between Kraepelin's disease concept and Freud's psychology. He followed Kraepelin in matters relating to severe illnesses—mostly schizophrenia and depression—and followed Freud in respect to neurosis. Cade had little tolerance for Freud's speculations, defining psychoanalysis as 'the art of describing the commonplace in terms of the incomprehensible, and commenting that 'Freudian psychology [had] cast a blight upon the minds of men that will last perhaps another fifty years.'[97] Cade's views are important because they led him to treat mania with lithium, which turned out to be the first psychiatric drug that actually worked.

What makes the story of lithium in psychiatry remarkable is first, the simple nature of the substance, and second, the fascinating character of its discoverer, John Cade.[98] Different from the large and chemically complex molecules that are the staples of modern medicine, lithium isn't even a drug according to our popular understanding of the word. It is, after all, a chemical element, fundamentally like 117 other elements in the periodic table. A light-weight alkali metal with three protons in its nucleus (atomic number 3), lithium sits immediately above sodium (atomic number 11) in the periodic table. Lithium is abundant in the seas, in spring waters and in rocks. Fittingly, in light of John Cade's nationality, Australia contains some of the largest deposits anywhere. It is widely used in the manufacture of glasses, as an ingredient in greases and as a component of household batteries. Despite being the best remedy for one of the most severe mental disorders, it has never been marketed by any pharmaceutical company. The reason? It is literally 'dirt cheap'.

---

[97] John F. J. Cade, 'Research in psychiatry.' *The Medical Journal of Australia*, vol II (7):213–219 (1951), p. 215.

[98] Cade's story is delightfully told in a one-hour film produced by Film Australia. The work artfully combines documentary images, interviews and staged reenactments. For details, see the listing at the end of this chapter.

Cade was the not first physician to recognize the curative properties of lithium. Second-century Greeks had recommended lithium-containing mineral waters for a variety of ailments, and Cherokee Indians were drinking spring waters for the same purpose long before any European set foot in America. The settlers learned from the Indians, and long before Cade's groundbreaking work, thirsty Americans were consuming large quantities of '7-Up Lithiated Lemon Soda' (later shortened to 7-Up). It was marketed, in part, as a drink that could boost your health. The choice was yours: Coca-Cola for its cocaine or 7-Up for its lithium.

Headquarters of the Atlanta Mineral Water and Supply Co., late nineteenth century [López-Muñoz et al., Molecular Sciences 19, 2018]

If he hadn't discovered lithium therapy, John Cade would have been remembered as a rather ordinary physician specializing in psychiatry at a small mental hospital. What catapulted him into the status of hero figure is the extraordinary manner of the discovery. It was by chance, but as Louis Pasteur famously declared, 'Chance favors the prepared mind,' and Cade was more than prepared; he was imaginative and persistent. He grew up as a child on the grounds of a mental hospital where his father worked as medical superintendent. Always close to nature in his youth, Cade was a life-long naturalist. In his leisure time, he published short notes about unusual phenomena. One was his interpretation of the kookaburra bird's laughter, another explained why the poop of a caterpillar is six-sided, and a third discussed whether white-backed magpies and black-backed magpies are two species or one. These examples illustrate Cade's keen observational sense, an attribute that served him well in his psychiatric research.

John Cade with lithium tablet [News Ltd/Newspix]

Early in his career, during World War I, Cade was sent to Asia as a medical director with Australian troops. He, together with several thousand fellow soldiers, was captured by the Japanese and interned at a notorious prison camp on the island of Singapore. Cade encountered many cases of mental collapse in the camp, including some that were marked by melancholia (depression) and mania (emotional excitation, flight of ideas, hyper-activity). He later wrote of them, 'I could see that so many of the psychiatric patients suffering from the so-called functional psychoses [those thought to be purely psychological] appeared to be sick in the medical sense. This fired my ambition to discover their etiology [cause].'[99]

After returning from the Malayan peninsula—weighing a mere ninety pounds—Cade took a job at a convalescent hospital in Bundoora, a suburb of Melbourne. Established on farmland in 1920, it was a place where returning servicemen recovered from post-traumatic stress and related mental disorders. In the beginning it housed a few dozen soldiers and almost as

---

[99] Frederick Neil Johnson, *The History of Lithium Therapy*, London: Macmillan (1984), p. 34. Cited in W.A. Brown (2019), p. 44. See suggested readings.

many horses, but by the time Cade arrived it had expanded to accommodate about 200 patients. The earlier 'farm' was now the Bundoora Mental Repatriation Hospital.

The Bundoora Reparation Mental Hospital, c. 1925 [Australian War Memorial]

As an admirer of Emil Kraepelin, Cade knew of Kraepelin's belief in internalized toxins as the cause of psychosis. If, as is likely the case, he had read Kraepelin's famous textbook, he would also have known of certain investigations (cited in the book) about body fluids in schizophrenic patients. One psychiatrist found enlarged 'red corpuscles' in the blood, another found 'cholesterin' in the cerebrospinal fluid, and a third researcher found sugar 'occasionally' in the urine. Kraepelin's colleague, Franz Nissl (affectionally known as Punctator Maximus) performed hundreds of spinal punctures looking for toxins in the cerebrospinal fluid.

Given the options of blood, urine or cerebrospinal fluid, John Cade chose urine. He started collecting urine samples early each morning. In addition to the patient samples, he also collected urine from a few healthy individuals, as a control. He conveniently stored the sample bottles on the top shelf of his family's refrigerator. Expecting to find high concentrations of a yet-unidentified toxin in the urine of at least some patients, he injected measured amounts of urine into the abdominal cavities of guinea pigs to see if they would exhibit any signs of illness, behavioral or otherwise. He'd grab a few experimental animals from an enclosure in the family's backyard, bring them to an unused pantry in one of the hospital wards and inject them.

Kitchen at the Bundoora Hospital; also John Cade's laboratory [López-Muñoz et al., Molecular Sciences 19, 2018]

Cade learned from his initial experiment that a guinea pig injected with 0.75 milliliter of urine per 30 grams of body weight—or more—would die. More interesting was the fact that animals given urine from manic patients died from considerably lower dosages than did animals given urine from healthy people or patients with other types of mental illness. Since the manner of death was similar in all cases, Cade concluded that all patients and all control subjects excreted a toxin, but the manic patients excreted *more* of it. What happened next is neatly summarized by Walter Brown, Cade's biographer,

> Cade embarked on a series of modest experiments that now have a mythic place in the history of psychiatry. These experiments did not follow an entirely logical or readily understood sequence, and Cade misinterpreted one of the critical results, but his effort to find the toxic substance led him, albeit via a circuitous and serendipitous route, to his groundbreaking discovery.[100]

Human urine is around 95 percent water, with the remainder consisting of breakdown products produced by protein metabolism. Urea, a nitrogen-

---

[100] W.A. Brown (2019), p. 64. See suggested readings.

containing compound, accounts for about half of all the breakdown material. Cade suspected, and his experiments confirmed, that urea is toxic, but contrary to his initial hypothesis, he did not find excessive amounts of urea in the urine of manic patients. Since the initial hypothesis was wrong, he revised the hypothesis. Maybe, he thought, manic patients have high levels of a substance that is not itself toxic, but which makes urea *more* toxic. He speculated that the enabling substance might be either creatinine or uric acid. To test the idea, he added creatinine to urea, but found no effect. Next, he added uric acid and found a slight effect, but not nearly enough to explain the lethality of 'manic urine'. Cade reasoned that he might see a bigger effect if he used a higher concentration of uric acid, but here he ran into a problem because uric acid ordinarily exists as a salt that does not easily dissolve in water or urine. Indeed, one type of kidney stone is made entirely of uric acid.

To get around the problem, he substituted uric acid for a chemically related salt, lithium urate. The result was not as he expected, for the addition of lithium urate seemed to *reduce*, rather than increase, the toxicity of urea. He again adapted, now switching from lithium urate to lithium carbonate, another lithium salt, but with lithium carbonate he found even less toxicity. Five of the ten animals injected with urea alone died, but none of the ten animals given urea plus lithium carbonate died. At this point, the proverbial light lit brightly in Cade's head. With his creative mind now fully engaged, he decided to test the effects of the lithium salts in a solution that contained absolutely no urea. Now the results were truly interesting. He described them thusly, 'After a latent period of about two hours the animals, although fully conscious, became extremely lethargic and unresponsive for one to two hours before once again being normally timid and active.'[101]

To summarize, Cade was looking for the toxin that makes people manic. Assuming that the toxin would show up in the patients' urine, he collected urine samples from patients and injected measured amounts into guinea pigs. As predicted, the guinea pigs died, but they also died when injected with urine from healthy people. He suspected that the toxic agent was urea, and since the patients' urine was more toxic than the urine of healthy persons, he thought that the patients' blood might contain a substance that boosted urea's toxicity. To test the idea, he added uric acid to urea and observed that, as expected, it increased the urine's toxicity, but it did so only slightly. He wanted to try higher concentrations of uric acid but found

---

[101] John F. J. Cade (1984), pp. 222–223.

that it did not dissolve well. To circumvent the problem, he used lithium salts instead of uric acid. Now, instead of dying, his guinea pigs became lethargic.

Years later, Cade was asked why he decided to try lithium salts as a treatment for mania after observing their effects in guinea pigs. He replied that it was the logical consequence of his thinking about toxins, but others see little logic in the sequence of experiments described above. Also, questions have been raised as to what, exactly, happened to the guinea pigs that were injected with lithium carbonate. Cade interpreted the effects as tranquilization, but it has been suggested that the animals were actually exhibiting the early signs of lithium poisoning. Fortunately, Cade judged the situation as he did, for otherwise we might not have lithium as a drug today. As for its toxicity, we will look at that again later in the chapter.

Cade understood that he would first have to give lithium to himself before giving it to any patient. But with what dosage? Cade's wife, Jean, was worried because she knew that there were potentially serious side effects. Although lithium had been a popular medicinal for centuries, the medical literature available to Cade mentioned a wide range of recommended dosages. In the end, he decided upon a dosage that was close to that which is currently prescribed, and with the dosage problem solved, he became a human guinea pig for his own experiment. Starting in February 1948, he injected himself with multiple doses of lithium carbonate and lithium citrate. Two weeks after the last injection, having suffered no ill effects, he began treating patients. His initial trial comprised ten patients with mania, six with *dementia praecox* and three with melancholia. In September of the following year, he reported the results in the *Medical Journal of Australia*.[102]

His report consists almost entirely of case histories, the first of which relates to 'WB, a male, aged fifty-one years, who had been in a state of chronic manic excitement for five years, restless, dirty, destructive, mischievous and interfering ... [He] had long been regarded as the most troublesome patient in the ward.' WB got lithium for two weeks. Afterwards, Cade observed that 'his response was highly gratifying ... He remained perfectly well and left hospital ... with instructions to take a maintenance dose of lithium carbonate, five grains [325 milligrams] twice a day ... He was soon back working happily at his old job.'

---

[102] John F. J Cade, 'Lithium salts in the treatment of psychotic excitement.' *The Medical Journal of Australia* 2(10): 349–352 (1949).

Nine other manic patients responded in a similar dramatic manner. Once their behaviors stabilized, they were released from the hospital. By the first anniversary of their treatments, five of the ten manic patients had left the hospital, including two patients who had been there during the previous five years. As expected, lithium produced no significant change in depressed patients, nor was there any 'fundamental improvement' in *dementia praecox* patients, although half of the latter became quieter and more cooperative.

Despite the spectacular short-term successes, there were troubling setbacks, starting with patient WB. Cade says in his report that at one point after his release from the hospital WB 'was becoming steadily more irritable and erratic', and a short while later, he 'ceased work just before Christmas.' WB was re-admitted to the hospital, at which point his relatives revealed that he had stopped taking the medication. Cade put him back on lithium carbonate and 'in a fortnight [he] again settled down to normal ... He is now (February 28, 1949) ready to return to home and work.' So goes the official story of WB and his lithium experience. But Walter Brown, author of an in-depth account of Cade's work, exposed further details pertaining to events that occurred in the interval between Cade's writing the report and its actual publication, that is, between the date of the last incident mentioned in the report—March 4—and the date of its publication on September 3. In the course of that half-year, several of Cade's patients suffered significant setbacks. WB's case is especially noteworthy.

According to Cade's clinical notes,[103] WB did not quickly return to work after his setback as Cade implied in the report. That is because he was experiencing 'anorexia, unsteadiness, general malaise and depression.' In fact, WB remained in hospital for at least five weeks. After his release, the treatments continued, but with frequent temporary halts. When off the medication, WB was 'manic, restless, euphoric, noisy, dirty, mischievous, destructive, [voicing] flight of ideas and thoroughly pleased with himself.' When on lithium, he was frail and dyspeptic. Then, after a period of utter exhaustion marked by three seizures, WB died. His death came a little more than two years after he first started on lithium.

We can't fault Cade for omitting WB's decline and death from his historic report, because those events occurred after the manuscript had been written and after it had been submitted to the medical journal. However, one wonders why Cade never mentioned these things when later retelling WB's story in interviews, lectures and publications. It is difficult to escape the conclusion that Cade did not want to tarnish the image of WB as the

---

[103] W.A. Brown (2019), pp. 77–78. See suggested readings.

poster boy of lithium therapy. Nor did Cade want to speak frankly about lithium's toxic effects, for that is what killed WB.

Lithium waters had been consumed as an all-purpose remedy since at least the mid-nineteenth century, and its troublesome side effects, typically upset stomach and dizziness, were well known. Cade was also aware of the fact that lithium could be lethal if taken excessively. Indeed, at the same time as Cade was preparing his breakthrough report, the reality of lithium toxicity was making headlines on the other side of the Pacific Ocean. Americans who had been put on low-salt diets because of heart disease or kidney disease were offered a substitute. Instead of sodium chloride—otherwise known as table salt—they were told they could put lithium chloride into their soups and onto their steaks. Apparently unaware of lithium's toxicity at the recommended concentration, people who chose the option suffered from nausea, blurred vision and tremors; some even died.

Whether Cade knew of the American lithium crisis is unclear, but he saw similar adverse effects in his patients. Thus, in his initial report he warned, 'It is therefore of the utmost importance that when a patient is on maximum doses he should be seen each day and that the nursing staff should be instructed to look for early symptoms of saturation.'[104] After WB died, Cade stopped prescribing lithium for his own patients, and a couple of years later, upon becoming superintendent at a large mental hospital, he banned its use altogether. Psychiatrists elsewhere were also wary. Fearful of adverse side effects, most doctors avoided lithium therapies. Attitudes changed only after the introduction of accurate methods for measuring lithium concentrations in the blood, and with that, the determination of safe dosages.

Apart from concerns over lithium's toxicity, psychiatrists had other reasons for ignoring Cade's work. It had been reported in the *Australian Journal of Medicine*, a journal which few foreigners read, and anyone who did happen to read it would have noticed that Cade's research methods were far from orthodox. Yes, his patients got better on lithium, but would they have improved just as much on placebo pills? Did they improve because of the lithium pills or because of all the attention they were getting? Readers also saw that Cade's conclusions rested entirely on evidence from ten case histories, and Cade himself had personally evaluated every one. Thus, the study lacked a comparison group, had no statistical validation, and was subject to investigator bias because Cade believed in the efficacy of his treatment.

---

[104] John F. J Cade (1949), pp. 351–352.

One person who did pay serious attention to Cade's 1949 paper was the Danish psychiatrist, Mogens Schou. Manic-depressive illness ran in his family and his younger brother had it, so Schou's interest in lithium was both academic and personal. Seeing something promising in Cade's report, Schou decided to confirm lithium's efficacy and safety through rigorous testing. To this end, he established a research group at the Risskov Psychiatric Hospital near the city of Aarhus. His tireless efforts over the next fifty years provided the compelling evidence that ultimately brought lithium into mainstream psychiatric practice.

Unlike Cade, who was not trained as a scientist and had little research experience, Schou was well acquainted with biological psychiatry through his father who was a psychiatric researcher and director of a large mental hospital. It helped, too, that his father's cousin was a Nobel laureate and professor of physiology in Copenhagen. Having spent two years doing basic biochemical research before setting up his own laboratory, Schou knew how to design a proper scientific experiment. Applying this knowledge to lithium therapy, he conducted a random, double-blind, placebo-controlled trial. Now the gold standard for any test of a proposed medical treatment, Schou's use of this design was one of the first in the field of psychiatry.

Every patient was given a pill once per day. Some received lithium carbonate, while others received a placebo that contained a different carbonate compound. After two weeks, the medications were switched—'randomly' according to the researchers—so that for the following two weeks some patients who had been receiving lithium now got the placebo, while others switched in the opposite direction. Every day, a psychiatrist on the ward logged a score for each patient signifying the clinical status of that patient on that particular day, but at no time did either the patient or the doctor know which substance was being ingested (double-blind).[105] Some nurses refused to give placebos to violent patients, so Schou countered by preparing the placebo pills in such a manner as to look, taste and feel like lithium pills. At its completion, the results showed that, on the whole, patients became less manic when switched to lithium, and more manic when switched to the placebo. Schou and his co-authors concluded that the results were 'in essential agreement with those of the Australian psychiatrists; lithium has an unquestionably beneficial effect on a number of manic patients.'[106]

---

[105] Note that Mark George's trial of TMS for depression, published in 1997, used the same experimental design; see p. 136.

[106] M. Schou et al. 'The treatment of manic psychoses by the administration of lithium salts.' *Journal of Neurology, Neurosurgery and Psychiatry* 17:250–260 (1954), p. 252.

Cade and Schou both showed that lithium can reduce the extreme emotions and heightened activities typical of manic patients, but only while the patients are on the drug. The majority of patients reverted to their manic states when taken off lithium. Schou's next big contribution, again in collaboration with co-workers, was to demonstrate the effectiveness of lithium in *preventing* manic episodes, the so-called prophylactic effect. This study included both manic patients and bipolar patients (mania and depression).[107] As before, the investigators used a double-blind experimental design. All patients began on continuous lithium treatment. After one year had passed, half of the patients were kept on lithium, while the other half was switched to a placebo. Differences between the two groups of patients soon became apparent. Twenty-one of the 39 patients on placebo pills had a recurrence, whereas none of the 45 patients still on lithium had a recurrence. After hearing of these results, psychiatrists everywhere kept their patients on lithium even after they seemed okay.

Perspective

It is surely ironic that one of the best drugs on the psychiatrists' prescription pad came not from the high-tech laboratory of a multi-national pharmaceutical company, but from the home refrigerator of an unassuming Australian psychiatrist working at a small suburban hospital. John Cade's discovery was the result of simple experimentation combined with a good measure of serendipity. Cade himself had no illusions. He was fond of pointing out that even 'the small boy, fishing after school in a muddy pond with string and a bent pin, occasionally hauls forth a handsome fish.'[108] And, in another context, 'I am not a scientist. I am only an old prospector who happened to pick up a nugget.'[109] None of this matters, of course, because no one doubts that it was him, and him alone, who made the truly great discovery. High-tech, rationally designed research has proven value, but there will forever be room for serendipity.

Lithium is commonly used today as a treatment for bipolar disorder. In contrast to many other psychiatric medications, it is very specific in its

---

[107] P.C. Baastrup et al., 'Prophylactic lithium: Double-blind discontinuation in manic-depressive disorders.' *Lancet* 2:326–330 (1970).

[108] John F.J. Cade, 'Research in psychiatry' (1951), p. 215.

[109] Jack L. Evans, 'Obituary.' *Australian and New Zealand Journal of Psychiatry* 15:275–277 (1980), p. 276.

actions. It stabilizes mood in bipolar disorder, but it is of little or no use in major depression, schizophrenia or other mental disorders.

Our knowledge of how lithium works is incomplete. While it affects numerous cellular processes, its ability to inhibit one particular enzyme, glycogen synthase kinase 3 (GSK-3), seems especially important. This molecule is implicated in several illnesses besides mania including epilepsy, Alzheimer's disease, and diabetes. It is known to participate in the regulation of neuronal excitability. Thus, it is possible that lithium works by reducing neuronal activity in brain regions responsible for manic behaviors. Apart from its effect on mood, lithium has also been shown to regulate the body's circadian rhythms, again through its inhibition of GSK-3.[110]

Suggested readings and a suggested film

Walter A. Brown, *Lithium: A Doctor, a Drug, and a Breakthrough.* New York, Liveright (2019).

Greg de Moore and Ann Westmore, *Finding Sanity: John Cade, Lithium and the Taming of Bipolar Disorder.* Sydney, Allen and Unwin (2017).

Film Australia, *Troubled minds: the lithium revolution.* New York, Films Media Group. Originally released as a short film (2004), it was later made available as a streaming video (2006).

---

[110] Gin S. Malhi and Tim Outhred, 'Therapeutic mechanisms of lithium in bipolar disease: Recent advances and current understanding.' *CNS Drugs* 30:931–949 (2016).

10 Chlorpromazine: the first antipsychotic drug

Doctors first learned about the new treatment for schizophrenia in 1952, three years after John Cade announced his lithium treatment for mania. Although both discoveries unfolded in an unusual manner, the circumstances were quite different. While Cade worked pretty much alone, far away from the centers of pharmacological research, the researchers who discovered chlorpromazine worked for a large biochemical company. Cade was looking for a toxic substance in manic patients, the chemists at Rhône-Poulenc company were seeking a better anaesthetic. In the end, Cade discovered a novel use for the element lithium, while the French chemists created an artificial molecule 50 times heavier than lithium.

Rhône-Poulenc wanted to develop a drug that could counter the actions of histamine, a natural compound present in the human body. Histamine has numerous beneficial functions, but it is also implicated in certain unpleasant and even dangerous reactions, including allergy, inflammation, sleeplessness and stress. In the 1940s, many pharmaceutical companies were trying to develop antihistamine drugs. Rhône-Poulenc was in the game with a drug called promethazine which they hoped to sell as a sedative and sleep inducer.

Meanwhile, Henri Laborit, a surgeon in the French navy, was thinking about how to combat his patients' physiological stress. Initially stationed in Tunisia, he was re-assigned to a military hospital in Paris, and it was there that he became friendly with Pierre Huguenard, a fellow surgeon with similar concerns. Both men ordinarily anaesthetized their patients with a gaseous chemical delivered through a facial mask. But one day Huguenard needed to operate on a woman's nose, and the mask did not fit. So, instead of the gas anesthetic, Huguenard used a cocktail containing a mix of Rhône-Poulenc's drug, promethazine, and pethidine, an opioid with the trade name Demerol. Afterwards, Huguenard told Laborit that the patient was not only relaxed but indifferent to what was being done to her. Laborit tried the same cocktail on several of his own patients, and he too noted the unusual psychological effect. Recognizing that it was promethazine, not the opioid, that had produced the indifference, he asked people at Rhône-Poulenc if they could create an antihistamine that was like promethazine but even more potent. Laborit wanted something that would render the patients oblivious to the surgeon's knife. Did he know that a few taxi drivers, dulled by antihistamines, had been driving through Parisian stop lights with barely a pause?

The chemist charged with improving upon promethazine found the trick he needed in his specialist's bag. After selecting a number of antihistamines already at hand, he added a single chlorine atom to each one. Confident that chlorine would increase the potencies of at least some of these compounds, he handed them all to Simone Courvoisier for testing. Courvoisier was head of the pharmacology group at Rhône-Poulenc. Ordinarily, she tested drugs using biochemical and physiological methods, but how to test for 'indifference'? For that, she designed a novel type of assay. First, she assembled an experimental environment that consisted of nothing but an elevated platform and an attached rope that hung beneath. On top of the platform, she placed some smelly food which she knew her hungry lab rats would want to eat. The rats had to climb the rope to reach the food. Unmedicated (control) rats quickly ascended the rope to access the reward, but the majority of rats that had been injected with a chlorinated antihistamine were slow to climb. Compound RP4560 stood out among the others, for rats injected with that compound lazied around at the base seemingly uninterested in eating. When later renamed, compound RP4560 became chlorpromazine.

Laborit found that chlorpromazine worked really well. He had wanted an agent that would stabilize multiple body systems, and chlorpromazine seemed to do just that. Not only did it produce the desired calming effect, it dampened down the sympathetic nervous system, steadied the heart and prevented vomiting. He convinced Rhône-Poulenc to sell it under the name Largactil, meaning 'large in action'. After Laborit published a short report on the drug, other surgeons began using it. Those doing open-heart surgeries found chlorpromazine especially useful because, as part of the procedure, they had to temporarily halt blood circulation. With the heart stopped, they cooled the body to reduce its metabolism and hence its need for oxygenated blood. However, the procedure often triggered a compensatory warming response that negated the desired effect. By inhibiting the body's temperature control system, chlorpromazine allowed the surgeons to maintain the body in a chilled state.

Laborit mentioned chlorpromazine's psychological effects to his psychiatrist colleagues, and a few of them decided to try it on their own patients.

Simone Courvoisier [Science History Institute]

Jacques L., a highly agitated 24-year-old got the first of twenty injections on January 19, 1952. While his condition improved, it was not clear how much of the improvement was due to chlorpromazine, because he was also given barbiturates and electroconvulsive shocks. Nevertheless, Jacques L's psychiatrists were sufficiently impressed to report the trial at the next meeting of the Société Médico-Psychologique.

Less than one month later, structured trials with chlorpromazine began at the Sainte-Anne mental hospital in Paris. Dr. Pierre Deniker was responsible for about one hundred male patients housed in a special, locked ward. It happened that Deniker's bother-in-law was an anesthetist, and it was through him that Deniker heard about chlorpromazine. According to a Canadian psychiatrist who knew him, Deniker was 'a real Parisian intellectual'.[111] Deniker's boss, Dr. Jean Delay, was also an intellectual, but aloof and patronizing. Deniker asked for permission to try chlorpromazine and Delay consented. A colleague later recalled the individuals selected for Deniker's drug trial, describing them as 'maniacal patients ... who for weeks would shriek and injure other patients; who had to be put in a straitjacket and even tied to the bed with straps.'[112] One patient in the drug trial was

[111] Interview with Heinz Lehmann in David Healy, *The Psychopharmacologists*. London, CRC Press (2001), p. 168.

[112] Jean Thuillier, *Ten Years That Changed the Face of Mental Illness*. London, CRC Press (1999), p. 111.

a 57-year-old laborer with a long history of mental illness. According to the case report, he had been recently admitted for 'making improvised political speeches in cafes, becoming involved in fights with strangers, and for the last few days has been [seen] walking around the street with a pot of flowers on his head preaching his love of liberty.'[113]

Deniker chose just eight patients for the trial. In the beginning, they were given small doses of chlorpromazine four to six times daily along with an ice bath to cool them down. On the whole, the patients got better, but when the hospital ran out of ice, Deniker decided to continue with chlorpromazine without the baths, *et voila*, they did just as well on chlorpromazine alone as they had on chlorpromazine plus baths.

Jean Delay (left) and Pierre Deniker

---

[113] Edward Shorter, *A History of Psychiatry: From the Era of the Asylum to the Age of Prozac.* New York, John Wiley & Sons (1997); p. 250.

A physician who was working with Deniker at the time recalls how things changed after the trial, 'The hemp waistcoats were put back in the cupboards, and the hydrotherapy pools were only used for personal washing.' In the hospital hallways, 'One no longer passed patients in shirts walking with their straitjackets open with straps undone on the way to the toilets' but instead encountered them 'strolling decently' in civvies. 'The most evident sign of this extraordinary therapeutic result could be appreciated even from the outside of the building of the men's clinic—there was silence [as opposed to screaming and shouting].'[114]

A final example of the drama surrounding the trial is related by the historian David Healy.[115] It concerns a barber from Lyon,

> who had been hospitalized for several years with a chronic psychosis and was unresponsive to his environment. When given chlorpromazine, he awoke from this stuporous state and told his doctor, Jean Perrin, that he now knew where he was and who he was, and that he wanted to go home and back to work. Perrin responded by challenging him to give him a shave. The open razor, water, and towels were produced, and the patient set about doing his job perfectly. Either Perrin had considerable nerve or the transformations were truly extraordinary.

It must be emphasized that these patients were severely ill. They heard the voices of persons long dead; they imagined secret groups plotting their downfall. Most psychiatrists viewed schizophrenia as a hereditary brain disorder for which there would never be a cure. And yet, they got better with chlorpromazine. The research team at Sainte-Anne's quickly put out six short, French-language publications. Pierre Deniker, the principal investigator, and Jean Delay, the department head, were both authors. Other men who had participated in the drug trial were co-authors on three of the papers, but the first listed author on all six papers—a place usually reserved for the most deserving author—was Delay. With these publications, and the even more efficient word-of-mouth, news of the discovery spread quickly throughout Europe. It took much longer to reach America, for reasons that will be explained below.

The tussle over authorship forms just part of the controversy surrounding credit for the discovery. No one doubts that Henri Laborit was the first to

---

[114] Jean Thuillier (1999), quoted in Edward Shorter's book review, *Journal of Psychopharmacology* 14(1), (2000), p. 89.

[115] David Healy (2002), p. 91. See suggested readings.

try it with humans, and even the first to note its psychological effects, but he did little to advertise that property. Jean Delay was the most senior psychiatrist at the mental hospital, but it was his underlings, especially Pierre Deniker, who carried out the first real trial. For years, Delay lobbied to be awarded the Nobel Prize (together with Deniker), all along insisting that Laborit did not deserve it. As it turned out, none of them was beckoned to Sweden.

Rhône-Poulenc was naturally pleased with Europe's enthusiasm for its new drug, and they looked forward to even more success in America, but enthusiasm was much delayed in America. The task of selling chlorpromazine in the United States was given— under license—to the pharmaceutical company, Smith, Kline and French. SK&F was eager to sell the drug, but not as an antipsychotic. In the 1950s, few American psychiatrists looked upon mental disorders in the context of brain abnormalities. They thought instead of unconscious psychological conflicts. One of Freud's disciples, Frieda Fromm-Reichmann, blamed the patient's mother for inflicting lasting psychological damage, writing that, 'The schizophrenic is painfully distrustful and resentful of other people due to the severe early warp and rejection he encountered in important people of his infancy and childhood, as a rule, mainly in a schizophrenogenic mother.'[116] Mania, major depression and other forms of psychosis were likewise spoken of in psychoanalytical terms. If there was anything that could possibly help these patients, it would be talk therapy, specifically psychoanalysis. Pharmacological treatments were generally dismissed as impossible. Given this climate of expert opinion, the prospect of getting governmental approval for a barely tested, French antipsychotic medication was bound to be an uphill battle, and indeed, no federal agency was interested in chlorpromazine.

In its attempt to shift public opinion, SK&F persuaded a few prominent psychiatrists to test chlorpromazine in their private practices. It happened, though, that the reporting of those trials emphasized the drug's undesirable side effects rather than its benefits, and they weren't wrong about the side effects. Chlorpromazine, like other drugs of its type, can cause tremors, jerky movements and stiffness in the limbs. Some patients experience restlessness and dizziness. Whether it was because of these lackluster reports or for other reasons, chlorpromazine generated little interest in America. Thus, SK&F delayed plans for a large-scale trial. They could afford to wait, because they saw other opportunities for chlorpromazine.

---

[116] Frieda Fromm-Reichmann, 'Notes on the development of treatment of schizophrenics by psychoanalytic psychotherapy.' *Psychiatry* 11:263–273 (1948), p. 265.

Apart from developing drugs for psychiatry, SK&F was also looking for an anti-emetic drug, that is, a medication for nausea and vomiting. The pharmacologists at Rhône-Poulenc had already noted that chlorpromazine had such an effect, but the SK&F's researchers wanted to see it for themselves. Caged rats were put on top of a large turntable and spun around. The rats became nauseous, but none vomited because rats cannot vomit. Instead, they opened their mouths widely, rubbed their chins against the cage floor and extended a paw, all signs of nausea in a rat. When the researchers reported that rats given chlorpromazine prior to being rotated showed less of these behaviors than unmedicated rats, the bosses were impressed. After weighing the poor prospects of an antipsychotic drug against the upside potential of an anti-emetic, they dropped the trade name Largactil and launched chlorpromazine as Thorazine, a new anti-emetic.

Although Rhône-Poulenc sold the rights for chlorpromazine in the United States, they retained the rights in Canada, where Largactil (still named as such in Canada) was selling no better than in the United States. Prospects for the drug were about to change, however, thanks to a visit by a Rhône-Poulenc salesman to the office of a Montreal psychiatrist named Heinz Lehmann. Even as a child in Germany, Lehmann was attracted to mental science. By the age of fifteen he had read all of Freud's books and chosen psychiatry as his life's work. After graduating from medical school, he and his father, a Jewish surgeon, fled Germany amidst rising tensions. Once settled in Montreal, he lived and worked at a mental hospital while teaching in the Department of Psychiatry at McGill University. Writing of this period, he recalled that 'most of the staff had gone to war. I was an immigrant, a refugee from Germany, and I had my difficulties with that. I had up to 600 patients alone; there were no residents or interns at the time and only one registered nurse to help.'[117] Hour upon hour, he walked alone through the wards talking to patients.

Just as John Cade had done, Lehmann searched by trial and error to find something that would help his suffering patients. He asked them all sorts of questions. He tested them on word associations. He produced huge skin blisters to stimulate the immune system and, along the same lines, he injected turpentine into the abdomen to stimulate white blood cells and induce a fever. A Swiss psychiatrist in the 1920s suggested continuous sleep therapy, so he tried that. Nothing worked. Thinking that he might find something akin to hallucinations in normal people, he experimented

---

[117] Interview with Heinz Lehmann in David Healy, *The Psychopharmacologists*. London, CRC Press (2001), p. 164.

with afterimages, flickering images and spinning lights. Endowed with a curious mind, Lehmann was drawn to research, yet in his opinion, 'What is most important, so far as I am concerned, is the contact-intensive training that you have to have. You have to have thousands of hours of contact with patients regardless of how much molecular biology is behind it, when you finally give them a pill.'[118]

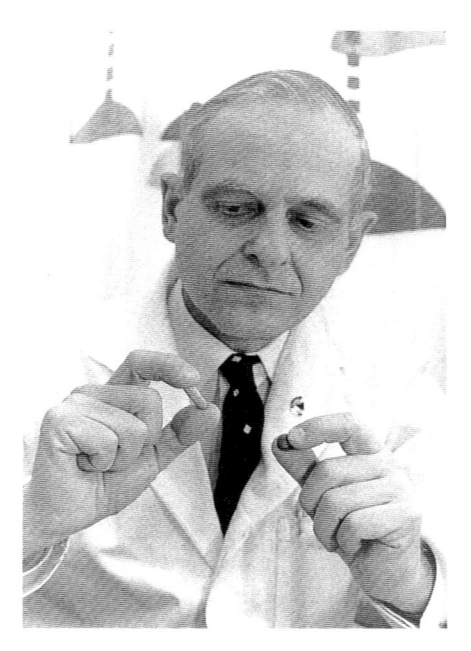

Heinz Lehmann [McGill University Archives, PR036882]

On that day in 1953 when the Rhône-Poulenc salesman dropped by Lehmann's office, Lehmann wasn't there, so the salesman left copies of the papers written by the Sainte-Anne doctors in Paris. Lehmann read them in the bathtub the following Sunday. Struck by what they reported, on the following Monday morning he asked his assistant to organize a trial with Largactil. Three months later, he and the assistant were ready to begin. Their study included seventy-five of the most highly agitated patients. Most of them had been diagnosed with schizophrenia, but there were also a few with depression or dementia. Lehmann recounts what happened after they were given chlorpromazine,

---

[118] Interview in D. Healy (2001), p. 171.

Two or three of the acute schizophrenics became symptom free. Now I had never seen that before. I thought it was a fluke—something that would never happen again but anyway there they were. At the end of four or five weeks, there were a lot of symptom-free patients. By this I mean that a lot of hallucinations, delusions and thought disorder had disappeared. In 1953 there just wasn't anything that ever produced something like this—a remission from schizophrenia in weeks.[119]

Clearly, chlorpromazine was just as effective in Montreal as it had been in Paris, but there were differences, and they account for the greater impact of the Montreal trial compared to the Parisian trial. First and foremost, Lehmann gave chlorpromazine to seventy-five patients, whereas Delay and Deniker had given it to only eight. Also, Lehmann published his results in an English language medical journal. The majority of North American psychiatrists read only English, so few of them had seen the papers coming out of France. Lehmann, however, was trilingual, having learned German as a child, English after migrating to Canada, and French from his Québécoise wife. Lehmann claimed, in his reminiscence, 'that is how it all started; it came about really because I married a French Canadian and we spoke French at home.'

The Canadian results aroused great interest in the United States. Soon, a second influential study was launched at the Camarillo State Hospital in California, where nearly 7,000 schizophrenia patients languished. A team of psychiatrists from the nearby University of California (UCLA) put chlorpromazine up against alternative treatments. The study design was simple enough. Each patient was randomly assigned to one of five experimental groups: psychotherapy, chlorpromazine, psychotherapy *and* chlorpromazine, electroconvulsive shock, or social and environmental support. Commenting on the final results, the team leader wrote that they 'demonstrate beyond reasonable doubt that drug therapy is the most effective single form of specific treatment.' As for the others, 'Electroconvulsive therapy cannot be considered to be desirable as an alternative or serious rival to drug therapy,' and 'Psychotherapy alone without drugs is an expensive and ineffective form of treatment that apparently adds little or nothing to conservative [nonmedical] therapies.'[120]

---

[119] Interview in D. Healy (2001), p. 160.
[120] P.R.A. May, *Treatment of Schizophrenia: A Comparative Study of Five Treatment Methods.* New York, Science House (1968), quotes on pp. 258, 262 and 267.

This author's brother was a patient at Camarillo State Hospital at the time. In a previous book, I remarked that thanks to this study, my brother 'was liberated from the frustrations of psychotherapy and the terrors of electroconvulsive shock. In their place, he received a medication that minimized the worst symptoms of his disease and provided him with many years of relative stability.'[121]

Chlorpromazine works well, but haloperidol works even better. Created by Janssen Pharmaceutica in 1958, haloperidol is 100 times more potent than chlorpromazine. Soon after its discovery, it quickly replaced chlorpromazine as the drug of choice in the treatment of psychotic illnesses, and it rose to become one of the top selling drugs of any kind. My brother took haloperidol for thirty years.

Janssen Pharmaceutica had always been a family operation. It started out importing Hungarian drugs for resale in Belgium, but when the founder's son took over, he completely changed the business model. Even as an undergraduate student in Belgium, Paul Janssen was ambitious. As part of his professional preparation, he traveled to the United States to learn from pharmaceutical companies and university pharmacology departments. At the end of his studies, he created a semi-independent research center with the directive to develop molecules with commercial potential. Endowed with great intelligence and a ridiculous work ethic, Paul Janssen is celebrated as the most prolific drug inventor of all time. In the beginning, the challenge was large and the progress slow.

> The odds against success were apparently enormous ... Trained personnel were virtually nonexistent and so was the budget. The only way out was somehow to concentrate on making new chemicals that could be synthesized and purified with simple methods and equipment, using the cheapest possible intermediates, and to efficiently investigate the pharmacology at minimal expense. The fact that I [Paul Janssen], the oldest member of our very small research group was 27 years of age, that we were all willing to work very long hours, seven days a week, and, being inexperienced, had no idea of the difficulties along the road but blind faith in ultimate success, were of course decisive factors in our favor.[122]

---

[121] Ronald Chase, *Schizophrenia: A Brother Finds Answers in Biological Science.* Baltimore, Johns Hopkins University Press (2013), p. 79.

[122] Jie Jack Li, *Laughing Gas, Viagra, and Lipitor: The Human Stories Behind the Drugs We Use.* New York, Oxford University Press (2006), p. 154.

Indeed, those factors must have contributed to his enormous success. By the time of his death, Paul Janssen had 5000 scientists working in his research laboratory. He himself is credited with 850 scientific publications, 100 patents and 77 prescribed drugs.

Paul A. Janssen [Janssen Pharmaceuticals]

Just as the chemists at Rhône-Poulenc discovered chlorpromazine while seeking a better antihistamine, so Janssen's team discovered haloperidol while looking for a better pain killer. Their customary strategy in situations like this was to select a drug that already worked, tweak the molecule by adding or removing atoms, and then testing every derivative for favorable effects. In this case, they began with pethidine, the opioid pain killer that Laborit had used for surgeries before chlorpromazine. Janssen's chemists started out by substituting a methyl group with a propiophenone group, only to discover that similar compounds had already been patented by other pharmaceutical companies. Their next step was substituting the propiophenone group for a butyrophenone group, a move that resulted in the creation of a totally new class of molecules, the butyrophenones. By the time that Janssen and co-workers finished tinkering with the butyrophenones, they had about 4000 unique molecules.

On a single day in 1958, Janssen's team synthesized 438 new butyrophenone compounds. As always with new candidate medicines, each was evaluated to see if it affected the size of the eye pupil in rats or the delay time before a mouse jumped off a hot plate. Compounds showing promise were then tested for interactions with other drugs. It was in these tests that haloperidol, the forty-fifth butyrophenone in the series, powered to the top of the line. The most interesting result came when they administered haloperidol in combination with amphetamine. Ordinarily, amphetamine causes lab animals to become highly agitated, but when the animals got haloperidol before getting amphetamine, they remained as calm as ever.

Outside the lab, there were indications of a causal relationship between amphetamine and psychosis. European cyclists, for example, had discovered that amphetamine could provide just enough 'agitation' to help them win major championships, including the Tour De France. Observers noted, however, that some of these athletes finished the race looking disoriented and, in some cases, slightly paranoid. Amphetamines were also widely used by Japanese soldiers in the second World War to enhance vigilance, but there too, unwanted psychological effects ensued. These days, the 'recreational' use of amphetamine derivatives —principally methamphetamine and MDMA (ecstasy)—has exploded into a public health crisis complete with paranoid delusions, hallucinations and extreme agitation.

Janssen saw what he was looking for in haloperidol, a compound that works against amphetamine. Indeed, the clinical trials that followed the laboratory tests clearly demonstrated its value in alleviating psychotic symptoms. Like chlorpromazine, haloperidol blocks hallucinations and delusions, reduces agitation and induces Parkinson's-like side effects. It is more calming than chlorpromazine, but less sedating (less sleep inducing). The main difference lies in its greater potency. Marketed under the name Haldol—and other brands—it has helped millions of people.

Ordinarily, one would assume that two drugs producing the same effects must act through the same mechanism. But chemically speaking, chlorpromazine and haloperidol are entirely different. Haloperidol is a butyrophenone, while chlorpromazine is a phenothiazine. Scientists puzzled over how two dissimilar molecules could have nearly the same psychological effects. Struggling with the conundrum, they came up with some key insights into how the brain works.

Every school kid knows—or should know—that messages in the brain pass from one neuron to another by means of chemical neurotransmitters. In the 1950s, however, in the decade when chlorpromazine and haloperidol were discovered, even top-level scientists did not know this. Yes, they knew about serotonin, norepinephrine, acetylcholine and dopamine, but they did not know what they were doing in the brain. Most scientists assumed that neurons communicate by means of electrical sparks, because only electricity would be fast enough. When asked about all those chemicals sloshing around the neurons, they replied that the chemicals were doing metabolic work. The neuroscience historian Elliot Valenstein wrote about these opinions in a book with the lovely title, *The War of the Soups and the Sparks.* 'Because neurotransmitters were not thought to exist in the brain, for a number of years it was not even possible to offer a reasonable explanation of what the [psychiatric] drugs might be doing there, even after their effects were discovered.'[123]

One researcher who did believe in chemical neurotransmission was Arvid Carlsson, professor of pharmacology at the University of Gothenburg in Sweden. It was a conviction that led him to discover that both chlorpromazine and haloperidol rely on the same mechanism of action. His path to the Nobel Prize (2000) was an unlikely one, given that his father, mother and older siblings were all historians and 'strongly oriented toward the humanities.' His choice of medicine as a career no doubt surprised his family but, as he later explained, 'The reason for this deviating behavior of mine was partly the kind of opposition often occurring in youngsters [and] partly some vague idea of science being more "useful" than the arts.'[124]

Carlsson, like other pharmacologists of the day, was interested in a drug called reserpine, a weak antipsychotic compound that reduces the levels of molecules known as monoamines, so named because each one contains a single nitrogen atom. In the brain, the main monoamines are serotonin, dopamine and norepinephrine. Carlsson believed that monoamines are neurotransmitters—as indeed they are—but other scientists were skeptical. Notwithstanding uncertainty about their exact functions, investigators came to believe that the monoamines were somehow implicated in psychosis. Since reserpine reduced monoamine levels *and* dampened psychotic symptoms, they figured that chlorpromazine and haloperidol probably acted in the same way. But they were wrong. When experiments showed that chlorpromazine and haloperidol do not lower monoamine levels, everyone had to re-think the explanation for how these drugs work.

---

[123] Elliot S. Valenstein, *The War of the Soups and the Sparks: The Discovery of Neurotransmitters and the Dispute Over How Nerves Communicate.* New York, Columbia University Press (2005), p. xi.

[124] Quotes from Arvid Carlsson's autobiographical sketch for the Nobel Prize in Physiology or Medicine 2000.

Arvid Carlsson and wife, Ulla-Lisa, upon learning of his Nobel Prize, 2000 [Reuters]

Arvid Carlsson discovered that antipsychotic medications work not by reducing monoamines but by interfering with their functions as transmitters. Ordinarily, when a neuron releases a monoamine molecule (one among thousands), it floats across a tiny gap to the opposing neuron where it is captured by an awaiting receptor molecule. If a molecule other than the monoamine is already occupying that receptor, the monoamine cannot land there, and neuronal communication is blocked. Carlsson and his co-worker, Margit Lindqvist, found that chlorpromazine and haloperidol are two such monoamine imposters. By sticking to the monoamine receptors, they disrupt neural circuits, in particular those responsible for hallucinations and delusions.

After comparing results across all monoamines, Carlsson found that dopamine is the monoamine most affected by chlorpromazine and haloperidol. Dopamine is an important neurotransmitter, implicated in Parkinson's disease, addictions, and other human disorders. Because Carlsson's research pointed to a shut-down of dopamine neurotransmission as the mechanism of action for antipsychotic drugs, speculation naturally arose that, conversely, schizophrenia might be caused by excessive activity in the dopamine communication system. Although it's an attractive hypothesis with some supportive evidence, few scientists believe that dopamine dysfunction is the only cause, or even the main cause. More likely, additional monoamines and multiple interacting systems are affected.

Perspective

Chlorpromazine started out as an antihistamine, later became a remedy for sleeplessness, a sedative (in surgeries), a physiological stabilizer (again in surgeries), an anti-emetic, and finally an antipsychotic. Chlorpromazine was one of the first synthetic products born of chemical tinkering. Its phenomenal commercial success paved the way for the modern pharmaceutical industry, which today churns out a seemingly endless list of psychiatric medications—and receives an ample profit in return.

After chlorpromazine came the similar but more potent haloperidol. Later still, came clozapine, a somewhat different type of antipsychotic. First sold in 1972, the initial success of clozapine ushered in dozens of similar drugs. They were named 'atypical' or 'second generation' drugs to distinguish them from chlorpromazine and haloperidol. Many of the atypicals block dopamine receptors—as do chlorpromazine and haloperidol—but they also target the neurotransmitters serotonin and glutamate. Psychiatrists attempt to prescribe drugs according to how well they match up against a particular patient profile, but the task is made difficult by the large number of licensed medications and the equally diverse manifestations of psychosis.

Overall, most patients respond well to most antipsychotic drugs. However, there are unpleasant side effects with all of the drugs, and for clozapine in particular, the side effects can be serious. No drug cures schizophrenia. Moreover, while the drugs may be good at reducing delusions, hallucinations and disordered thinking, they do little or nothing to alleviate the so-called negative symptoms of apathy, loneliness and stifled emotions. Finally, patients tend to dislike the drugs, so they sometimes stop taking them, and that causes the symptoms to reappear.

Suggested readings and a suggested film

David Healy, *The Creation of Psychopharmacology.* Cambridge, Mass., Harvard University Press (2002).

Green Lion Productions, *Untangling the Mind: The Legacy of Dr. Heinz Lehmann.* New York, NY: Filmakers Library (2000).

Judith P. Swazey, *Chlorpromazine in Psychiatry: A Study of Therapeutic Innovation.* Cambridge, Mass., MIT Press (1974).

Jean Thuillier, *Ten Years that Changed the Face of Mental Illness.* Translated by Gordon Hickish. London: Martin Dunitz (1999).

11 The first antidepressants

Nearly everyone gets depressed from time to time, but whether you *have* depression depends on the definition. Just as the meaning of melancholia has changed considerably from the time when it was virtually synonymous with madness, so too has depression taken on a new meaning in recent times. By the early eighteenth century, depression had come to imply intense sadness and self-loathing often accompanied by despair and thoughts of suicide. People with symptoms like that are seriously ill. They often require hospitalization and are prone to becoming psychotic. The antidepressive drugs discovered in the 1950s—those featured in this chapter—were intended for people with this type of depression. Back then, negative mood states of a less serious nature were largely ignored. When Prozac and other drugs of its type arrived, they helped men in boring jobs, lonely housewives and bankrupted investors, but not those on the verge of suicide. To clarify the distinction between these patient groups, psychiatrists coined the term 'major depressive disorder' to cover severe conditions, leaving less serious conditions with the tag 'minor depression', or simply 'depression'. Whereas it is assumed that major depression has a biological basis, the cause or causes of minor depression are less certain. To summarize, although many people experience occasional, minor depression, relatively few people become seriously ill with major depressive disorder.

Lithium and chlorpromazine changed the psychiatric landscape by proving that chemicals can dramatically improve the lives of mental patients. With mania and schizophrenia now manageable by means of medication, dulling sedation and electroconvulsive shock fell to the wayside. Doctors eagerly awaited additional drugs for treating other conditions, and pharmaceutical companies stood ready to cooperate. It was a natural pairing that brought forth lasting alliances between businesses and psychiatrists. Company chemists generated a seemingly endless number of compounds of unknown value, and the psychiatrists tested them for efficacy. Many of these compounds were initially intended as treatments for medical conditions such as tuberculosis and inflammation but were given to the psychiatrists just in case. It is only a slight exaggeration to suggest that the pharmaceutical companies first created drugs, then searched for matching diseases. It was mostly a matter of trial and error.

There are currently more than 70 drugs for depression licensed for sale worldwide (according to Wikipedia). Two of these, imipramine (Tofranil) and fluoxetine (Prozac), will be discussed here, along with iproniazid (Marsilid), which was important in the early stages of drug development, but was later withdrawn over concerns of its toxicity. Laboratory research played a significant role in the discovery of the antidepressants, and once they were proven effective, efforts were made to understand their mechanisms of action. Ultimately, scientists proposed a specific hypothesis that explains the biological basis of depression. However, as we will see, questions have been raised about whether, in fact, the hypothesis is true.

The story begins at the end of World War II, when Germany grounded its fleet of Messerschmitt fighter planes. These planes, as well as the German rockets, were fueled by hydrazine, a colorless, highly inflammable liquid. With hostilities ended, vast stores of hydrazine sat unused and unwanted by anyone but the Swiss pharmaceutical company Hoffmann-La Roche, which bought large quantities at cheap prices. The Swiss were thinking tuberculosis, not mental illness. They already had two closely related drugs in hand, both synthesized from hydrazine and both performing well in clinical trials. Although intended primarily for tuberculosis, Hoffmann-La Roche conducted smaller trials with the same drugs to explore possible applications in psychiatry. However, few of the patients in these trials were depressed. Most had schizophrenia, and the drugs didn't help them.

Word got around that some of the patients being treated for tuberculous got decidedly happy, even mildly euphoric, after receiving one of the two candidate drugs but not the other. They were talking about a compound called iproniazid, and the reports of its effect on mood prompted Dr. Nathan Kline, at the Rockland State Hospital in New York, to conduct trials with psychiatric patients. Kline was an active researcher and a vocal backer of new ideas—usually those of his own making. Jumping at the opportunity to try iproniazid, he set up trials both at the hospital and in his private practice. He surprised colleagues by reporting at a medical conference in 1957 that 47 percent of his chronically depressed patients had improved after five weeks on iproniazid, and 70 percent showed a 'measurable response' after treatment for five months. Kline characterized iproniazid as a 'psychic energizer' and urged Hoffmann-La Roche to conduct further research with the goal of marketing iproniazid as an antidepressant. He was disappointed to learn that Hoffmann-La Roche was in no hurry to proceed. 'Here indeed was a fairly unique situation!' wrote Kline. 'A group of clinical investigators [was] trying to convince a pharmaceutical house that they had a valuable product rather than the other way around.'[125]

Nathan Kline [Nathan S. Kline Institute for Psychiatric Research]

In the end, of course, Hoffman-Roche did come around to Kline's way of thinking. They renamed iproniazid as Marsilid, sold it as an antidepressant and chalked up about 400,000 prescriptions in the first year. Many patients who would otherwise have needed electroconvulsive shock therapy were kept stable on Marsilid. The drug was also helping individuals with less severe depressions, those of the 'ordinary' variety. The historian Edward Shorter dug up evidence suggestive of the latter usage in the fact that 'a horse named Marsilid won in the ninth at Belmont racetrack outside of New York city on September 4, 1959.' Shorter explains, 'It is tempting to think

---

[125] Nathan Kline, 'Monoamine oxidase inhibitors: An unfinished picaresque tale.' In Ayd, F. J., Jr. and Blackwell, B., eds., *Discoveries in Biological Psychiatry*. J. B. Lippincott: Philadelphia (1970), p. 200.

that its owner might have been among Dr. Kline's grateful patients.'[126] Although highly effective as a treatment for depression, the U.S. Federal Drug Administration halted sales of Marsilid in 1961, following reports of jaundice and high blood pressure associated with its use.

Marsilid had only a short run as a prescribed drug, yet it had a lasting influence on the discovery of even better drugs. Thanks to the investigations of Nathan Kline and other research-oriented psychiatrists, scientists came to believe that iproniazid (Marsilid) worked by interfering with a specific biochemical process in the brain. Never before had there been such a detailed—and plausible—explanation for the effects of a psychiatric drug.

To better understand the science side of antidepressant drug development, we must go back to the state of affairs in the mid-1950, before Kline's large-scale trial of iproniazid. At the time, Kline was interested in reserpine, a substance mentioned in the previous chapter for its ability to lower levels of monoamine neurotransmitters. For centuries, reserpine had been extracted from the dried roots of a flowering milkweed plant, *Rauwolfia serpentina.* It had been used to treat high blood pressure, fever, snake bites and, yes, insanity. Kline decided to run a proper test of reserpine's efficacy in the treatment of mental disorders. His first trial, involving 700 schizophrenia patients ended in disappointment, so he tried reserpine with anxious patients and, later, with obsessive-compulsive patients, but the results were no better. Then one day, while chatting with an acquaintance after a lecture, Kline heard something that greatly affected his thinking about reserpine. Here is Kline's recollection of what the colleague said:

> [Another psychiatrist] and he [the colleague] had found that if experimental animals were given iproniazid [Marsilid] prior to reserpine that instead of becoming calm and somewhat sedated they actually became hyperalert and hyperactive. The possibility of using this combination on retarded and depressed patients immediately led me to speculate whether this was the psychic energizer for which we had all been looking.[127]

The illustration on the next page shows an example of the effect observed by Kline's colleague. Kline was impressed. If iproniazid could counteract reserpine's sedative effect, it must produce the opposite effect when admin-

---

[126] Edward Shorter, *Before Prozac: The Troubled History of Mood Disorders in Psychiatry* (2008), p. 112. See suggested readings.

[127] Nathan Kline (1970), pp. 197–198.

istered alone.[128] It was at this point that he began the clinical trials that ultimately demonstrated iproniazid's strong 'energizing' properties.

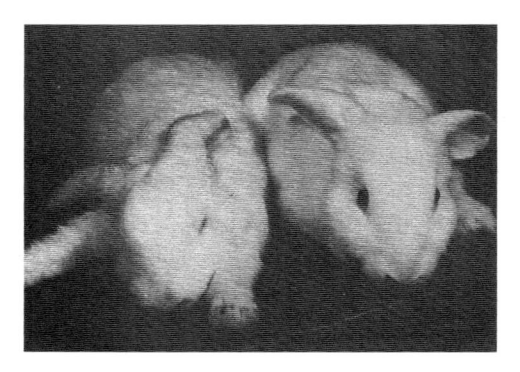

Both animals were given reserpine but only the animal on the right was pretreated with iproniazid [Brodie and Shore, Annals New York Academy of Sciences 66, 1957]

Meanwhile, laboratory scientists were making their own discoveries concerning the pharmacology of reserpine and iproniazid. First came the finding that iproniazid blocks monoamine oxidase, the enzyme that metabolizes, or breaks down, monoamine neurotransmitters in the brain (serotonin, norepinephrine, dopamine). Three years later, it was discovered that reserpine, the downer substance, depletes the brain of these same neurotransmitters. These findings led scientists to two conclusions: First, depression is caused by the depletion of one or more monoamine transmitters, and second, depression can be relieved by boosting the levels of those same neurotransmitters. Thus was born the monoamine hypothesis of depression. The next big antidepressant discovery provided more support for the hypothesis.

Around the time that iproniazid was being developed at Hoffman-Roche, a second antidepressant drug, imipramine, was in the early stages of development at a competitor company, Geigy in Switzerland. Geigy started out as a chemicals and dye trading company in the eighteenth century. Later it merged with Ciba, another dye company. Later still, Ciba-Geigy merged with Sandoz to become Novartis. Anyway, the original idea at Geigy was to tinker with the chlorpromazine compound in hope of finding a better antipsychotic. If a new molecule looked promising, it was sent to Dr. Roland Kuhn at the Münsterlingen Cantonal Asylum. This was a large, attractive

---

[128] Note the parallels between reserpine-iproniazid antagonism and haloperidol-amphetamine antagonism (Chapter 10).

hospital situated beside the picturesque Lake Constance. Kuhn had access to thousands of psychiatric patients, every one a potential subject for his experiments. Although Kuhn trained in psychoanalysis, his enquiring mind was open to alternative theories and new methods of treatment, especially new drugs. Driven by a distaste for the then-fashionable electroconvulsive therapy—and no doubt by the prospect of monetary rewards—Kuhn eagerly accepted a partnership with Geigy. During the period 1946 to 1980, he tested as many as 67 different substances on as many as 2789 patients.[129]

Roland Kuhn and staff at the Psychiatrischen Klinik Münsterlingen, 1961 [Fotoalbum Marlies Verhofnik]

An agent working for Geigy brought Kuhn a list of about 40 newly synthesized molecules. 'Which one would you like to try first?' the man asked. Kuhn chose a compound labelled G22355, because its chemistry was closest to chlorpromazine. Actually, G22355 and chlorpromazine differ only in respect to two atoms. The crucial difference, as it turned out, was the elimination of chlorpromazine's single sulfur atom. Kuhn did not imagine G22355 as an antidepressant. In fact, he had no idea what type of patient G22355 might be good for, if any. It was only after getting disappointing results from a trial of around 300 schizophrenia patients that he asked his assistants to try it on some depressed patients. 'After treating our first three

---

[129] Marietta Meier, Mario König and Magaly Tornay, *Testfall Münsterlingen : Klinische Versuche in der Psychiatrie*, 1940–1980. Zürich: Chronos Verlag (2019).

cases, it was already clear to us that the substance G22355, later known as imipramine, had an antidepressive action.'[130]

The world first heard of Kuhn's breakthrough at the Second World Congress of Psychiatry, held in Zurich in September 1957. Well, not really the entire world. There were actually no more than a dozen people in the audience. One of those in attendance recalls the occasion,

> Kuhn is a rather tall man, slender, very soft spoken, very cultured, very dignified and very erudite. He gave a very, very nice description of the clinical manifestations of the illness he was treating. He didn't say, 'this is a good antidepressant'. He said, 'this is a good drug for depressed patients who have these symptoms'. That was basically his message.[131]

One week prior to the opening of the World Congress, Kuhn published the contents of his upcoming presentation in the *Swiss Medical Weekly*, a German language newsletter. The following is his account of what transpired with his patients after receiving G22355,

> The facial expression loses rigidity, modulation and expression abilities return. The patients become livelier, the depressive whispering becomes louder, patients become more communicative, and moaning and whining can no longer be heard. If the patient was discontented, querulous or irritated, he changes into a friendly, content and amenable person ... Patients who had great difficulties in getting up in the morning, get out of bed early with their own initiative, at the same time as other patients.[132]

Geigy branded imipramine as Tofranil and started selling it in 1958. Soon thereafter, Marsilid (iproniazid) was withdrawn due to reports of toxicity, and sales of Tofranil boomed. Still, Kuhn refused to say that imipramine was 'a good antidepressant' because he knew that it did not help all patients. He estimated that the drug was of little or no help to 20–25 percent of

---

[130] Roland Kuhn (1970), p. 211.

[131] Interview with Frank Ayd in David Healy, *The Pharmacologists*. London, CRC Press. (2001), p. 96.

[132] Translation of Kuhn's 1957 paper in Walter A. Brown and Maria Rosdolsky, 'The clinical discovery of imipramine.' *American Journal of Psychiatry* 172: 426–429 (2015), p. 427.

his depressed patients. It is was an important observation, one later shown to be equally valid for other so-called antidepressant drugs. The term 'depression' covers many different psychological conditions, each with its own symptoms, and no drug fits all cases. Each of the 70 licensed medications for major depressive disorder presumably acts on a distinct bit of brain biochemistry. The situation raises the question whether depression is a single mental illness. Similar concerns have been raised about other diagnostic categories, as explained in Chapter 15.

Laboratory studies that looked into imipramine's mechanism of action found evidence consistent with the monoamine hypothesis which, as stated, attributes depression to low levels of monoamine neurotransmitters.[133] Scientists formulated the monoamine hypothesis after finding that iproniazid (Tofranil) increases monoamine levels by blocking the enzymes (monoamine oxidases) that degrade those transmitters. It came as somewhat of a surprise, therefore, that while imipramine (Tofranil) also increases monoamine levels, it does so through a different mechanism. Shortly after a monoamine neurotransmitter is released into a synapse, the 'leftover' molecules are pumped back into the releasing neuron so that they can be reused. Imipramine works by slowing down the reuptake,[134] thereby prolonging the transmitters' presence at the synapse and maintaining their physiological actions. Imipramine mostly affects the reuptake of norepinephrine, less so serotonin and dopamine. In summary, both iproniazid and imipramine enhance monoamine neurotransmission, but by different means. One does so by blocking metabolism, the other by blocking reuptake.

Good as they are, these breakthrough drugs are not perfect. Like Marsilid which was withdrawn due to its toxicity, Tofranil also has nasty side effects. Patients with pre-existing cardiac conditions are especially at risk. Less dangerous effects—but still undesirable—include dry mouth, mental confusion and fever. Iproniazid, imipramine, chlorpromazine and dozens of other psychiatric drugs are molecules built upon a basic structure of three interconnected chemical rings, hence 'tricyclic'. Currently, about one-quarter of all antidepressants are of the tricyclic variety. It was known from the beginning that they affect the reuptake of norepinephrine and, to a lesser extent,

---

[133] The monoamine hypothesis for depression is unrelated to the dopamine hypothesis for schizophrenia, even though dopamine is a monoamine. The hypothesis for depression invokes a *depletion of monoamines*, whereas the hypothesis for schizophrenia invokes an *overabundance of dopamine.*

[134] Reuptake occurs when the transmitter is taken back by the same neuron that released it. Uptake refers to absorption or binding by a neuron other than the releasing neuron.

serotonin and dopamine. But pharmacologists looking into the side effect problem discovered that the tricyclic drugs also block the reuptake of histamine and acetylcholine, and it is these latter actions that cause the side effects. With these facts in hand, the Eli Lilly company began looking for an antidepressant that would work exclusively by inhibiting the reuptake of serotonin without affecting either histamine or acetylcholine. A team of three investigators dug in; twenty years later, they came up with Prozac.

Left to right: David Wong, Ray Fuller, and Bryan Molloy [Eli Lilly and Company]

Ray Fuller acquired his interest in psychiatry during his college years, not from classroom instruction but from working at a state mental hospital. After taking advanced studies in biochemistry, he joined Eli Lilly and started working on antidepressants. Bryan Molloy was one of Fuller's colleagues at the Eli Lilly Research Laboratories. Knowing that Molloy was a specialist in acetylcholine, the neurotransmitter responsible for the cardiac side effects of tricyclic antidepressants, Fuller persuaded Molloy to join him on the project. The third member of Molloy's team was David Wong, who had traveled a long road before arriving at Eli Lilly.

Wong was born and raised in Hong Kong, briefly attended the National Taiwan University, and immigrated to the United States. After completing his undergraduate education at Seattle Pacific University, Wong went to Oregon for his graduate studies and to the University Pennsylvania for postdoctoral training. He wound up working for Eli Lilly because, as he explained, 'My grandmother was a diabetic, and I remembered seeing the

Lilly logo on a bottle of insulin. Then, when I was in graduate school, I saw a big Lilly sign at a medical conference. I said, "That's the company I'm going to work for."'[135] When he asked his new boss what they wanted him to work on, the boss replied, 'You are a well-trained biochemist. You should be able to decide on your own.'[136] As it happened, he was interested in monoamine reuptake.

Certain of the team's colleagues discouraged their research, fearing that enhancing serotonin function might actually increase depression rather than reducing it, but Fuller reminded critics of the rabbits that got 'depressed' after reserpine depleted serotonin. He also pointed to reports describing unusually low levels of serotonin in the brains of suicide victims (persons dying of suicide have significantly less serotonin than do those dying of heart attacks). So, the Lilly team insisted, if low serotonin means depression, high serotonin should mean something like elation. The challenge was to find a molecule that would selectively reduce serotonin reuptake while having little or no effect on norepinephrine or acetylcholine, both of which were associated with side effects.

Fuller assigned David Wong the task of finding a method for measuring the amount of serotonin reuptake. Actually, they already had a method, but it was time-consuming and imprecise. Their method was similar to the one that Julius Axelrod had used to demonstrate the phenomenon of monoamine reuptake, for which he was awarded the Nobel Prize. Axelrod began by asking what happens to the norepinephrine that is released by nerve endings. To find out, he injected his experimental animals with a radioactive version of norepinephrine. After waiting minutes or hours, he killed the animals and measured the radiation signal in the blood and various organs. As expected, most of the radioactive norepinephrine wound up in in body tissues rather than the blood. The question remained, exactly *which* tissues? To find out, Axelrod surgically removed several small nerves attached to the eye muscles before injecting radioactive norepinephrine. Whereas he had previous detected radioactivity in these muscles, he found none after removing the nerves. He concluded that norepinephrine must be taken up by the same nerves that release it (reuptake), not by muscles or glands. As a final proof, Axelrod demonstrated—in unoperated animals—that he could release radioactive norepinephrine from nerves by electrically stimulating them.

---

[135] *Response*, Seattle Pacific University online web magazine for alumni, Winter 1998.
[136] David T. Wong in *Nature Reviews Drug Discovery* 4:622 (2005).

Axelrod's experiments immediately suggested a method for measuring reuptake, but it was not one that lent itself to the type of rapid testing that David Wong needed for his antidepressant research. Wong was struggling to overcome the bottleneck when he attended a lecture given by Dr. Solomon Snyder of Johns Hopkins University. In that lecture, Snyder, a former student of Julius Axelrod, described a pared down version of Axelrod's assay. Instead of tediously dissecting out nerves, Snyder prepared a slushy solution of nearly pure nerve endings that could be placed in a Petri dish and quickly assessed for radioactivity. He first removed the brain and ground it up in a glass homogenizer fitted with a motor-driven Teflon pestle. Next, he filtered the solution, poured the slush into a centrifuge and spun it down to a pellet of concentrated cellular material. The pellet—called a synaptosome—was composed almost entirely of nerve endings and the bits of synapses to which they were attached. It was heavily enriched with monoamines.

Solomon Snyder's presentation won over Wong, who quickly installed the synaptosome as the workhorse of his drug discovery program. The move eventually paid off with the discovery of a drug that did exactly what they wanted it to do—it blocked serotonin reuptake while leaving norepinephrine and acetylcholine unaffected. In January 1988, a marketing specialist launched fluoxetine under the trade name Prozac. It was an immediate success—actually a blockbuster. Just two years after the launch, Prozac was the bestselling antidepressant drug in the United States. Worldwide sales in that year alone earned Eli Lilly 2.58 billion dollars. The popular press sensationalized Prozac to the point where everyone was talking about it, whether they were on the drug or not. Some folks wrote books heralding the drug as their salvation (*Prozac Nation, Prozac Diary*), whereas others warned of its dangers (*Prozac Backlash; Talking Back to Prozac*). In follow-up studies, fluoxetine was found to be much safer than any tricyclic antidepressive, but generally no more efficacious.

Perspective

The discovery of antidepressant drugs meant real relief for millions of people, but it left unresolved questions. We can start by asking, Why the need for so many different antidepressant drugs? According to the prevailing hypothesis, all these drugs work, in one way or another, by boosting monoamine function. Some drugs block monoamine oxidase, others block reuptake. Some boost serotonin, some boost norepinephrine, and a few boost dopamine.

If it were as simple as that, we should be able to manage all cases of depression using just Tofranil for norepinephrine, Prozac for serotonin, and maybe something for dopamine. But this hasn't happened, leading some scientists to ask whether there might be a problem with the monoamine hypothesis. Indeed, critics have pointed out several weaknesses. It is worrisome, for example, that antidepressant drugs raise monoamine levels in a matter of hours, yet it can take weeks before there is any significant reduction of clinical depression.

Even when a pharmacological study confirms that a particular drug increases monoamine levels—either epinephrine or serotonin—around 30 percent of patients with major depression experience *no improvement* after taking the drug. But, you ask, didn't the rabbits get 'depressed' when on reserpine, a substance known to deplete monoamines? And, didn't Marsilid help them by boosting epinephrine? The answer to these queries is yes, but we don't know what those rabbits were actually *feeling.* They may have shown little activity and they may have looked drowsy, but were they *depressed*? Can we really say that an animal—any animal—has moods like human moods? Nathan Kline once said that he had observed human subjects become depressed after being given reserpine, but Kline also tried giving reserpine as a *treatment* for human depression. Researchers who examined the entire literature on the effect of reserpine in humans concluded that reserpine does not cause depression.[137] Since the monoamine hypothesis was founded on the belief that reserpine causes depression by depleting monoamines, evidence to the contrary casts doubt on the validity of that hypothesis.

The brain is a complex organ. Multiple things can go wrong with it. As for depression, several ideas have been proposed to replace, or add to, the monoamine hypothesis. According to one hypothesis, depression results from the disruption of certain neural circuits that play a key role in the regulation of mood (see chapter 13). Alternatively, it has been proposed that depression is caused by chronic stress, which damages the hippocampus and reduces neurogenesis (see chapter 14). At a finer level of analysis, there could be malformed neurotransmitter receptors, or structural damage in

---

[137] Alan A. Baumeister, Mike F. Hawkins, and Sarah M. Uzelac, 'The myth of reserpine-induced depression: Role in the historical development of the monoamine hypothesis.' *Journal of the History of the Neurosciences* 12(22):207–220 (2003).

nerve cells. There is evidence for each of these ideas, but none has been proven correct.

A popular notion holds that the brain is awash in neurotransmitters and that a healthy mood is all about getting the levels just right. It's more complicated than that.

Commenting on the state of science in so far as it concerns psychiatry, the distinguished neuroscientist Ralph Gerard once remarked, 'For every twisted thought there is a twisted molecule.' At least for depression, it appears that there may many 'twisted molecules' responsible for several varieties of 'twisted' thought. Perhaps that is why we need seventy different antidepressants.

Suggested readings

David Healy, *The Antidepressant Era.* Cambridge, MA, Harvard University Press (1997).

Emmanuel Jesulola, Peter Micalos and Ian J. Baguley, 'Understanding the pathophysiology of depression: From monoamines to the neurogenesis hypothesis model – are we there yet?' *Behavioural Brain Research* 341:79–90 (2018).

Edward Shorter, *Before Prozac: The Troubled History of Mood Disorders in Psychiatry.* New York, Oxford University Press (2008).

12 Endophenotypes

In this chapter we jump into modern findings about brain mechanisms underlying mental illness. As noted at the conclusion of the previous chapter, the brain is incredibly complex at all levels of organization, from enzymes to tiny structures like synapses to long distance neural networks. Consequently, the number of structural problems and physiological malfunctions *possibly* responsible for mental illness is huge, all the more so because there are different types of mental illness. Research in this area is highly productive—at least numerically—with several hundred studies on the subject of neural mechanisms published every week in the scientific literature. Our challenge lies in selecting the meaningful studies from the irrelevant studies, the great discoveries from the simply mundane.

Already in this book, we have considered damaged arachnoid membranes (Chapter 2) and swollen ventricles (Chapter 3), both of which are biomarkers of mental illness. Although each is indicative of illness, neither contributes to scientific explanation or clinical application because neither participates in the work of the brain. Only neurons can generate fears, compulsions, hallucinations, paranoia, et cetera. Other biomarkers, even those in the brain, can be ignored if they are *caused by the illness*. For example, biomarkers that result from medication, lifestyle changes and the like are useless for most purposes. What we want are brain abnormalities that *cause the illness*, or more exactly, cause the symptoms of the illness. Ideally, we need symptom-causing abnormalities that link directly to genetics, because we know—from heritability analyses—that every one of the major mental illnesses is, to a large extent, heritable. The biomarkers that satisfy these criteria are called endophenotypes. We will consider two endophenotypes in this chapter, two more in the next chapter.

Before endophenotypes entered the stage, the action was all about biomarkers, and mostly in relation to schizophrenia. Arguably the most devasting of all mental illnesses, schizophrenia accounts for the majority of hospitalizations and is highly costly for society. German anatomists first reported microscopic biomarkers for schizophrenia at the close of the nineteenth century, principally in misshaped neurons but also in glia cells.

However, those claims were ultimately rejected due to lack of confirmation, leaving one author to write, in 1972, 'It is widely stated that in schizophrenia there is no visible pathology, nor do we really know whether there is irreparable damage in schizophrenics.'[138]

Forsaking anatomy ('visible pathology'), researchers turned to biochemistry in their search for biomarkers. But here again they came up with false leads, among which high levels of non-metabolized neurotransmitters (norepinephrine and epinephrine) and high levels of bufotenine (a metabolite of indolylalkylamines); vitamin deficiencies and abnormal amounts of a copper-containing enzyme (ceruloplasmin) in blood. But it was urinary 'pink spots' that drew the most attention.

Pink spots were first seen in 1952. Researchers collected urine samples from 19 schizophrenia patients and 10 healthy individuals. The samples were concentrated down to a single drop and applied to a strip of paper. Once spread out and dried, a pink spot appeared in 15 of the patient samples, but in none of the healthy samples. What was it? Biochemists found that it contained dimethoxyphenylethylamine, a substance that is structurally similar to dopamine, but not a dopamine breakdown product as initially thought. The pink spot was said to be present in acute cases but not in chronic cases, common in hallucinating patients but not in paranoid patients. Early reports lit up the psychiatric community, but the lights dimmed as subsequent results were inconsistent at best. In the end, the pink spot turned out to be just an occasional insignificant correlate of schizophrenia, in other words a false lead. Researchers failed to take into account the fact that schizophrenia patients drink more coffee, smoke more cigarettes and get fewer vitamins that non-patients, plus of course their medications.

In the face of such nonsense, two veteran twin researchers entered the fray. James Shields learned how to conduct twin studies from Eliot Slater after Slater returned to the U.K. from Ernst Rüdin's lab in Munich. He teamed up with Irving Gottesman, an American who started out in academic psychology but turned to genetics because someone close to him had schizophrenia. Gottesman and Shields began their collaboration at the Genetics Institute of Maudsley Hospital in London. Searching through around 45,000 admission records in the period 1948 to 1964, they found 57 cases in which one or both members of a twin pair had schizophrenia. Their 433-page report documented a double-hit rate of 58 percent for identical twins

---

[138] A. Pauline Ridges, 'Biochemical research into schizophrenia in relation to pink spot excretion.' *Journal of Orthomolecular Psychiatry* 1:18–27 (1972).

compared to only 12 percent for fraternal twins.[139] Apart from its value as a convincing demonstration of genetic inheritance, Gottesman and Shields' study led directly to the concept of psychiatric endophenotypes.

Irving Gottesman [University of Minnesota]

Gottesman and Shields pondered how to connect genetics with the myriad of psychological and behavioral symptoms in schizophrenia. The symptoms are readily observable but complex, while the genetic risk factors are obscure and difficult to study. For Gottesman and Shields back in 1972, it was a gap seemingly too large to fill—and for the most part it still is. Looking for something that might lie *in between* genes and psychology, they came up with endophenotypes.[140]

An endophenotype in psychiatry is a biomarker that connects genes on one side with symptoms on the other side.[141] The word, 'endophenotype' has two roots, endo and phenotype. Phenotype (think phenomenon) refers to the observable traits of an organism, while endo means within or hidden. So, we are talking about hidden features like a biochemical flaw, a neurophysiological abnormality, or a structural brain defect. Endophenotypes are observable, but not obvious. Because an endophenotype is a single, tangible characteristic rather than the bundle of psychological and behavioral symptoms that together define the illness, it can be easier to find the few genes responsible for the endophenotype than the many genes responsible

---

[139] As explained in chapter 5, a double-hit is when both members of a twin pair have schizophrenia (or some other trait).

[140] Gottesman and Shields did not invent the concept of endophenotype. It was first used to explain the geographical distribution of grasshoppers.

[141] I.I. Gottesman and T.D. Gould (2003). See suggested readings.

for the illness as a whole. The same reasoning applies to complex illnesses like diabetes, arthritis and heart disease, which have also benefited from the discovery of endophenotypes.

Walter Jacobi and Herbert Winkler get partial credit for one of the first confirmed endophenotypes in schizophrenia, because it was their discovery of swollen ventricles that prompted other investigators to suggest that the ventricles may have expanded to fill space created by dying or dead nerve cells. Modern studies have confirmed the loss of brain mass, mostly in respect to what neuroscientists refer to as 'gray matter'. Gray matter contains the neurons' cell bodies and dendrites, whereas 'white matter' contains axons, the neurons' long extensions. Gray matter and white matter differ fundamentally in appearance, function and distribution. Both are altered in schizophrenia and likely other mental illnesses as well. We start, as scientists started, with gray matter, keeping white matter for the next chapter.

Early investigators cut post-mortem brains into thin sections. Using a microscope for magnification and a mirror system for projecting images onto a sheet of white paper, they measured the size of selected gray areas by rolling a metering device around the boundary. Initial results were mixed with regard to shrinkage. Some studies reported that schizophrenia brains had less gray matter than normal brains—in certain regions—but other studies found no significant differences. With the introduction of CT-scanning it became possible to examine the living brain. Each 'slice' generated a 2-dimensional image containing about 25,000 pixels. Researchers assumed that the optical density of each pixel reflected the amount of neuronal tissue in the pixel area. In one study, they tabulated the density of every fourth pixel along an arbitrary line. The results, they reported, 'support the hypothesis that there are primary structural deficits in some schizophrenic patients, and these deficits are centered in and around the anterior areas of the left (dominant) hemisphere.' [142]

But it was only after the introduction of magnetic resonance scanning (MRI) that scientists found convincing evidence. Instead of 2-dimensional pixels, the modern MRI delivers 3-dimensional voxels (volumetric pixels). There are around one million voxels in a typical brain, with each voxel representing a volume of brain tissue about the size of a black pepper corn. In addition to its vastly improved resolution, current magnetic imaging methods provide contrasting intensities for gray matter and white matter.

---

[142] Charles J. Golden et al., 'Structural brain deficits in schizophrenia.' *Archives of General Psychiatry* 38:1014–1017 (1981), p. 1014.

A comprehensive review of 317 MRI studies published between 1998 and 2012 (a meta-analysis) delivered the final verdict on gray matter losses.[143] In total, more than 9000 schizophrenia patients and an equal number of healthy subjects participated. Most of the losses were found in the outermost portion of the brain, the cerebral cortex. On average, it amounts to around 4.8 percent relative to healthy controls. The largest reductions occur in the prefrontal lobe (minus 6.1 percent) and the temporal lobe (minus 4.1 percent). In contrast, gray matter losses in the cerebellum are 'only' 1.5 percent, relatively small but statistically significant. Other regions lying beneath the cortex are also affected, for example gray matter reductions of 6.3 percent in the hippocampus and 4.8 percent in the amygdala. All of these losses increase over time as the illness progresses.

Losing gray matter is a serious thing, even though it is the neuron's dendrites that are lost, not the cell body (the latter would imply a loss of the entire cell). Dendrites are absolutely essential for proper functioning because they are at the receiving end of neuronal messages. In schizophrenia, no neuron loses all of its dendrites. Rather, branches die off, carrying with them the vital synapses. Given that the largest losses are in the prefrontal lobe and the temporal lobe—regions known to mediate cognitive tasks—it easy to appreciate how the loss of gray matter might account for the symptoms of schizophrenia. Already in 1919, Emil Kraepelin proposed,

> If it should be confirmed that [*dementia praecox*] attacks by preference the frontal areas of the brain, the central convolutions and the temporal lobes, this distribution would in certain measure agree with our present views about the site of the psychic mechanisms which are principally injured by the disease.[144]

Most patients take drugs to control their symptoms, and these medications affect gray matter. Although the reductions are generally greater in patients receiving antipsychotic medications than in those not receiving any medication, even drug-free patients lose a significant amount relative to healthy controls. Curiously, when researchers examined the effect caused by different antipsychotic medications of the 'atypical' variety, they found

---

[143] Sander V. Haijima et al., 'Brain volumes in schizophrenia: A meta-analysis in over 18,000 subjects.' *Schizophrenia Bulletin* 39:1129–1138 (2013).

[144] Emil Kraepelin, *Dementia Praecox and Paraphrenia*, trans. Mary Barclay. Edinburgh: E.& S. Livingstone (1919), p. 219.

that patients on clozapine had more severe and more extensive losses than did patients on risperidone.[145]

Remember, endophenotypes are supposed to bridge the gap between genes and mental symptoms. The best way to demonstrate this is to show that a candidate endophenotype is present not only in persons with the illness, but also in closely related family members who likely share the same risk genes. An investigation that examined the issue with respect to the loss of gray matter found that high-risk relatives of patients with schizophrenia do have significant gray matter reductions. The largest losses were seen in the prefrontal cortex and the area around the hippocampus.[146]

We turn now to a different type of endophenotype for schizophrenia. Unlikely though it may seem, this endophenotype is in the eyes, or more precisely, in eye movements. The connection to schizophrenia lies in the fact that eye movements are controlled by the brain. Three slender nerves carry messages from the brain to the eyes, where they contact one or more small muscles to move the eyes. Both voluntary and involuntary movements are controlled in this manner. Certain unusual eye movement phenomena qualify as endophenotypes because they associate with schizophrenia and they are hereditary. Despite their apparent independence from anything psychological, they offer insights into symptom-related brain mechanisms.

Eye movement abnormalities in mental patients were first noticed by a pair of Americans, one a psychiatrist, the other an experimental psychologist. Allen R. Diefendorf was an assistant physician and pathologist at the Connecticut Hospital for the Insane, while Raymond Dodge was a professor at Wesleyan University, also in Connecticut. They met up in the fall of 1908 after becoming aware of their mutual interests. It was an ideal collaboration based on two different sorts of expertise. Diefendorf knew about mental patients. Dodge was an authority on eye movements.

Diefendorf and Dodge both had connections with Germany. Dodge studied in Germany for his Ph.D. during a time that saw the birth of experimental psychology. His academic work utilized novel methods, and it relied on precise measurements, so he needed special-purpose instruments. As a result, Dodge acquired skills in instrument design and construction that served him well in his later collaboration with Diefendorf. Diefendorf may

---

[145] Nian Liu et al., 'Characteristics of gray matter alterations in never-treated and treated chronic schizophrenia patients.' *Translational Psychiatry* 10:136 (2020).

[146] Lena Palaniyappan, Vijender Balain and Peter F. Liddle, 'The neuroanatomy of psychotic diathesis: A meta-analytic review. *Journal of Psychiatric Research* 46:1249–1256 (2012).

never have visited Germany, but he learned a great deal about German psychiatry through his boss, Adolf Meyer, who had observed it firsthand. Following Meyer, Diefendorf became an admirer of the leading German psychiatrist of the time, Emil Kraepelin. Diefendorf's parents were originally Dutch, and from them he learned to speak and read German as a child. It was an aptitude that served him well in later life, for it allowed him to translate Kraepelin's textbook into English. Diefendorf's translations of the sixth and seventh editions (1902, 1904), ultimately became the principal means by which psychiatrists outside of Germany learned of Kraepelin's work.

Raymond Dodge [National Library of Medicine, USA]

Readers of Kraepelin's textbook—consulted even now in Diefendorf's translation—are struck by its scientific tone, so unlike the works of his contemporaries. Kraepelin believed that mental illnesses originate in the body, or at least they reveal themselves in biological signs. His description of schizophrenia includes a total of nineteen bodily indicators, among which dilated pupils, skin lesions, strong perspiration, low body temperature and, in women, irregular menstruation. He recommended that psychiatrists measure the skull, track body weight and note changes in muscle tension. For diagnosing disorders of mood, he built a device for recording the patient's handwriting. From these recordings, he measured the speed of writing and the pen pressure (in grams weight), finding that he could diagnose depression and mania based on these properties alone. Having absorbed Kraepelin's scientific bias, Diefendorf must have been delighted to find in Dodge a devotee of German instrumental expertise.

While studying for his Ph.D., Raymond Dodge spent long hours in the lab and probably had no contact with either Kraepelin or any other psychiatrist. His research concerned how people move their eyes when reading. He found that the eyes regularly alternate between full stops (fixations) and rapid movements. Once back in the United States, he applied his skills to the construction of an instrument for determining the duration of fixations and the velocity of eye movements. The ingenious contraption recorded—on a single photographic plate—a succession of images, each of which marking the position of the eye at a moment in time. The images themselves were of a light reflecting off the cornea. As the eye moved, the reflected light also moved, leaving a string of bright spots on the film. The device was basically a long box with a camera at one end and a film plate at the other end. In order to capture multiple images, Dodge contrived to have the film plate fall smoothly at a fixed rate. He did that by controlling the escape of air from an ordinary bicycle pump. Dodge's photochronograph revolutionized the study of eye movements.

Shortly after hearing of Dodge's work from across the Connecticut River, Diefendorf sought his collaboration for a study of eye movements in mental patients. We don't know how he came up with the idea, but probably he observed something unusual in his patients. The study got under way in 1908 after Diefendorf recruited 21 manic-depressive patients, four patients with *dementia praecox* (schizophrenia), four epileptics, four patients with progressive paralysis of the insane, and one 'imbecile'. Their eye movements were compared with those of nine healthy subjects. The investigators had no difficulty in obtaining the patients' cooperation, noting in their published report, 'For both of us the most surprising feature of the experiments was the conduct of the patients during the tests. We anticipated a considerable variety of troubles, particularly from the maniacal patients, and safeguarded the apparatus in a number of entirely unnecessary ways ... [W]e succeeded

The Dodge photochronograph [Diefendorf and Dodge, 1908]

in getting excellent records from patients that in the wards appeared utterly impossible.'[147]

One test required the subjects to move their eyes to an object that suddenly appears in their vision. The study found that manic patients respond unusually quickly—relative to healthy subjects—and their eye movements are unusually fast, in contrast to depressed patients who move them relatively slowly. A second test required subjects to track the movement of a swinging pendulum. Significantly—in light of later discoveries—the authors noted that 'the most marked variations are found in the pendulum pursuit movements in *dementia praecox*, where a marked hesitation to fall into the swing of the pendulum was found even in the mildest cases. While this peculiarity is apparently not absolutely restricted to *dementia praecox*, it was found in other patients only where the disease-process has produced

---

[147] Allen Ross Diefendorf and Raymond Dodge, 'An experimental study of the ocular reactions of the insane from photographic records.' *Brain* 31:451–489 (1908), p. 453.

marked deterioration.' Errors in this task indicated, in their words, 'a general disorganization of the central systematizations.'[148]

Dodge's photochronograph worked well enough, but it was cumbersome. Modern methods are simpler and more accurate. They also allow testing in a greater variety of visual tasks. One tracking method relies on the fact that the front of the eye is electrically positive relative to the back of the eye. If a pair of electrodes is attached to the skin adjacent to both eyes, a small voltage is detected, and that voltage changes as the eyes move. Movements in the horizontal plane, but not the vertical plane, can be accurately monitored in this manner. Alternatively, high-definition video provides digitized records of eye movements in all directions. Armed with these new methods, plus the use of larger sample sizes and statistical analysis, modern researchers have re-investigated the phenomena first reported by Diefendorf and Dodge. (The studies discussed below are not related to eye movement desensitization and reprocessing [EMDR], a technique occasionally used in psychotherapy.)

Our brains allow us to execute several distinct types of eye movements, each of which can be investigated using appropriate techniques. Diefendorf and Dodge studied two types. One, the so-called saccadic eye movement, ranks among the fastest movements performed by any part of the body. The saccade is automatically triggered whenever an object suddenly appears in the visual field at a position away from the current point of focus. Because our lives could depend on identifying that object as rapidly as possible, evolution has given us the saccade. It quickly brings the object onto the central part of the retina (the fovea), where our vision is most acute. Diefendorf and Dodge were studying saccades in the experiments noted above, those in which they recorded anomalies of reaction times and velocity. They found anomalies in manic patients and depressed patients, but not in schizophrenic patients. Later research—summarized below—uncovered a more demanding task, also based on saccadic eye movements, upon which schizophrenia patients perform poorly.

The second task examined by Diefendorf and Dodge had subjects tracking a moving pendulum. Today, subjects typically watch a computer-generated image oscillating back and forth across a screen. To succeed in this task, known as 'smooth pursuit', the eyes must remain continuously fixed on the moving object. Only humans and other primates (monkeys, apes et cetera) can do it. Diefendorf and Dodge reported that patients with schizophrenia perform poorly in the task. The patient's eyes move

---

[148] A. R. Diefendorf and R. Dodge (1908), p. 469.

too slowly to keep up with the moving target, so they attempt to catch up by making frequent saccadic movements. A review of 57 studies published between 1994 and 2008 found strong evidence confirming Diefendorf and Dodge's conclusion that schizophrenia patients have problems with smooth pursuits.[149] Investigators are currently uncertain to what extent antipsychotic medications contribute to the deficit, but we know that none of Diefendorf and Dodge's patients were on such medications—because they hadn't yet been discovered.

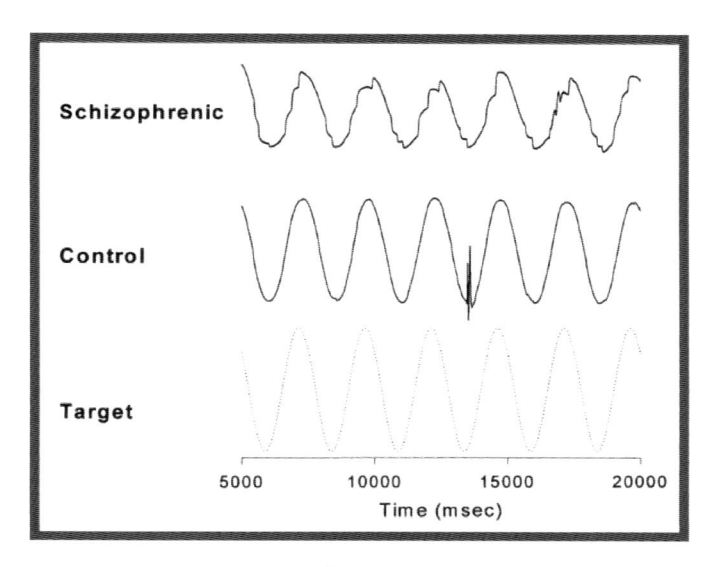

Eye movements in smooth pursuit task [P.S. Holzman, Neuropsychopharmacology 25 (3), 2001]

So far, we have considered saccades and smooth pursuit eye movements. Even more revealing are the *anti*saccades, which are teachable but unnatural movements. Certain reflexes, such as the knee jerk and the Babinski reflex (on the sole of the foot) are totally controlled by neural circuits within the spinal cord, so they happen without the person's willing participation. But other reflexes, including saccades, are routed though the brain, so it was reasonable that someone would design a task that requires subjects to control their own saccades. After an American vision scientist demonstrated that healthy volunteers could do it, a group of Japanese researchers thought of testing schizophrenia patients on the same task. It was a long shot, but

---

[149] G.A. O'Driscoll and B.L. Callahan, 'Smooth pursuit in schizophrenia: A meta-analytic review of research since 1993.' *Brain and Cognition* 68:359–370 (2008).

logical given that part of the neural control of eye movements resides in the frontal lobe, which also happens to be implicated in schizophrenia.

Junko Fukushima and his team asked their subjects to focus on a spot placed in the center of his or her vision.[150] The experimenter then made an object appear off to one side, say to the *right*. Ordinarily, a person would immediately move the eyes toward the right, but for the antisaccade task the subject is told in advance to move the eyes in the opposite (mirrored) direction from the introduced object, in this case to the *left*. It is called an *antisaccade* because the subject must suppress his or her natural reaction to look at the object.

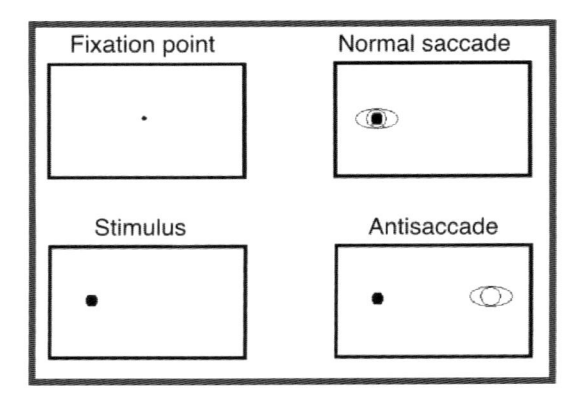

The antisaccade task [Elizabeth Calvin et al., Colorado Journal of Psychiatry and Psychology 2(1), 2017]

All ten of the healthy subjects in the Japanese study performed the task with little difficulty, committing only a single error in multiple trials. By contrast, 6 of 12 patients looked in the wrong direction on 20 percent or more of trials. Even when the patients looked in the correct— antisaccade—direction, they were slower than the healthy subjects. Similar results were subsequently found in larger studies. For example, 267 schizophrenia patients and 244 healthy controls were tested in 2014.[151] In that study, the patients errored, on average, on 44 percent of trials, compared to 18 percent for healthy subjects. Heritability was tested by examining the patients' first-degree relatives. They also errored significantly more than did healthy controls, though on average approximately one-third less than pa-

---

[150] Junko Fukushima et al., 'Disturbances of voluntary control of saccadic eye movements in schizophrenic patients.' *Biological Psychiatry* 23:670–677 (1988).

[151] J.L. Reilly et al., 'Elevated antisaccade error rate as an intermediate phenotype for psychosis across diagnostic categories.' *Schizophrenia Bulletin* 40(5):1011–1021 (2014).

tients. Age, sex and race were all discounted as explanatory factors. Nor were error rates affected by antipsychotic medications, anxiety or restlessness.

These experiments raise the obvious question, what have eye movements to do with schizophrenia? Yes, both eye movements and schizophrenia originate in the brain, but motor behaviors and mental illness are hugely different. Researchers thought there might be something wrong with the eye muscles in schizophrenia, but that is not the case. To gain further insight, they turned their attention to the neural mechanisms of eye movement control, particularly in regard to the execution of saccades. Because our survival depends on keeping objects of interest in focus, evolution has optimized the process by enlisting multiple brain circuits for cooperative work. The brain areas involved include the visual cortex, the superior colliculus and the cerebellum— all in the back of the brain—plus the basal ganglia and the thalamus deep in the brain and, as mentioned, the frontal lobes. It is remarkable that each of these areas communicates with the others in the *milliseconds* preceding the saccade. Collectively, they locate the stimulus, determine its significance, and calculate the muscular actions required to bring it into focus. Once the calculations have been completed, the brain sends finely tuned messages down to specific eye muscles—ordinarily one muscle in each of two groups—and the saccade is executed. Saccades are a normal part of everyday life, whereas antisaccades are an oddity of experimental science. Even so, healthy people can do them with ease, whereas schizophrenic patients cannot. Why can't patients do antisaccades?

The answer may lie in a specialized region of the frontal lobe, known as the 'frontal eye field', which works in conjunction with the superior colliculus in issuing the final command for a saccade. The neural circuit has been studied in monkey brains as they perform saccades and antisaccades. In the lead-up to a saccadic eye movement, neurons in both the frontal eye field and the superior colliculus fire rapidly, but these same neurons remain silent if the monkey is instructed to perform an antisaccade. Excitation is cancelled in the antisaccade task due to the arrival of a strong inhibitory signal. Presumably, the same thing happens in healthy human subjects as they perform the antisaccade task, but schizophrenia patients seem unable to generate this inhibitory signal, possibly due to the unavailability of the inhibitory neurotransmitter, gamma-aminobutyric acid (GABA), which is substantially reduced in schizophrenia brains.

Because endophenotypes are supposed to bridge the gap between genes and mental symptoms, any candidate endophenotype must be shown to be hereditary. Importantly, both biomarkers mentioned in this chapter—gray matter losses and antisaccade errors—satisfy the criterion. Note that neither gray matter losses nor antisaccade errors are *necessarily* hereditary. In principle, they could be caused by patient lifestyles or patient medications, but research shows otherwise. Nonetheless, the fact that the endophenotypes are hereditary does not exclude additional environmental influences. Like all traits, the endophenotypes are influenced by both genes *and* the environment.

Perspective

Although the focus in this chapter has been on schizophrenia, research shows that both the gray matter endophenotype and the eye movement endophenotype apply equally well to bipolar disease.[152] Since the anomalies are rare in healthy people but can be reliably detected in psychotic patients, gray matter losses and eye movement abnormalities could find a place in the diagnosis of psychotic illness.

Moreover, because endophenotypes are traits that lie in between genes and symptoms, it is possible for them to be present before the appearance of any symptoms. This appears to be the case for the endophenotypes discussed in this chapter.[153] Detecting an illness very early in its development is desirable, because with early detection comes the possibility of a medical intervention that can prevent full-blown expression. Commenting on the prospect, the authors of a recent article in the *American Journal of Psychiatry* spoke of moving 'from fantasy to reality.' Standing in the way, they say, is the current 'lack of sensitive and specific diagnostic criteria for [nonsymptomatic] schizophrenia, validated biomarkers, and proven therapeutic strategies.'[154] Endophenotypes are exceptionally well qualified to serve as 'validated biomarkers'. What was once the 'fantasy' of early intervention could soon become a 'reality', thanks to endophenotypes.

---

[152] Elena I. Ivleva et al., 'Gray matter volume as an intermediate phenotype for psychosis: Bipolar-schizophrenia network on intermediate phenotypes (B-SNIP).' *American Journal of Psychiatry* 170:1285–1296 (2013).

[153] Lynn E. DeLisi et al. (2008), see suggested readings; Ilya Obyedkov et al., 'Saccadic eye movements in different dimensions of schizophrenia and in clinical high-risk state for psychosis.' *BMC Psychiatry* 19:110 (2019).

[154] Jeffrey A. Lieberman, Scott A. Small and Ragy R. Girgis, 'Early detection and preventative intervention in schizophrenia: from fantasy to reality.' *American Journal of Psychiatry* 176:794–810 (2019).

Suggested readings

Lynn E. DeLisi et al., 'Understanding structural brain changes in schizophrenia.' *Dialogues in Clinical Neuroscience* 8(1):71–78 (2006).

Irving I. Gottesman and Todd D. Gould, 'The endophenotype concept in psychiatry: etymology and strategic intentions.' *American Journal of Psychiatry* 160:636–645 (2003).

13 The disconnected brain

In the year 1891, the best-known neurologist of the nineteenth century found himself embroiled in a scientific dispute with a young man who would later become the most famous psychiatrist of the twentieth century. The roots of the argument lay in a remarkable discovery made earlier by yet another man, Paul Broca. Broca was a French physician with wide scientific interests, including the study of skulls for understanding human racial groups. Broca was also a brain anatomist, intrigued by issues of function. One day, a stroke victim with speech problems came for a consultation. The man understood perfectly well what the doctor was saying, but he himself was unable to speak. Later, when the patient died, Broca dissected the brain and found a spot of obvious damage at the bottom of the left frontal lobe, near the posterior border and next to the temporal lobe. An additional eleven cases followed, all with the same speech deficit and the same lesion in what is now known as 'Broca's area'.

The famous neurologist mentioned above was the German neurologist, Carl Wernicke. He too was passionate about brain research and, like Broca, he examined his patients' brains after death. He confirmed the location of Broca's area and its association with speech deficits, but he found something different in his own patients who had other types of speech problems. In contrast to Broca's patients, who could not speak, Wernicke's patients spoke perfectly well, but had trouble understanding what people were saying. Wernicke found that his patients had healthy looking frontal lobes, but unmistakable lesions in the left temporal lobe, within a region now known as Wernicke's area. So, there were now two distinct speech pathologies—called 'aphasias'—each apparently caused by a different anatomical lesion.

For some time previously, Wernicke had been arguing that different functions must be located in different parts of the brain. Naturally, therefore, he took satisfaction in announcing that a seemingly single faculty of mind, namely speech, needs at least two separate centers. The theory of localization of function was not his alone, but he was its main proponent and its most vociferous defender against contrary views. His enthusiasm led

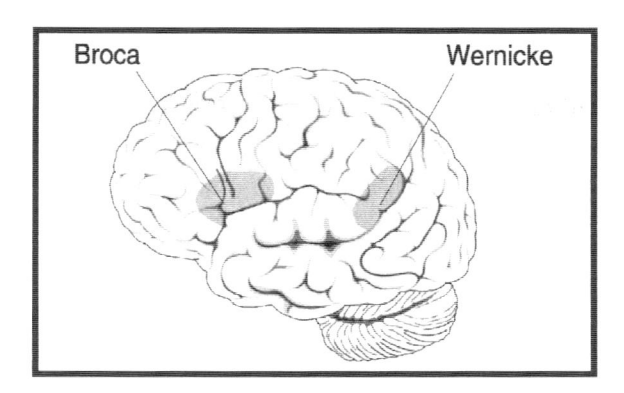

Two separate brain areas for speech production and speech comprehension [National Institute of Health, USA]

him to formulate hypothetical explanations for numerous neurological and psychiatric disorders. Detractors referred to his ideas as 'brain mythology'.

Knowing that there is one speech area responsible for producing speech and another for understanding speech, Wernicke reasoned that there must be a neural connection between the two, and further, there must exist a particular type of aphasia caused by the destruction of the physical connection. He speculated that patients in whom that connection was broken would understand speech relatively well but would utter inappropriate words. He proposed the syndrome based on his examination of two patients, both of whom were still alive when he published the speculation. Later, other neurologists noticed something similar. Their patients understood speech, and they spoke reasonably well, but they too made frequent errors, especially when asked to repeat a sentence spoken by someone else. Wernicke named this new type of language deficit 'conduction aphasia', implying that it is caused by a failure of electrical conduction between Broca's area and Wernicke's area.

The second person referenced above, 'the most famous psychiatrist of the twentieth century,' was, of course, Sigmund Freud. While his reputation rests on the invention of psychoanalysis, he began his career as a neuroscientist. The first of his numerous books, published in 1891, was a critique of Wernicke's ideas on language, and in particular, Wernicke's interpretation of conduction aphasia. So far as we know, Freud had no aphasic patients, nor did he ever examine the post-mortem brain of an aphasic person. Nevertheless, he confidently asserted the following:

> We reject the assumptions that the language apparatus consists of separate centers which are divided by cortical regions without function, furthermore that the images that serve speech are stored at particular cortical sites which are called centers... [T]he associations and transmissions upon which the language functions are based take place with a complexity that is beyond comprehension.'[155]

Freud sided with the critics who opposed Wernicke's idea of local control over brain functions. He did not believe that any psychological disorder could be the result of damage to any particular nervous pathway. Instead, Freud assumed that the brain operates as a whole, with the mind dependent on unimaginably complex interactions amongst the brain's innumerable yet equivalent parts. Unwilling to confront the conundrum, Freud turned away from neuroscience and toward psychology.

Today, we commonly speak of localized functions in the brain. We say that the hippocampus is for memories, the frontal lobe is for planning, the amygdala is for emotions, the cerebellum is for balance. We also have the *visual* cortex, the *somatosensory* cortex, the *motor* cortex and the *auditory* cortex. While these are simplifying notions, there is a good measure of truth in them. Wernicke was largely right, Freud mostly wrong. And yet, for the greater part of the twentieth century, professionals tended to side with Freud. One prominent researcher argued that 'integration cannot be expressed in terms of connections between specific neurons ... the mechanisms of integration are to be sought in the dynamic relations among the parts of the nervous system rather than in details of structural differentiation.'[156] The author of these comments conducted experiments that proved—he said—the 'whole brain' concept. Others pointed to serious flaws in his methods and arguments.

The tide turned in favor of localization in the 1960s as laboratory research accelerated and clinical data accumulated. Wernicke's conduction aphasia came under renewed scrutiny, and the predicted disconnection was found to lie in the arcuate fasciculus, not the nearby insula as Wernicke had thought. But Wernicke's misidentification was a minor error compared to the uncontested confirmation of a physical disconnection between Broca's area and Wernicke's area. It didn't take long before psychiatrists began to

---

[155] Claus-W. Wallesch, 'History of aphasia: Freud as an aphasiologist.' *Aphasiology* 18:4, (2004), p. 394.

[156] Karl S. Lashley, *Brain Mechanisms and Intelligence.* Chicago, Illinois: Chicago University Press (1929), p. 176.

ponder whether other disconnections might impair mental life. Before we look at what their research revealed, we need to understand the anatomical basis of connectivity in the brain and how centers become disconnected.

Even the first neuroanatomists must have noticed, after slicing up the human brain, that the outer regions differ from the inner regions. Later, after the invention of microscopes, they saw many small objects (nerve cells) in the outer regions (the cerebral cortex), but very few just below. The presence of so many nerve cells in the cortex made it look gray, whereas the inner portion glistened white. Upon closer examination, the anatomists saw that the white matter has a fibrous quality. It is, in fact, composed of nerve cell axons, also known as nerve fibers. The majority of fibers are bundled into well-defined pathways, or tracts, which together constitute about 60 percent of the brain's volume.

Nerve fibers (white matter) in the human brain. Lateral view with the front of the brain at the left [Prevue Medical]

A question of fundamental importance then arose: What is the relationship between the neurons in the cortex and the fibers beneath? A breakthrough occurred in 1865 when the German anatomist Otto Deiters succeeded in removing a single, fully intact neuron from surrounding tissues. With that, it became perfectly clear that a neuron comprises three principal parts: the cell body, the finely branched dendrites, and one long axon. The axons branch only at their terminals, as each tiny branch (up to 10,000 in some cases) snuggles up close to a dendrite. It is at these points of near-contact—called synapses—that the axon-bearing neuron communicates with the dendrite-bearing neuron. Long after Deiters, neuroscientists learned what makes the white matter white. They found that each axon is tightly wrapped by a fatty substance named myelin. Like all fats, myelin reflects white light.

Because axons have an essential role as lines of communication, any damage to the structural integrity of either the axon or its myelin sheath is bound to be disruptive. Once research revealed the loss of gray matter in schizophrenia (Chapter 12), the obvious next question was whether white matter is likewise affected. Early studies produced variable results, with some reporting reductions—in certain brain areas—whereas others reported no differences between patients and healthy controls. The main cause of disagreement was the fact that neither X-ray scans nor conventional MRI 'sees' white matter distinctly. That shortcoming thwarted progress until it was eliminated, in 1985, by a French doctor with knowledge of nuclear physics.

Magnetic resonance imaging (MRI) works by buzzing a strong magnet around the body at a frequency that matches (resonates with) the electromagnetic properties of atoms within the body. Actually, the buzz resonates with the single proton that lies within each hydrogen atom. As soon as the magnet shuts off, the proton gradually returns to its normal state, and while this is happening the proton emits radio frequency waves that the machine translates into images. The body is mostly composed of water and, of course, each molecule of water contains two hydrogen atoms, so the MRI mostly detects water.

Denis Le Bihan, the man who empowered MRI for the analysis of white matter, was a medical resident in a radiology clinic when a colleague challenged him to solve a problem that was plaguing his cancer diagnoses. Specifically, the colleague wanted the MRI machine to recognize the difference between a liver tumor and an angioma (abnormal growth in a blood vessel). Le Bihan remembered from his studies that Albert Einstein explained the diffusion of floating pollen grains by the random movement of molecules within the grains. And, Le Bihan had 'some fuzzy intuition that, perhaps, water molecular diffusion measurements would result in lower values in solid tumors because of [chemical] hindrance to water molecular movement compared to flowing blood.'[157] Water is made of molecules, H_2O, which of course diffuse just like pollen grains. Since the MRI machine de-

---

[157] Denis Le Bihan (2014), p. 569. See suggested readings.

tects H2O molecules, it is able to track the movements of water, and that is what allows it to distinguish white matter from gray matter, for reasons to be explained below. Application of the same principles also allow physicians to distinguish solid tumors from angiomas—in the liver and elsewhere.

Diffusion MRI distinguishes white matter from gray matter based on the speed of water diffusion, which depends on physical context. Inside neuronal cell bodies, water diffuses slowly because the space is cluttered with organelles like the nucleus and mitochondria, plus proteins and dissolved molecules. By contrast, water diffuses more rapidly in axons because there are fewer obstacles. Diffusion is even greater in the ventricles due to the large volume of pure cerebrospinal fluid. Images obtained with diffusion MRI are dark where diffusion is rapid, bright where diffusion is slow. Therefore, the ventricles appear pitch black, and white matter (axons) appears significantly brighter than gray matter (cell bodies and dendrites).[158] Credit Einstein, if you wish, for his contribution to diffusion magnetic resonance imaging, but psychiatry owes more to Denis Le Bihan, the man whose insights opened a window onto neural disconnections in mental illness. Prior to his discovery of diffusion MRI, in 1985, only a handful of scientific papers had dealt with white matter in psychiatric illnesses; afterwards (to November 2020), there were more than 4350 articles and books on the subject.

Contrary to findings in regard to gray matter, studies looking for possible losses of white matter came up mostly negative. Axons do not die and disappear unless the entire nerve cell dies, and that doesn't happen either in schizophrenia or in any other psychiatric disorder. More interesting was the finding of tiny cracks in the myelin sheath around axons. The observations marked a giant step forward in the discovery of disconnections.

Imagine an axon as a long tube filled with water. Ordinarily, the water diffuses back and forth along the length of the axon, but it doesn't leave the axon because the axon is tightly wrapped in fatty myelin. However, if there are breaks in the myelin, water does leak out, and the movement shows up in diffusion MRI. When startled researchers found many instances of this kind of diffusion in psychiatric patients, they immediately understood its significance because, if water is leaking out of the axons, electrically charged ions are surely leaking out as well. This is important because the main biological function of the myelin sheath is to block the passage of ions; stopping the leakage of water is secondary. Leakage of ions signals trouble

---

[158] White matter got its name from the appearance of axons in the ordinary light microscope, on account of the myelin sheath. It is pure coincidence that axons also appear whiteish (bright) in diffusion MRI.

for the brain's electrical system. Think of telephone and internet cables, which are tightly covered in plastic or rubber to prevent just such a leakage of electricity. If the insulation on one of those cables should become damaged, the signal carried by the cable—your friend's voice or that popular Netflix movie—will crack and pop and possibly go silent. Similarly in the brain, leaky axons mean unreliable, disconnected communications.

In schizophrenia patients, myelin-related disconnections affect several important brain structures and their partner regions.[159] The uncinate fasciculus, a bundle of nerve fibers that connects the frontal lobe to the temporal lobe is hit especially hard. So too is the cingulum bundle, which connects components of the limbic system, including the amygdala and the hippocampus, two structures with key roles in memory formation and emotion. Inter-hemispheric pathways such as the corpus callosum are also damaged. Since our cognitive and emotional lives depend on the smooth functioning of the structures mentioned here, one can easily imagine the devastating impact of disrupted connectivity. But again, the question arises whether it is the psychosis that causes the damage or the medications that are used to treat the psychosis. Studies indicate that the disconnections are a product of the disorder itself, because myelin breaks begin to appear at about the same time as the symptoms and therefore prior to medication, or at least prior to consistent medication. As the illness progresses, the disconnections worsen.

White matter abnormalities are also seen in mental illnesses other than schizophrenia. Disconnections in patients with bipolar disorder are similar to those seen in schizophrenia, that is, they primarily affect the frontal lobe, limbic areas and inter-hemispheric pathways. In depressed patients, damage to the inter-hemispheric pathways is even more prominent, affecting especially connections between the left and right prefrontal cortices. A particular type of white matter abnormality is seen in elderly patients. These are exceptionally bright spots, known as white matter hyperintensities, which represent sites where water molecules move easily through large holes in the myelin sheath. Scattered around the brain, they ordinarily cause no harm, but large numbers may signal approaching depression and intellectual decline.

---

[159] S.W. Joo et al., 'Altered white matter connectivity in patients with schizophrenia: An investigation using public neuroimaging data from SchizConnect.' *PLOS ONE* 13(10):e0205369 (2018). Shu Liu et al., 'Polygenic effects of schizophrenia on hippocampal grey matter volume and hippocampus-medial prefrontal cortex functional connectivity.' *The British Journal of Psychiatry* 216:267–274 (2020).

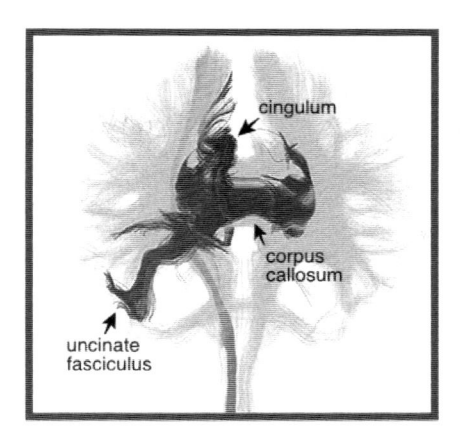

White matter tracts most frequently disrupted in patients with chronic schizophrenia [Modified from Wheeler and Voineskos, Frontiers in Human Neuroscience 8, 2014]

The combined evidence of structural brain damage, noted above, strongly suggests interference with functions but does not prove it, even when specific pathway disruptions match up with predicted functions, such as with hippocampal connections and amygdala connections. The best way to link structural damage to functional damage is by means of physiology, and the study of brain physiology in humans poses obvious problems. Fortunately, the MRI machine has answered the call. First, we visualized gray matter losses with conventional MRI, then white matter damage with diffusion MRI, and most recently physiological disconnections with the appropriately named functional MRI (fMRI). The MRI machine is a versatile device that can tell us much about the human brain.

Functional MRI was invented by a collection of creative scientists working at multiple locations. It was an undeclared competition in which everyone raced to finish first. One pioneer characterized the early 1990s as the 'heady days', remarking that 'this kind of scientific opportunity comes along rarely, if at all in a scientist's career ... I was a graduate student so my own feeling was perhaps like a novice surfer, looking for something—anything—to ride, and suddenly experiencing a swell of perfectly formed 50 foot waves.'[160]

fMRI measures, in real time, the amount of energy being used in different parts of the brain. Neurons consume energy—to power ion pumps—whenever they fire an action potential or 'spike'. Most neurons in the human brain fire action potentials at a low rate even while a person is

---

[160] P.A. Bandettini (2012), p. 581. See suggested readings.

resting, but once the brain needs to react to an external stimulus or engage in a task, certain neurons begin firing more quickly. The more active the neurons, the more energy they consume. The energy comes in the form of oxygen, which is taken from the hemoglobin of passing red blood cells. As each molecule of hemoglobin gives up its oxygen to the neurons, its magnetic state changes, and it is that change of state that the MRI machine detects. The machine does not detect changes in individual hemoglobin molecules, but rather the compounded changes that occur within tiny veins. The method is called BOLD, short for blood oxygen-level-dependent imaging. By focusing on the veins servicing a brain site of interest, neural activity at that site is effectively measured. BOLD is used to find brain areas that process sensory information, that move limbs, and that complete cognitive tasks. It can monitor areas active during gambling, help in the development of better drugs, and (sometimes) tell if you are lying. BOLD can also tell us about connections and disconnections.

Obviously, if a task, a response, or even a thought requires neural activation in more than a single region—as they nearly always do—then several areas will simultaneously 'light up' in BOLD pictures. Researchers assume that simultaneous activity means anatomical connectivity, either directly by means of a fiber bundle or indirectly through intervening structures. The issue in psychiatry is whether those connections are the same in patients as in healthy persons. If not equal, they could be weaker (hypoconnected) or stronger (hyperconnected), depending on the network's function and the type of illness.

Studies of individuals with autism spectrum disorders performing one specific task are particularly interesting. Autism is a complex disorder with many symptoms that vary from person to person, but all individuals have problems in understanding what other people are thinking and feeling. Experts say that autistic children lack a 'theory of mind', meaning that they cannot relate to the beliefs, desires and intentions of other people. In a classic test, a group of children watch as Sally puts a marble into a basket. After Sally leaves the room, Annie removes the marble from the basket and puts into a box. The children are then asked, 'Where will Sally look for the marble when she comes back into the room?' Most children answer, 'in the basket,' because they understand that Sally will have a false belief. The children who answer, 'in the box,' cannot relate to Sally's beliefs and are likely to be autistic.

Researchers used a modified version of the false-belief test—one that works in the confines of the MRI machine—to identify brain areas active during performance of the test. Beginning with healthy adults, they found several areas, ranging from the prefrontal cortex to the posterior cingulate cortex. Each individual area had already been implicated in either social functions or cognition. After it was found that they jointly participate in the false-belief task, the entire group of sites was designated the 'frontal-posterior network'. Next, researchers studied activation of the network in people with autism spectrum disorder. They found that neural activity in the frontal-posterior network was substantially less coordinated in young adults with autism than in their normally developing peers. As the authors of one study put it, the results "shed light on the disruption in brain functioning in general and connectivity in particular in autism when challenged by complex tasks like theory of mind.'[161]

Before BOLD—and still now—brain activity was monitored by gluing electrodes to the skull. Early investigators were surprised to find high levels of electrical activity even in subjects that were lying perfectly still. Later, it was found that the brain uses nearly as much energy at rest as it uses during the performance of a difficult mental task, 95 percent as much to be exact. Now, with the help of BOLD, we know that only neurons in certain brain regions are active during rest. The active regions constitute a connected network known as the 'default network' or 'default mode network', and the smaller frontal-posterior network mentioned above is part of it.[162]

As a person switches from performing a task to resting, some areas of the brain shut off, while activity in the default network *increases*. So, you ask, what could the network be doing while I'm resting? It is doing just what you are doing: mind-wandering. At rest, we—our minds together with our brains—think mostly about ourselves, about other people and about our social relationships. For example, 'I hope Johnnie didn't hurt Eddie's feelings ... Mary and Henry must be fighting again ... I think she loves me,' and so on. Note that a lot of this is theory-of-mind stuff.

It should come as no surprise, given the introduction above, that functional connections within the default network and between the default network and other networks are disrupted in autism. The extent of disruption is related to the size of the child's deficit in social communications. Children with few social deficits have small disruptions, whereas those with signifi-

---

[161] Rajesh K. Kana et al., 'Aberrant functioning of the theory-of-mind network in children and adolescents with autism.' *Molecular Autism* 6:59 (2015), p. 10.

[162] M.E. Raichle and A.Z. Snyder, 'A default mode of brain function: A brief history of an evolving idea.' *Neuroimage* 37(4):1083–1090 (2007).

cant social deficits have large disruptions.[163] The nature of the 'disruptions' changes with age, in that children have *over*-connected default networks, while autistic adolescents and autistic adults have *under*-connected default networks.

Other conclusions have been drawn from studies of the insula, a brain structure that continues to fascinate neuroscientists long after Carl Wernicke incorrectly identified it as the source of conduction aphasia. The internal anatomy of the insula resembles that of the cortical lobes (frontal, temporal, et cetera), but in contrast to its look-alikes that sit atop the brain, the insula lies deep within the lateral sulcus, a crevice that separates the frontal lobe from the temporal lobe. As regards function, the insula is sensitive to a wide array of stimuli and everyday events ranging, according to one authority, from 'bowel distension and orgasm, to cigarette craving and maternal love, to decision making and sudden insight.'[164] Some neuroscientists think that its core function is self-awareness. These and other properties implicate the insula in autism spectrum disorders.

Researchers looked for anatomical abnormalities in the insula but found none, and when they first examined connectivity using functional MRI, the results were inconsistent. Some studies reported that the insula is under-connected with the rest of the brain, while other studies found that is over-connected. Then came recognition of the age effect, as first encountered in relation to the default network. The brain begins its development in the embryo, and it is not completely formed until late adolescence. For reasons unknown, it appears that the time course of brain development is altered in autism, such that it grows faster than normal growth in early years, but slower than normal in later years. The proposed developmental scenario explains why the brains of autistic children are relatively over-connected, whereas they are relatively under-connected in adolescence and afterwards.

Connectivity, like autism, is strongly influenced by gene activity, and both change dramatically during early life as the brain grows into the hugely complex machine that supports our mental and physical lives. The machine works only if it has in place all the correct neural connections—at their optimal strengths. How these connections get made is one of the wonders of biological development, but we know that it requires precise timing and the unfailing recognition of chemical cues. Thus, it is tempting to think of

---

[163] Aarthi Padmanabhan et al., 'The default mode network in autism.' *Biological Psychiatry: Cognitive Neuroscience and Neuroimaging* 2:476–486 (2017).

[164] A. D. Craig, 'How do you feel—now? The anterior insula and human awareness.' *Nature Reviews Neuroscience* 10:59–70 (2009). Quote in Abstract.

autism as a disorder caused by the improper development of brain pathways.

The contrasts between autism and schizophrenia are interesting. The first symptoms of autism appear early, often within the first year of life, whereas in schizophrenia they appear in late adolescence. Autism is seen as a disorder of development, whereas schizophrenia is thought to be degenerative. Accordingly, while disconnection abnormalities are common to both disorders, they arise through different processes. In schizophrenia, they result from damage to the axonal sheath, whereas in autism they result from an altered developmental program.

Major depression presents yet another picture, where the default network is more active and more connected than in healthy people. This observation is consistent with the fact that the default network is active during introspection and rumination, two mental activities all too familiar to depressed patients. One would think, therefore, that dampening activity in the default network might relieve depression, and that is apparently true. In chapter 8, we learned about electroconvulsive shock (ECT) and transcranial magnetic stimulation (TMS) as treatments for depression. Research shows that when these treatments succeed in reducing symptoms, they also lower connectivity in the default neural network. Because patients with strong connections and a highly active default networks respond best to ECT and TMS, it has been suggested that network connectivity could be used to predict the likelihood of successful treatment in individual cases.[165]

Perspective

Thanks to the wonderful instruments that allow us to see inside the living brain, and the awesome power of modern computers for digesting mountains of data, scientists have found disrupted connectivity in the brains of psychiatric patients. Disconnections, as a general phenomenon, do not constitute an endophenotype, but broken myelin and disrupted neural networks—each considered separately—do qualify as endophenotypes. Just as the loss of gray matter and errors in the antisaccade task (Chapter 12) pass the test of heritability, so too do the biomarkers discussed in the present chapter. Heritability for leaky axons and out-of-sync neural networks has been demonstrated through family studies, twin studies and genetic studies.

---

[165] Zhiliang Long et al., 'Prediction on treatment improvement in depression with resting state connectivity: A coordinate-based meta-analysis.' *Journal of Affective Disorders* 276:62–68 (2020).

Endophenotypes are more interesting than mere biomarkers because they point to specific mechanisms possibly responsible for symptoms. For example, schizophrenia is an illness that typically appears in late adolescence when the brain is undergoing significant changes. One big change is the programed loss, or pruning, of synapses during childhood. Approximately one-third of all existing synapses are pruned. According to one credible hypothesis, schizophrenia is tied to excessive synaptic pruning at this critical time. Fewer synapses would mean less gray matter, and that is exactly what is seen in adult schizophrenia brains. Therefore, focussing on the genes responsible for the loss-of-gray-matter endophenotype might help in pinpointing the ultimate cause of schizophrenia.

Similarly, focussing on the genes responsible for wrapping myelin around axons could help in dissecting causal factors for schizophrenia, autism and perhaps other mental illnesses. Human babies are born with no myelin, but soon thereafter myelin production begins in a specific type of (nonneuronal) brain cell. By the age of three most axons have some myelin, and recent work suggests that the sheath continues to mature and be modified throughout adolescence and early adulthood.[166] Since healthy myelin is essential for maintaining neural connectivity, and disconnections are implicated in mental illness, attention has turned to the genes that make myelin. One study has found 17 gene variants that associate with both schizophrenia and leaky axons.[167]

Suggested readings

Denis Le Bihan, 'Diffusion MRI: What water tells us about the brain.' *EMBO Molecular Medicine* 6(5):569–573 (2014).

D. H. Geschwind and P. Levitt, 'Autism spectrum disorders: developmental disconnection syndromes.' *Current Opinion in Neurobiology* 17:103–11 (2007).

Neil D. Woodward and Carissa J. Cascio, 'Resting-state functional connectivity in psychiatric disorders.' *JAMA Psychiatry* 72(8):743–744 (2015).

---

[166] Jill M. Williamson and David A. Lyons, 'Myelin dynamics throughout life: An ever-changing landscape?' *Frontiers in Cellular Neuroscience* 12:424 (2018).

[167] Ivan Chavarria-Siles et al., 'Myelination-related genes are associated with decreased white matter integrity in schizophrenia.' *European Journal of Human Genetics* 24(3):381–386 (2016).

14 The plastic brain

What adjective comes to mind when you think of the brain? Is it *wrinkled*, because you've seen pictures? *Mushy*, because it cuts like tofu? Maybe *heavy* and *dense*. Actually, it is all of these things, but it is also *plastic*. Which is not to say that the brain is made of plastic, but rather, that it changes its shape like plastic. Fortunately, our brain doesn't need to be melted down before changing its shape. Life experiences, and sometimes simply will power, gets the job done.

Beginning in the embryo and continuing until late adolescence, the brain grows according to a predetermined plan, then late in life it deteriorates. All along the way, on every single day throughout our entire lives, it changes. The changes occur mostly at synapses, so they are tiny and invisible, unless examined with an electron microscope. Nevertheless, these small structural changes affect our minds, sometimes for the better, sometimes not. Neural plasticity has implications for psychiatry, including opportunities for reversing or repairing detrimental changes.

Hans Lukas Teuber, an American neuropsychologist, founded the Department of Psychology (later the Department of Brain and Cognitive Sciences) at the Massachusetts Institute of Technology in 1964. Revolutionary at the time, Teuber believed that to understand the mind, one must understand the brain. One of the first professors that he hired was his former student, Joseph Altman. Teuber had been studying the psychological effects of gunshot wounds suffered during WWII, and Altman was researching how the brain recovers from such injuries. Specifically, Altman wanted to know whether glia cells proliferate. Glia cells do not process information, but among other functions they were thought to clean up, and possibly repair, damaged nerve cells. As predicted, therefore, Altman found many new glia cells in the damaged brains of experimental animals. More surprising, startling in fact, he also found new nerve cells. The brains had changed by adding new neurons.[168]

---

[168] Joseph Altman, 'Are new neurons formed in the brains of adult mammals?' *Science* 135:1127–1128 (1962).

Nerve cells are born when neural stem cells divide (mitosis). Since no dividing cells had been seen in any adult mammalian brain prior to Altman's discovery, it was assumed that all neurons are born during early development. Altman begin his experiment by injecting adult rats with thymidine, a component of DNA. All new cells need to synthesize DNA, so they need thymidine, and they get it from blood. The thymidine that Altman injected into his rats was special, however, because he had made it radioactive. Later, when he found radioactive cells in post-mortem brain slices, he knew that they could only have been born subsequent to the injection. The reason why new neurons had not been noticed previously is because the stem cells that make them reside far away from where the new neurons eventually come to rest, and while migrating, the newly born cells undergo a drastic change of appearance from small and inconspicuous to fully formed neurons.

Joseph Altman [Shirley A. Bayer]

Altman announced his discovery in a series of papers published in the 1960s, but few scientists paid attention until 1998, when other investigators found neurogenesis in the adult *human* brain. Still, some scientists didn't believe it. They said the methods were inappropriate and the evidence inadequate. Then a group of researchers in Sweden, together with international collaborators, seized upon a clever test of Altman's claim. As mentioned, new cells need new DNA and thus, new thymidine. Now thymidine, like all organic compounds, contains carbon, which ordinarily has 6 neutrons and

6 protons (carbon-12). During the Cold War (1955–1963), however, above-ground bomb testing released enough energy to convert much of carbon-12 into an alternative isotope, carbon-14 (8 neutrons and 6 protons). Prior to the tests, carbon-14 was extremely rare, and it again became rare shortly afterwards, but in the meanwhile, huge amounts of carbon-14 entered the atmosphere and spread worldwide. Plants took up carbon-14, humans ate the plants, and all new biological cells born during that period incorporated carbon-14. When people who were adults in the bomb-testing years died fifty years later, they still had brain cells labelled with carbon-14, proving that the neurons had been born in their adult brains.

It was not just that neurogenesis occurs in humans— exciting in itself—but where, exactly, it occurs. The single beneficiary of new neurons, it turns out, is the hippocampus. A recent study counted newly born neurons in post-mortem brain slices.[169] Individuals with healthy brains at the time of death had tens of thousands of new hippocampal neurons per cubic millimeter. The number declined with increasing age at the time of death. By contrast, subjects who died with Alzheimer's disease had fewer new neurons than even the oldest of the healthy subjects, regardless of age.

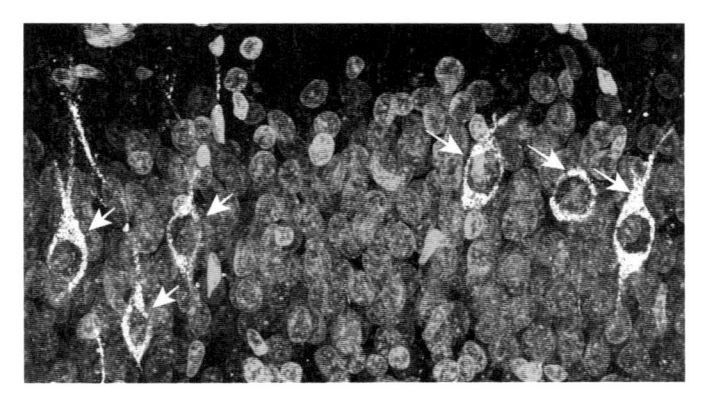

Newly born nerve cells (arrows) in the hippocampus of a 68-year-old man [Moreno-Jiménez, E.P., Nature Medicine 25, 2019]

Since the hippocampus plays an important role in the formation of memories, some scientists believe that neurogenesis participates in the process. Although unproven, it is possible that a decline in neurogenesis late in life accounts, at least in part, for memory losses. Low levels of neurogenesis

---

[169] Elena P. Moreno-Jiménez et al., 'Adult hippocampal neurogenesis is abundant in neurologically healthy subjects and drops sharply in patients with Alzheimer's disease.' *Nature Medicine* 25:554–560 (2019).

might also contribute to the risk of mental illness. In particular, it has been proposed that depression results from reduced levels of neurogenesis. Noteworthy therefore, are experiments indicating that the drug fluoxetine (Prozac) increases neurogenesis *and* relieves depression—but so far only in rodents. Ethical concerns prevent us from testing the relationship between neurogenesis and human depression, but even for rodents, fluoxetine is not necessarily working just by increasing neurogenesis, because fluoxetine still has an antidepressant effect in aged mice that are no longer capable of increasing the rate of neurogenesis.[170]

Another example of neuroplasticity comes from the laboratory Michael Merzenich, a professor at the San Francisco campus of the University of California. Merzenich designed experiments—first with monkeys and later with humans—that resulted in a rewiring, or rearrangement, of neural connectivity within the brain area responsible for touch sensations. It was a stunning series of experiments that jolted the world of neuroscience.

Michael Merzenich [onthebrain.com]

On a spot literally at the top of the brain, there lies a strip of cerebral cortex known as the 'sensory map'. Every neuron lying within the area is specialized for detecting touches on a particular part of the body. Once activated by a touch, the responding neurons tell the rest of the brain about what has happened *at that spot*. The sensory map is laid out like

---

[170] Laura Micheli et al., 'Depression and adult neurogenesis: Positive effects of the antidepressant fluoxetine and of physical exercise.' *Brain Research Bulletin* 143:181–193 (2018).

any ordinary map, that is, with neurons responding to stimulation of the hand lying near neurons responding to stimulation of the wrist, which in turn lie adjacent to neurons responding to touches on the lower arm, and so on. Previous to Merzenich's work it was thought that the map is fixed in early life, unchangeable and identical in every individual. Merzenich showed otherwise.

Working with monkeys, he began each of his investigations by determining the precise arrangement of the sensory map. With the animal anesthetized and a micro-electrode inserted into the cerebral cortex, he touched parts of the body while monitoring the activity of individual neurons. If, for example, a neuron responded to touches of the hand but not to touches of the wrist, the arm or any other part of the body, he knew that the neuron was in the hand portion of the map.[171]

After carefully mapping out the hand area in one monkey brain, he found that the middle finger of one hand was represented by an area of cortex measuring about 1 mm^2. With the animal under anaesthesia, he then cut the nerve innervating the middle finger. Following recovery, he found that the cortical area formerly occupied by neurons responding only to touches of the middle finger was now filled with neurons responding only to neighboring fingers. The map had changed!

In another experiment, Merzenich again began by mapping the sensory cortex. He then trained the monkey to gently touch a spinning disk with a specific fingertip in order to receive a banana pellet reward. The monkey had to act within 10 seconds of a start signal and he/she could not use excessive pressure. After thousands of trials extending over 109 days, the monkey was performing very well. When Merzenich re-mapped the touch-sensitive cortex, he found that the area devoted to that one fingertip had expanded from 0.32 mm^2 before stimulation to 0.92 mm^2 afterwards, nearly a 3-fold increase in size. Again, the map had changed.

The plasticity evident in these experiments likely reflects changing patterns of connectivity between low level sensory pathways and cortical neurons. Connections that are no longer being used—such as those serving a finger that has lost its nerve, become weaker or die off entirely, whereas those that are frequently used, such as those involved in learning a task that brings a food reward, are strengthened or added. Only the most active connections survive.

---

[171] Merzenich's experiments are described in Doidge (2008), pp. 66–70. See suggested readings.

Single cell mapping with micro-electrodes, as done by Merzenich and colleagues, is generally not possible in humans, but magnetoencephalography is a non-invasive method that is nearly as precise as micro-electrode mapping. In one such investigation, the cortical finger areas of musicians were mapped, specifically in musicians playing stringed instruments like the violin, cello and guitar.[172] Researchers predicted that the map area for left-hand fingers would be larger than the corresponding right-hand area because fingers on the left hand need to move rapidly and accurately across several strings, whereas the right hand only has to move the bow back and forth. The predictions were correct: left-hand finger representations occupied more space on the sensory map than their right-hand counterparts. Moreover, the size of the difference was correlated with the number of years the musicians had been practicing.

In a separate investigation, a different group of investigators examined the hippocampi of London taxi drivers.[173] Since the streets are maddingly complex in London, taxi drivers must undergo extensive training, and they need to pass a stringent test to get a license. The navigational skills of the London taxi drivers made them ideal subjects for testing whether the human hippocampus, like the hippocampi of birds and rodents, holds memories of spatial locations. The researchers scanned the brains of taxi drivers, using magnetic resonance imaging, and measured the hippocampus from the obtained images. The results showed that the posterior part of the hippocampus was about 5 mm^2 larger in taxi drivers than in non-drivers. Moreover, there was a strong correlation between the time spent as a taxi driver and the size of the posterior region, similar to what was found in the musicians' study described above. So, the human hippocampus—like the human somatosensory cortex—is plastic.

Having witnessed firsthand the wonders of brain plasticity, Merzenich searched for practical, real-life applications. He began by designing computer games for schizophrenia patients, hoping to re-wire critical circuits. However, when patients reported no benefits, he changed the name of his company and its focus. Posit Science Corporation now sells software for improving cognitive functions in psychologically healthy individuals. Merzenich has also written a book that offers 'clear, specific, scientifically

---

[172] T. Elbert et al., 'Increased cortical representation of the fingers of the left hand in string players.' *Science* 270:305–307 (1995).

[173] D. Maguire et al., 'Navigation-related structural change in the hippocampi of taxi drivers.' *Proceedings of the National Academy of Sciences*, USA 97(8):4398–4403 (2000).

proven advice for how you can rejuvenate, remodel, and reshape your brain at any age.'[174]

If the reader doubts that will power alone can change the brain—as stated at the beginning of this chapter—he or she needs to hear of the experiment conducted by a pair of exercise physiologists interested in building strong muscles.[175] Three groups of healthy youngsters were tasked with increasing muscle strength in their left fifth fingers (the 'pinkies'). Subjects in the 'contraction' group placed their hands in a device that held the finger in a fixed position while electrodes monitored muscle activity. These subjects trained by repeatedly squeezing their abductor muscle as hard as they could, while adhering to a rigid schedule of exercise. The second group was called the 'imagining' group. They also placed their fingers in the restraining device, but rather than contracting the abductor muscle —they were explicitly told *not* to do that—they simply *imagined* contracting it. A third group was told to stay at home and refrain from any sporting activities. At the end of four weeks, all subjects were tested for muscle strength.

As expected, the contracting group experienced, on average, a 30 percent increase in muscle strength. Equally impressive, however, was the 22 percent increase in the imagining group. The stay-at-home subjects had no significant change. Since the imaginers had held their fingers perfectly still during training, the researchers attributed the strengthening effect not to any change in the muscle, but rather to changes in the nervous system. The researchers could not determine what, exactly, had happened, but they proposed that additional neurons became connected to the finger-contracting muscle. Regardless of the mechanism, it is difficult to escape the conclusion that participants in the imagining group got stronger *just by thinking about it*.

Likewise, when a tennis player imagines hitting the ball with strokes that he or she might have to play in game situations, that player will come to a real game better prepared to make winning shots. Competitive runners find that they can endure pain if, before the race, they imagine positive responses. And some legendary pianists, including such stars as Glenn Gould, Vladimir Horowitz and Arthur Rubinstein, practiced pieces entirely in their heads before performing them in public.

---

[174] Quote from publicity blub for Michael Merzenich's book, *Soft-Wired.* San Francisco CA: Parnassus (2013).

[175] G. Yue and K. J. Cole, 'Strength increases from the motor program: comparison of training with maximal voluntary and imagined muscle contractions.' *Journal of Neurophysiology* 67(5):1114–1123 (1992).

Prolonged thinking about *anything* changes the brain. It leaves a memory trace that is identical in its physical nature to the memories of Grandma's name, the taste of strawberries and the motor skills for riding a bicycle. Experiences of all kinds are stored in the brain. The more emotionally laden the experience, the more securely is it stored. When scientists say that depression, for example, is 45 percent hereditary, the remaining 65 percent is due to remembered experiences. The influential experiences may be hidden from consciousness, like Bertha Pappenheim's dog experience, but they survive as physical traces in the brain. The nature of the contributing experiences is fairly obvious in posttraumatic stress disorder and anxiety, but less clear in schizophrenia and depression.

The memories that reside in our brains also fill our minds. That delicious duality motivates psychiatrists and neuroscientists to explore the biological mechanisms of memory. In experimental animals, they have literally *seen* the neurons that hold specific memories, and they have manipulated those same neurons to activate and suppress memories. So far, only animal memories have been tinkered with, but psychiatry is paying close attention. Before we examine what this might mean for psychiatric treatments, we will review some basic facts about the biology of memory.

Sigmund Freud, master of the mind, was among the first scientists to offer an explanation of how memories are established in the brain. In a letter sent to a friend in 1895, Freud jotted down his ideas. That letter, and those ideas, remained virtually unknown to the public until 1950, when they were published under the title, 'Project for a Scientific Psychology.' One passage in that complex document reads like a summary of twentieth century knowledge,

> It will now be clear what assumptions about the neurons are necessary in order to cover the most general characteristics of memory. This is the argument. The neurons are permanently altered by the passage of an excitation. Their contact-barriers [synapses] are brought into a permanently altered state by excitation. This alteration must consist in the contact-barriers becoming more capable of conduction. We can then say: Memory is represented by the facilitations existing between neurons.

Early in the twentieth century, the German biologist Richard Semon, unaware of Freud's 'assumptions', wrote about memories as 'latent modifications in the irritable substance.' Semon imagined that every remembered experience is represented in the brain by a small number of highly connected neurons; he called that physical memory an 'engram'. He further proposed that connectivity within the engram accounts for the fact that we can recall an entire event by activating just a single component of the original experience. So, for example, noticing a particular flower arrangement might recall an entire wedding celebration. Although neither Freud nor Semon was able to marshal any real evidence in support of their conjectures, subsequent research has proven them essentially correct. Important elements of that research were conducted by the American psychiatrist, Eric Kandel.

Kandel's motivation for studying memory was both personal and professional. Born in Vienna, he and his family lived close to Sigmund Freud's home, and like Freud, Kandel is Jewish. Also, like Freud, Kandel left Vienna after Hitler's troops marched into the city on March 14, 1938. Years later, in an autobiographical essay written on the occasion of his Nobel Prize, Kandel recalled that,

> every one of my non-Jewish classmates – the entire class with the exception of one girl – stopped talking and interacting with me. In the park where I played I was taunted and roughed up ... I cannot help but think that the experiences of my last year in Vienna helped to determine my later interests in the mind, in how people behave, the unpredictability of motivation, and the persistence of memory.

After graduating from medical school in the United States, Kandel faced a difficult decision: continue with his psychoanalytic training or switch to neuroscientific research. Convinced that memories play a key role in the genesis of mental illness, he chose research. He wanted to know how Semon's engrams are created and how they get fixed in the brain. Next, he had to choose the subjects for his experimentation. After dismissing the human brain as off limits, he considered using rats— popular at the time—but rat brains were too complex for the experiments he had in mind. In the end, he selected *Aplysia californica,* a large sea slug. This unassuming mollusc has a simple nervous system, large nerve cells and, crucially, the capacity to form memories. In a series of brilliant experiments conducted over the span of two decades, Kandel discovered the essential mechanisms responsible for learning and memory, applicable to all animals including humans. Late in his career, but still very active, Kandel turned to the mouse and expanded his findings in the areas of genetics and molecular biology. All of this while bringing his insights closer to what really mattered, the betterment of psychiatric care.

Eric Kandel

Not until 1998, at the peak of his fame, did Kandel write his first article for the *American Journal of Psychiatry*. Few of the journal's readers were comfortable with contemporary neuroscience, and fewer still knew anything about the biology of memory. Specifically addressing these practitioners, Kandel boldly announced his intentions in the title of his article, 'A New Intellectual Framework for Psychiatry.' Kandel's framework rests on five pillars that together constitute 'the current thinking of biologists about the relationship of mind to brain.' Kandel's first principle, and probably the most important, is that, 'All mental processes, even the most complex psychological processes, derive from operations of the brain.' After reviewing experimental findings, he plainly states that 'there can be no changes in behavior that are not reflected in the nervous system and no persistent changes in the nervous system that are not reflected in structural changes on some level of resolution.'[176]

Kandel's visionary work inspired others to move toward practical applications of memory research. One scientist who took up the torch is Susumu Tonegawa, a professor at the Massachusetts Institute of Technology and a master manipulator of memories. Before learning the tricks of that trade, he won a Nobel Prize for figuring out how the body makes millions of different antibodies. Endowed with prodigious energy, a brilliant mind and a highly competitive attitude, Tonegawa quickly got up to speed with the latest techniques after plunging into neuroscience. A key technique—borrowed

---

[176] Eric R. Kandel, 'A new intellectual framework for psychiatry.' *American Journal of Psychiatry* 155:457–469 (1998), quotes on pp. 460, 464.

from other researchers—enabled him to insert a foreign genetic element into selected neurons, specifically into neurons that are electrical active during a learning experience. Later, at a time of his choosing, he could re-activate the same neurons by targeting them with a laser beam.

In one such experiment,[177] Tonegawa and colleagues trained mice to freeze in the presence of a loud tone that had been previously paired with electrical shock. This simple piece of learning created an ensemble of memory neurons, an engram. The scientists inserted one of their foreign genetic elements into those neurons—and only those neurons—that had formed the engram. Later, as the rats were happily exploring an unfamiliar territory, the investigators used the genetic element in combination with a laser beam to selectively activate the labelled neurons (cause them to fire action potentials). Within seconds of switching on the laser beam, the mice remembered what they had learned about the tone predicting the shock, and they stopped in their tracks. This technical tour de force demonstrated that memories are stored in small groups of neurons.

Skilled researchers can also erase or modify specific memories. These manipulations are not (yet) possible in humans, but an experiment conducted by Tonegawa and colleagues suggests what might someday be done with depressed patients. Who knows what goes through the mind of a mouse when it is restrained, but judging its behaviours, it seems depressed. It quickly gives up trying to escape and, simultaneously, loses its usual taste for sugary water. The MIT scientists managed to switch the mouse's response from something like depression to something like pleasure. The experiment utilized six groups of mice, each of which contained 16–18 animals. For simplicity, it will be presented as involving just two mice, both males.

Tonegawa and colleagues began by inserting their special genetic element into a small population of neurons that became excited after the *male* mouse was placed in contact with a *female* mouse.[178] The scientists assumed that the male mouse found the experience 'pleasant', and they further assumed that the labelled neurons now held a memory of that pleasure. As in the previously described experiment, the presence of the genetic element meant that researchers could activate these neurons by illuminating them with a laser beam. So, later, when the mice were again restrained, the pleasurable memory was recalled in one of the mice (by activating the en-

---

[177] X. Liu et al., 'Optogenetic stimulation of a hippocampal engram activates fear memory recall.' *Nature* 484:381–385 (2015).

[178] S. Ramirez et al., 'Activating positive memory engrams suppresses depression-like behaviour.' *Nature* 522:335–339 (2015).

gram neurons) but not in the other mouse. As predicted, the first mouse—in whom the 'pleasure' memory had been recalled—struggled to escape from its imprisonment and eagerly slurped up sugary water, whereas the second mouse—the one that did not get the memory recall—behaved as previously, that is, by giving up the struggle and ignoring sweetened water. The authors propose that 'direct activation of [hippocampal] engram cells associated with a positive memory offers a potential therapeutic node for alleviating a subset of depression-related behaviours.'

Is this a realistic scenario for erasing bad memories in humans, dropping foreign molecules into nerve cells and implanting a light pipe in the brain? Obviously not, or at least not yet, but there may be an alternative to physical intrusion. To see how these alternative methods could work, we need to consider how short-term memories are converted to long-term memories. Most memories are short-term, meaning that they survive for only a few seconds. For long-term memory storage (days to years), additional protein must be produced and inserted into the synapses that hold the memory. If, for one reason or another, an experience fails to initiate protein synthesis, the memory is destined for a short life. This conditional aspect of memory formation led Karim Nader to think about what happens when we bring to mind a long-held memory. He wondered if the memory, once recalled, now needs a new round of protein synthesis to save it for long-term storage, and what happens if it doesn't get the fresh proteins.

Nader was a post-doctoral fellow at New York University, working in a laboratory investigating fearful memories. His training had been in psychology, so he did not fully understand the complex molecular machinery that is involved in long-term memory formation. If he had, according to his own recollection, he would not have conducted the remarkable experiment that brought him international acclaim.[179] He began by training rats to fear a tone that had become associated with a mild electrical shock (as in Tonegawa's experiment). When he presented the rats with the same tone twenty-four hours later (long-term for a rat), they immediately froze, indicating that they remembered the tone's painful association very well. Immediately after the recall test, Nader injected some of the rats with a substance that blocks protein synthesis in the brain; a second group of control rats was injected with cerebrospinal fluid. Twenty-four hours later, he again presented the fearful tone in another test of recall. Nader found that those rats which had been injected with cerebrospinal fluid froze after hear-

---

[179] K. Nader, G.E., Schafe and J.E. LeDoux, 'Fear memories require protein synthesis in the amygdala after retrieval.' *Nature* 406:722–726 (2000).

ing the tone (they remembered), whereas the rats injected with the protein synthesis blocker acted as if they had never encountered an electrical shock (they forgot). Nader's conclusion: A recalled memory can be erased by preventing protein synthesis. Psychiatrists asked whether traumatic memories could be similarly erased in humans.

Blocking protein synthesis is dangerous, and even in rats, the drug must be directly injected into the brain. It's not something we want to do with humans, and it may not be necessary. Recalled memories need new proteins because they are physically weak. So weak, in fact, that even with new proteins, a recalled memory seldom returns to long-term storage in its original form. Imagine that you witness a violent assault perpetrated right in front of your home. Although you may have failed to notice the assailant's orange-colored shoes at the time, let's say that a description of the shoes appears in a newspaper story months afterwards. Naturally, the article recalls your personal memory of the event. What happens next, when the memory returns to long-term storage, is very interesting because in the returned memory *you see* the orange shoes. False memories of this type present problems for judges and juries in criminal trials, but equally, they provide opportunities for psychotherapists. An experiment conducted at New York University shows how this might work.[180]

Healthy subjects were shown two colored objects. They received a mild electrical shock when shown one of the objects, the 'scary' one, but not when shown the 'safe' object. Naturally, they formed a fearful memory of the scary object, but not of the safe object. The next day, subjects in the experimental group saw the same scary object many times *without any shock*. For these subjects, the fearful memory was recalled, but then immediately *updated* by showing that the once-feared object was not actually scary. Subjects in the control group were also shown the scary object without any shocks, but they got the updating treatment six hours after the memory recall. One year later, the subjects were invited into the lab and outfitted with electrodes for measuring sweat. As expected, none of the subjects produced sweat when shown the safe object. However, when shown the scary object, the control subjects—whose memories had been updated long after the memory recall—produced lots of sweat, whereas subjects who had been updated immediately after the recall sweat hardly at all. The researchers had capitalized on the vulnerability of recalled memories to convert a once fearful memory into a benign memory.

---

[180] Daneila Schiller et al., 'Preventing the return of fear in humans using reconsolidation update mechanisms.' *Nature* 463:49–53 (2010).

In chapter 4, we learned that Sigmund Freud modeled his therapeutic technique on the 'talking cure' practiced by Josef Breuer's patient, Bertha Pappenheim. He was impressed with how Anna's mood improved on occasions when Breuer encouraged her to recall her traumatic experiences. Viewed in the context of contemporary memory research, Anna's talking cure—later named free association—appears as a technique for updating troublesome memories by recalling them in a non-threating environment.

Perspective

The experiments mentioned in this chapter highlight the power of modern brain science and its allied discipline, psychology. Beyond that, they illustrate the tangled relationship between mind and brain, and the fact that the two are inextricably bound up in our synapses. Despite the heavy reliance on animal studies for much of our knowledge in this field, it would be foolish to deny its relevance to humans. Every advance in neuroscience in an advance in understanding mental illness.

While the ability to manipulate memories has been demonstrated in animal studies, it remains to be seen whether the methods can be adapted for use in humans and whether they can be effective in psychiatry. Erasing or editing a few specific memories might help in alleviating phobias and post-traumatic stress disorder, but applying the same methods to disorders of a more complex nature, such as schizophrenia and depression, will be challenging. One way forward might be to address constellations of memories that are collectively marked by attributes relevant to psychological symptoms. Examples might include anxious memories or memories relating to particular events or people.

Early in his career, Sigmund Freud correctly imagined how memories are stored in the brain. Later he listened while his patients recited painful memories. Freud transformed himself from neuroscientist to psychotherapist. Did he ever contemplate editing the physical substate of memory?

Suggested readings

Norman Doidge, *The Brain that Changes Itself.* New York: Viking (2007).

Elizabeth A. Phelps and Stefan G. Hofmann, 'Memory editing from science fiction to clinical practice.' *Nature* 572:43–50 (2019).

15 An old diagnosis gets a bad prognosis

In Hans Christian Anderson's folktale, The Emperor's New Clothes, a pair of swindlers sell the emperor a magnificent, invisible outfit. The emperor steps out expecting to be greeted by an admiring crowd, but the room is silent until a gasping child cries out, 'The emperor has no clothes!' The story teaches the pitfalls of vanity and the fact that authority silences opposition.

Think now about Emil Kraepelin, the German psychiatrist whose name has appeared so often in this book. He has been described as the father of clinical psychiatry. The *Encyclopedia of Psychology* identifies him as the founder of modern scientific psychiatry, and, according to the distinguished medical historian Edward Shorter, 'It is Kraepelin, not Freud, who is the central figure in the history of psychiatry.'[181] It would be fair to conclude that Kraepelin's authority—within psychiatry—was as great as the emperor's. Moreover, Kraepelin's crowning achievement, schizophrenia, was a brilliant idea that no one dared to criticize. But now people are asking embarrassing questions.

Kraepelin first described schizophrenia in 1893. Some people say that he discovered schizophrenia, but it was really more of an invention. The real discovery—the one that merits inclusion in this book —is that schizophrenia is not the illness that Kraepelin thought it to be. It may not even be an illness. The emperor has no clothes. Kraepelin's schizophrenia is not an illness.

Schizophrenia is the quintessential madness, a highly debilitating condition that has long served as the testing ground for theories and treatments. In recent years, however, Kraepelin's grand conception has suffered one blow after another, to the point where many psychiatrists today question whether it serves any useful purpose. The reformers are picking up the shattered pieces of Kraepelin's edifice and reassembling them in ways that make us reconsider the very notion of discrete mental illnesses.

Immediately after writing that Kraepelin is the 'central figure' in the history of psychiatry, Edward Shorter defended the judgment, stating that Kraepelin 'provided the single most significant insight that the late nine-

---

[181] Edward Shorter, *A History of Psychiatry*. Toronto: John Wiley & Sons (1997), p. 100.

teenth and early twentieth centuries had to offer into major psychiatric illness: that there are several principal types ...'[182] That is not to say there were no types of psychiatric illness before Kraepelin. In early times, there were two types: mania and melancholy. The number grew to six in 1801 when Philippe Pinel recognized mania with delirium, mania without delirium, melancholia with elevated moods, melancholia with depressed or anxious moods, dementia and idiocy. For the remainder of the nineteenth century, French psychiatrists obsessed with identifying and classifying even more types.

> The classification of data under clear and distinct rubrics was the *sine qua non* of enlightened scientific method in France at the end of the eighteenth century. With respect to psychiatry, that meant—and continued to mean throughout the nineteenth century—drawing up and periodically overhauling ... classificatory systems of mental disease, in which each disease was defined by the cluster of symptoms it regularly presented, and the ensemble was presumed to exhaust all the pathological possibilities.[183]

The enterprise of psychiatric classification spread around the world. Benjamin Rush, the leading American psychiatrist in the early 1800s, thought that madness was either partial (disorders like hypochondriasis, tristimania and amenomania) or general (disorders like mania, manicula and manalgia). The Scottish psychiatrist, David Skae, named mental disorders after the part of the body from which the malady arose, for example mania of masturbation, mania of pregnancy, sunstroke mania and metastatic mania. Some authors used Latin names, some used vernacular names, and some organized their disease types in complex schemes copied from Carl Linnaeus's biological taxonomies. Every classification was different.

Most troubling for practicing psychiatrists was the multitude of diagnostic terms meant to encompass the most severe cases. These were named madness or insanity in Britain, craziness in America, *manie* in France and *Wahnsinn* in Germany. On top of that, an Austrian doctor coined a new term, *Psychose*, in 1845. Initially a term for purely psychological disorders, psychosis later came to imply brain damage. Asylums dealt with their psychotic patients as best as they could, usually with physical restraints, iso-

---

[182] Ibid.

[183] Jan Ellen Goldstein, *Console and Classify: The French Psychiatric Profession in the Nineteenth Century*. Cambridge, England: Cambridge University Press (1987), p. 5.

lation and punishment. Meanwhile, in the universities, professors argued over whether psychosis constitutes a single disorder or multiple related disorders. One year after the word *Psychose* was introduced, a textbook listed no less than thirteen synonyms, all commonly used in clinical practice.

Enter Emil Kraepelin. Hard-working and highly ambitious, his career first took off after being appointed head of an asylum in Heidelberg. Later, as director of a large psychiatric hospital in Munich, he gained international fame. Although he was a man of wide interests, his passionate attention was focused on psychosis. His widely consulted textbook expressed the view that mental illnesses are real diseases, just like any physical disease. Each mental illness has its own psychological profile but also a unique biological basis. The way forward, he wrote, is to design treatments that address the underlying causes, most probably germs and toxins. But first, psychiatry had to properly identify the various diseases.

Emil Kraepelin and the psychiatric clinic at Heidelberg, c. 1900 [Heidelberg University Library, Graph. Slg. A_0775]

Kraepelin approached psychiatry as a scientist, and he likely learned to think that way from his older brother, Karl. The family lived in a region of northern Germany surrounded by patches of untamed nature. Karl, who later became a botanist, took Emil for walks in the woods. He showed Emil how to identify the different plants. Each species, he explained, possesses certain unique features which together constitute its essence. Later, when the young doctor confronted insanity in all its bewildering variety, he recalled his brother's teachings. What sets this patient's illness apart from that other patient's illness? What are its essential features? He may have recalled Karl telling him about giraffes. Karl would have told him, 'If you see an animal with long legs, a long neck and patchy coloring on its skin, you'll know it's a giraffe *because these are its essential features.*' Kraepelin believed that mental illnesses also have essences, and that the essences are more meaningful than any collection of clinical symptoms. He devoted his research toward identifying the essential features of each mental disorder. For this, he used the tools at his disposal, namely measuring sticks, cameras, blood tests, thermometers and, of course, patient interviews.

The sixth edition of Kraepelin's textbook is his masterpiece. At nearly one thousand pages in length, the book is both a practical guide for psychiatrists and a highly readable description of every known mental disorder. Included amongst those descriptions are two new illnesses which—according to Kraepelin—accounted for all cases of psychosis. It was a grand simplification, greeted with relief by contemporary psychiatrists. The two illnesses were manic-depressive insanity, a disorder of affect, and *dementia praecox* (later, schizophrenia), a disorder of intelligence. We focus here on *dementia praecox*, which translates as premature dementia.[184]

In seventy-eight pages, Kraepelin describes the many characteristic features of *dementia praecox*, including weak wills, bizarre behaviors, incoherent thoughts, movement abnormalities, speech abnormalities, delusions and hallucinations. It is remarkable, however, that he never provides his readers—mostly asylum psychiatrists—with specific criteria for a diagnosis. Despite the myriad of symptoms described in vivid detail, the single definitive feature turns out to be incurability. Kraepelin states that patients with schizophrenia get worse over time and never recover. It is a criterion that is easily assessed, but obviously of limited value for evaluating new patients. Nonetheless, it was, for Kraepelin, the essence of schizophrenia. By contrast, the essence of manic-depressive insanity—which had symptoms similar to those of schizophrenia—was a disease characterized by partial or complete recovery.

Kraepelin was the first psychiatrist to fully describe schizophrenia, but he was not the first to notice it. As was the case with Leo Kanner and Hans Asperger's discovery of autism, others had been aware of the symptoms long before Kraepelin wrote at such length about them. Not only did several psychiatrists describe schizophrenia before Kraepelin, some had even given it the same name. Heinrich Schüle mentioned *das pubische Ir-*

---

[184] Kraepelin first wrote about *dementia praecox* in the fourth edition of his textbook (1893), but the description was not fully elaborated or set next to manic-depressive insanity until the sixth edition (1899). *Dementia praecox* and schizophrenia refer to the same illness, so the terms are interchangeable.

resein (pubic insanity); Albert Charpentier wrote about *les démences de la puberté* (dementias of puberty); Benedict Morel used the term *démence précoce* (precocious dementia); Thomas Clouston described an 'adolescent insanity and its secondary dementia'. And Arnold Pick had even used the identical term, *dementia praecox*.

Regardless of precedents, Kraepelin's work had an immediate impact around the western world. Psychiatrists welcomed the opportunity to sort out the bewildering assortment of patients. In any case of obvious psychosis, the doctor had only to choose between schizophrenia and manic-depressive insanity. Nowhere were the consequences greater than in America, where the asylums were full to the brim with psychotic patients. Recall that the sixth edition of Kraepelin's textbook was published in 1899. Just a year later, when a survey was conducted at the Connecticut Hospital for the Insane, it found that 31 percent of 2,600 patients admitted during the years 1898–1900 had been diagnosed with *dementia praecox*. The high percentage of *dementia praecox* cases at this particular hospital may have been slightly inflated by the presence of Dr. Allen Diefendorf of eye movement fame (Chapter 12)—an ardent supporter of Kraepelin's ideas—but a similar survey at the Manhattan State Hospital in New York revealed that 29 percent of new patients were diagnosed with *dementia praecox* in the years 1904 and 1905. Similar and even greater percentages persisted across the United States until well past mid-century.[185]

Scholars knowledgeable of the history of schizophrenia are struck by the fact that the definition of schizophrenia, already vague in Kraepelin's writings, has never been made precise. At one point, the definitions of schizophrenia were so vastly different around the world that it led to large discrepancies in the rates of diagnosis. For example, researchers compared admissions at the Brooklyn State Hospital in the years 1966–1967 with records from the Netherne Hospital in Surrey, England during the same period. Noting in particular the diagnosis assigned to each of 145 consecutive admissions at each hospital, they found that doctors in Brooklyn entered a diagnosis of schizophrenia in 35 percent of cases, whereas in Netherne the comparable figure was 57 percent.[186]

As problems with the definition of *dementia praecox* became evident, changes were made. The first in a long series of changes came from Eu-

---

[185] Figures from R. Noll (2011), chapter 4. See suggested readings.

[186] John E. Cooper et al., 'Cross-national study of diagnosis of the mental disorders: Some results from the first comparative investigation.' *American Journal of Psychiatry* 125 (10, supplement):21–29 (1969).

gen Bleuler, a respected Swiss psychiatrist. He dropped the criterion of incurability—because he found it untrue—and switched the emphasis from biology to psychology. Instead of toxins and brain degeneration, he wrote about the 'splitting of functions' (different from multiple personalities). The illness was no longer a hereditary dementia but rather a disorder characterized by disorganized thought and disorganized speech. Following upon these insights, Bleuler suggested that the name by changed from *dementia praecox* to schizophrenia.

A further unravelling of schizophrenia can be tracked through successive editions of the Diagnostic and Statistical Manual of Mental Disorders (DSM), the document consulted by nearly all American psychiatrists when assessing patients. In each of the Manual's five editions, the psychoses appear in a different light. Surprisingly, you will find no mention of either schizophrenia or manic-depressive insanity in the first edition, published in 1952. Instead, you see 'schizophrenic *reactions*' and 'manic-depressive *reactions*'. The term reaction was drummed up by a Swiss-born American by the name of Adolf Meyer. While studying medicine in Europe, Meyer spent several months visiting Kraepelin's clinic in Heidelberg. Once back in America, his enthusiasm for Kraepelin's ideas convinced many psychiatrists to accept schizophrenia (still known as *dementia praecox*) as a useful diagnosis. A few years later, Meyer had a change of mind. No longer sold on Kraepelin's scientific approach, he switched allegiance to Freud's psychoanalytic ideas. In contrast to Kraepelin's concept of schizophrenia and manic-depressive insanity as illnesses rooted in biology, Meyer and his fellow psychoanalysts saw them as mental disturbances, or abnormal responses to social and psychological pressures; hence, 'reactions'.

The 'reactions' were ultimately dropped in DSM-II (1968), leaving clinicians to ponder this revised description of schizophrenia,

> Disturbances in thinking are marked by alterations of concept formation which may lead to misinterpretation of reality and sometimes to delusions and hallucinations ... Corollary mood changes include ambivalent, constricted and inappropriate emotional responsiveness and loss of empathy with others. Behavior may be withdrawn, regressive and bizarre.

The historian Richard Noll notes that the vagueness of the diagnostic criteria in DSM-II implied that schizophrenia had become merely 'a synonym for severe functional impairment ... a label for grossly impaired persons who could not meet the "ordinary demands of life" '.[187]

DSM-III (1980) adopted a new approach based on the work of the German psychiatrist, Kurt Schneider. Schneider was interested in exactly what symptoms Kraepelin and colleagues had seen in the patients whom they had diagnosed with schizophrenia. To find out, he looked at the doctors' notes, still held at Kraepelin's former clinic in Heidelberg. From the many symptoms that the men had recorded, Schneider selected five that he felt were most characteristic of the illness. He called these the 'first-rank' symptoms of schizophrenia. Therefore, relying on Schneider's analysis, DSM-III stated that schizophrenia is an illness defined by one or more of the following symptoms:

- Thought broadcasting

- Thought insertions by another person

- Thought withdrawals

- Delusions of being externally controlled

- Voices communicating with or about the person

Besides schizophrenia, DSM-III contained 262 other disease categories, one of which was a concession to those who questioned the absolute separation of schizophrenia and manic-depression. To meet these concerns, a new disease category, schizoaffective disorder, was invented to fill the gap. Schizoaffective disorder is still listed in the current DSM manual. It applies to patients who have psychotic symptoms like delusions, hallucinations or disordered thoughts *plus* mood symptoms like mania and depression.

DSM-IV (1994) retained the first-rank symptoms, but in addition, psychiatrists were told that if they wanted to diagnose a patient with schizophrenia, they had to say which *type* of schizophrenia. They could choose between catatonic, disorganized, paranoid, residual or, if uncertain, undifferentiated schizophrenia. Alternatively, they could go with schizoaffective disorder. If they still had not found what they were looking for, it was suggested that they consider schizophreniform disorder, which was for short-term symptoms.

The latest edition of the Manual, DSM-5 (2013) has abandoned subtypes and 'eliminated the special status of Schneiderian first-rank symptoms.' Now, 'Schizophrenia is defined by a group of characteristic symptoms, such

---

[187] R. Noll (2011), p. 274. See suggested readings.

as delusions, hallucinations, and negative symptoms (i.e., diminished emotional expression or avolition); deterioration in social, occupational, or interpersonal functioning; and continuous signs of the disturbance for at least 6 months.'[188]

Bestseller, 2013

Summing up the history of schizophrenia as defined by the DSM, a kindly interpretation might be that the authors tried really hard to get it right. Still, the complicated nature of the diagnostic criteria allows for dubious outcomes. Consider, for example, where the manual specifies that a patient must have at least two symptoms from a list of five possible symptoms. It follows that one person qualifies if he or she has diminished emotional expression and delusions, while another person with hallucinations and disorganized speech also qualifies. In effect, two people with different sets of symptoms will both be diagnosed with the same illness.

More troublesome even than the diagnostic criteria is the assumption that schizophrenia is a real illness. Real giraffes have well-defined, objectively observed markers that are distinct from those of any other animal, and the list of markers never changes. Kraepelin taught that mental illnesses are real in the same manner. But the markers for schizophrenia are subjective and constantly changing. In the absence of a clear definition, the DSM struggles to distinguish schizophrenia from its nearest neighbors. Thus, serious concerns have been raised over the classification of the psychoses, and deeper questions have been asked about the entire system of psychiatric

---

[188] D.W. Black and J.E. Grant *DSM-5 Guidebook: The Essential Companion to the Diagnostic and Statistical Manual of Mental Disorders*, Fifth Edition. Washington, DC: American Psychiatric Association Publishing (2014). Quotes on pp. 71, 72.

classification. The empirical basis of these concerns derives from clinical observations, drug prescription practices, endophenotype data and genetics.

Anecdotal and clinical evidence suggests that certain hallmark symptoms of schizophrenia, such as hallucinations and delusions, are also present in patients diagnosed with schizoaffective disorder or bipolar disorder. A group of researchers decided to investigate whether, in fact, patients diagnosed with schizophrenia differ from individuals diagnosed with either schizoaffective disorder or bipolar disorder.[189] The study of 933 patients began with interviews and clinical tests to determine exactly what symptoms each patient had. When the symptom profiles of schizophrenia patients were then compared with those of bipolar patients, the researchers found 'a high degree of overlap in clinical characteristics.' And, with respect to patients with schizoaffective disorder, the researchers found that 'in some cases [the symptom profiles] mirrored those of psychotic bipolar disorder.' The results point to a basket of symptoms shared by all illnesses recognized as psychotic.

Further evidence of the blur separating supposedly distinct psychotic disorders comes from studies of the drugs that doctors prescribe for this group of illnesses. That is, drugs that work for a particular patient, are often prescribed regardless of what the label may say about the drug's intended uses. In 1995, for example, 78 percent of antipsychotic prescriptions were for conditions *not* approved by the United States Federal Drug Administration (FDA). Off-label usage was still at 67 percent in 2008.[190] Most of these cases concerned a prescription for either chlorpromazine or haloperidol, both of which were given to patients with bipolar disorder, despite being approved for schizophrenia alone. Once known as 'anti-schizophrenia' medications, chlorpromazine and haloperidol are now 'antipsychotic' medications.

Studies of endophenotypes (Chapter 12) tell a similar story. A network of European investigators compared gray matter in schizophrenic patients and bipolar patients, drawing subjects from four psychiatric centers.[191] Although the loss of gray matter was greater and more widespread in

---

[189] Carol A. Tamminga et al., 'Clinical phenotypes of psychosis in the bipolar-schizophrenia network on intermediate phenotypes (B-SNIP).' *American Journal of Psychiatry* 170:1263–1274 (2013).

[190] G.C. Alexander et al., 'Increasing off-label use of antipsychotic medications in the United States, 1995–2008.' *Pharmacoepidemiology and Drug Safety* 20:177–184 (2011).

[191] Eleonora Maggioni et al., 'Common and distinct structural features of schizophrenia and bipolar disorder: The European network on psychosis, disorders and cognitive trajectory (ENPACT) study.' *PLOS ONE* 12(11):e0188000.

schizophrenia than in bipolar disorder, there was significant loss in both disorders. The antisaccade task has also been identified as an endophenotype in both schizophrenia and bipolar disorder. In a recent study,[192] schizophrenia patients had an error rate of 44%; schizoaffective patients, 35%; bipolar patients, 32%. Each of these scores is significantly greater than the 18% error rate of healthy participants.

The first hint of a genetic overlap came from an English family with three seemingly identical boys (triplets), all three of whom developed psychological problems in their teen years. At maturity, one of the boys worked as an electronics technician, whereas neither of his brothers was able to hold any type of job. Psychiatrists, using criteria derived from Kraepelin's 1899 textbook, diagnosed the electronics technician with manic-depressive psychosis, his two brothers with schizophrenia. Years later, a group of psychiatrists puzzled over the fact that these apparently identical triplets had been diagnosed with two different psychotic illnesses. After a thorough re-examination of the data, both clinical and genetic, they confirmed the genetic identify of the men as well as the original diagnoses of manic-depressive psychosis in one case, schizophrenia in the two other cases. The study authors wrote, 'Our conclusion must be that the brothers have different forms of the same condition and that it represents a variety of square peg which will uneasily fit into a round Kraepelinian hole.' They added, 'While it now seems probable that the area between Kraepelin's two entities [schizophrenia and manic-depressive psychosis] is not unoccupied territory, a clear outline of what exists there is shrouded from view by mists of uncertainty.'[193]

The heritability of both schizophrenia and bipolar disorder is estimated to be around 80 percent. That being the case, and given the indications of overlap mentioned above, one might expect that the same genes are mutated in both illnesses. To test whether this is true, researchers needed to look at genes in an unprecedented number of patients. Scientists are ordinarily very competitive, but when the need arose for a very large patient sample, these researchers buried their individual ambitions and teamed up to form the Cross-Disorder Group of the Psychiatric Genomics Consortium, a collaboration involving 800 investigators working in 38 different countries.

---

[192] James L. Reilly et al., 'Elevated antisaccade error rate as an intermediate phenotype for psychosis across diagnostic categories.' *Schizophrenia Bulletin* 40(5):1011–1021 (2014).

[193] Peter McGuffin, Adrianne Reveley and Anthony Holland, 'Identical triplets: Non-Identical psychosis?' *British Journal of Psychiatry*: 140:1–6 (1982), p. 5.

Their broad reach enabled them to collect DNA from tens of thousands of psychiatric patients.[194]

In Chapter 6, we learned about genome-wide association studies (GWASs) and the search for site-specific variations in the DNA code, called single-nucleotide polymorphisms (SNPs). The Cross-Disorder Group relied on the same GWAS methodology. To see whether schizophrenia and bipolar disorder have a common genetic basis, they calculated a statistical measure known as the correlation coefficient, which describes the relationship between two sets of data, in this case the SNPs found in schizophrenia patients and the SNPs found in bipolar patients. The correlation was .68, which happens to be nearly the same as the correlation between height and weight. One-third of the shared SNPs are in genes active in the central nervous system. As a check on the specificity of the observed correlations, the Cross-Disorder Group calculated correlations between each of the two psychiatric conditions and Crohn's disease, a gastrointestinal disorder. Like the psychiatric diseases, Crohn's disease is also highly heritable, and it sometimes occurs together with depression or autism. Nevertheless, the genetic correlations between Crohn's disease and either schizophrenia or bipolar disorder are close to zero.

Altogether, the study described above investigated genetic overlap among five major psychiatric disorders. In addition to schizophrenia and bipolar disorder, it examined shared genetic markers in autism spectrum disorder, major depressive disorder and attention deficit hyperactivity disorder. They found strong SNP correlations between several pairs of disorders, and 36 variant genes overlapped across all five disorders.[195] Thus, there is compelling evidence of shared genetic elements in multiple mental illnesses.

Kraepelin assumed that mental illnesses are real things, part of the natural world. He no doubt believed that schizophrenia, like giraffes and carbon atoms, was always there and would always be there, forever unchanged. Yet years later, he doubted the distinction between this illness and manic-depressive insanity, the second type of psychosis highlighted in his textbook. In 1920, near the end of his life, he cautioned,

---

[194] Cross-Disorder Group of the Psychiatric Genomics Consortium, S. H. Lee et al., 'Genetic relationship between five psychiatric disorders estimated from genome-wide SNPs.' *Nature Genetics* 45(9):984–994 (2013). This paper has more than 200 individual authors.

[195] Huiying Zhao and Dale R. Nyholt, 'Gene-based analyses reveal novel genetic overlap and allelic heterogeneity across five major psychiatric disorders.' *Human Genetics* 136:263–274 (2017).

> We shall have to get accustomed to the notion that our much used clinical checklist does not permit us to differentiate reliably manic-depressive insanity from schizophrenia in all circumstances; and that there is an overlap between the two ... [I]t is becoming increasingly obvious that we cannot satisfactorily distinguish these two diseases. The suspicion remains that we are asking the wrong questions.[196]

Perspective

Psychiatrists in the Western world spent the better part of the twentieth century searching for the right questions, not just for schizophrenia and manic-depressive insanity but for other diagnoses as well. However, their questions focused on improving the criteria for diagnosis, rather than asking whether the historical disease types are really distinct. If they are not, as suggested in this chapter, we need to consider alternative approaches to diagnosis. There have been a number of suggestions, including those described below.

One proposal is to drastically reduce the number of recognized disorders, currently around 150 in DSM-5. This could be done by acknowledging overlaps between similar disorders. A start in this direction has already begun with the creation of autism spectrum disorder, which incorporates the former diagnoses of autistic disorder, Asperger's syndrome, Rett's syndrome and childhood disintegrative disorder. Similarly, the new definition of substance abuse incorporates the former diagnosis of substance dependency along with several specific disorders named after the abused substance. It has been suggested that obsessive-compulsion disorder, panic disorder, social anxiety disorder could be collapsed into a single spectrum disorder. And lastly, schizophrenia, schizoaffective disorder and bipolar disorder could be combined into a single psychosis spectrum disorder.

Those psychiatrists advocating for the creation of broadly defined spectrum disorders often include in their recommendations a system for scoring the severity of symptoms, from mild to disabling. Currently, diagnoses are categorical, meaning that the patient either has the disorder or does not have it. Epidemiological and other research would benefit from the provision of graded severity estimates, and psychiatrists might find that it facilitated the fine-tuning of treatment options in individual cases.

---

[196] Emil Kraepelin, 'The manifestations of insanity,' transl. D. Beer. *History of Psychiatry* 3: 499–529 (1992). Quote on pp. 527–528.

Diagnoses now rely almost entirely on psychological symptoms (moods, thoughts, beliefs), which psychiatrists discover through interviews and third-persons accounts. Psychiatrists reach their conclusions based on judgements which may or may not be accurate. Ideally, diagnoses would be based on methods that provide objective, quantitative measures. Examples might include data on gray matter volumes, white matter anomalies, gene variants, and behavioral tests such as the antisaccade eye movement task. These methods are not yet fully reliable, so they are not ready for widespread adoption, but that time may soon arrive.

Lastly, we might want to consider abandoning conventional diagnosis altogether. Rather than worrying about whether a person has *this* illness or *that* illness, we could focus instead on the person's functional problems. Is he able to control his anger; does she fail to establish close personal relationships? Does she suffer from voices heard in her head; does he have constant mood swings? Each symptom could be specifically addressed through psychotherapy, medication or physical therapy, as appropriate.

Suggested readings

Ronald Chase, *The Making of Modern Psychiatry.* Berlin, Logos Verlag (2018).

S. Guloksuz and J. van Os, 'The slow death of the concept of schizophrenia and the painful birth of the psychosis spectrum.' *Psychological Medicine* 48(2):229–244 (2018).

Richard Noll, *American Madness: The Rise and Fall of Dementia Praecox.* Cambridge, Harvard Univ. Press (2011).

Godfrey D. Pearlson et al. 'Does biology transcend the symptom-based boundaries of psychosis?' *Psychiatric Clinics of North America* 39(2):165–174 (2017).

Index